Beyond Held Hostage

Beyond Held Hostage

Healing and Restoration

Aubrey Dawn Weinzetl

Beyond Held Hostage

By Aubrey Dawn Weinzetl

Published by Aubrey Dawn Weinzetl, Sioux Falls, SD

www.aubreydw.com

Aubrey.heldhostage@gmail.com

ISBN 9798987989319

Library of Congress Control Number: 2023905346

Editors: Krystle Van Roekel, Valerie Weinzetl, Douglas Weinzetl

Cover Image: Bonnie Sandvold

Cover Layout: Aubrey Dawn Weinzetl

Book Layout: Aubrey Dawn Weinzetl

Dedication

To my nephew and niece, Jeremiah and Adelyn, I am so honored to be your spiritual mother. You have both been a blessing to me. I will forever cherish our memories and our times together. I pray that you would walk in relationship with God and in full obedience to Him, and that you would hear His voice and His gifts would be evident in your lives. I pray that His face would always shine upon you, and that you would continue to grow in Him. In Jesus' name, Amen.

I love you both so very much.

CONTENTS

Foreword:

As a teenager, I always wanted to write a book. Around 2008, God began to share with me that I would write one, but life happened, and I thought it was a promise that had been taken away. After my divorce was finalized, God began to bring that promise back to life. He told me that I needed to write about my life and let Him use everything that had happened for the good of others and not just myself. In January of 2022, I began writing Held Hostage, a story about some of what I have experienced in my life. I changed the names in the book, first because I believe it shows honor to my ex, and second because it felt weird to use my name with a different man's name, so I decided to change both. It took two months to write Held Hostage, but it was a very difficult time spiritually. I was being vulnerable, knowing that what I shared could be used against me, sadly in the world we live in, I would be judged because of my life. The book was published in July of 2022 and with it came a release and deep knowing that God was going to use my life for His glory.

In May 2022, God revealed that I would write a second book (which turned into so much more). The heart of Beyond Held Hostage is the explanation of the steps to healing, why those are the steps to take, and then how to apply these steps to your own life. The writing of Beyond Held Hostage started in September 2022, and as I write this it's in its last phase of editing. God told me that I would need to be even more open and vulnerable in this book. It has been months of spiritual warfare, as God breathed into it and led it in directions I never dreamed of. I said yes to God and was obedient to Him, but with this obedience was the awareness that some will use what God has told me to do as a means for judgment against me. Although I expected people to make assumptions and have questions about me, I was not expecting that my family would also be brought into this. So, I want to take some time to give understanding concerning my life and clarify some information, mainly because, for those of you who have been abused or are still in situations of abuse, I want you to be aware that you may have people make judgments about you for it, but even if that does happen, to not let it keep you from getting healing and freedom.

I have heard many people say, "Well if I was the one being abused, I wouldn't stay in the marriage and I wouldn't take what they are doing to me." The truth is, when you go through the grooming process, then the abuse, and then trauma, your brain and body changes. Boston Clinical Trials puts the information as such: Scientific research shows that when abuse or trauma takes place, your brain is affected in three different areas.[1] "During a traumatic experience, the reptilian brain takes control, shifting the body into reactive mode. Shutting down all non-essential body and mind processes, the brain stem orchestrates survival mode. During this time the sympathetic nervous system increases stress hormones and prepares the body to fight, flee or freeze."[2]

For most individuals, their mind and body go back into normal mode, but "…20 percent of trauma survivors who go on to develop symptoms of post-traumatic stress disorder (PTSD) — an unmitigated experience of anxiety related to the past trauma — the shift from reactive to responsive mode never occurs. Instead, the reptilian brain, primed to threat and supported by dysregulated activity in

---

[1] Michele Rosenthal, "The Science Behind PTSD Symptoms: How Trauma Changes The Brain," Boston Clinical Trials, June 27, 2019. https://www.bostontrials.com/how-trauma-changes-the-brain/#!/
[2] Michele Rosenthal, "The Science Behind PTSD Symptoms: How Trauma Changes The Brain," Boston Clinical Trials, June 27, 2019. https://www.bostontrials.com/how-trauma-changes-the-brain/#!/

significant brain structures, holds the survivor in a constant reactive state."[3]

Here are a couple of websites that will help benefit your understanding of what is possibly going on with you, or with someone else close to you: https://www.wholewellnesstherapy.com/post/trauma-and-the-brain

and https://www.bostontrials.com/how-trauma-changes-the-brain/#!/

When you are abused, betrayed, or traumatized, your brain changes, as does your thought processes. Things you once said, 'I would never,' or 'how could I let that continue' to become your reality because of what has happened in your brain. Thankfully though, we do not have to stay in a place of brokenness, because our brains can heal and change. Hence, the Beyond Held Hostage became a reality. God wants to use it to break the chains that hold people hostage and heal them to the point that it never even happened. We are talking about complete healing and restoration, realignment, and new beginnings.

So, a word of warning, be careful of the assumptions you make towards a person who is in an abusive situation or has been betrayed but remains in the relationship. Their brain and body are being affected in ways you don't understand. Also, if you are one who has said, 'I would never stay and let them do that,' be careful, because your words are without merit. I hope you never experience abuse, betrayal, and trauma; but if you do, there is no way to know how you would respond when faced with a similar situation. It will depend on what your brain does and if you are able to come out of it right away, or if you become part of the twenty percent. Also, when it comes to staying with a person who is abusive or who betrays their spouse, this individual could be experiencing Stockholm syndrome, have been conditioned to accept the relationship because of religious beliefs, or beliefs about themselves and their identity. The truth is, there are many reasons why a person would stay, and if others forced them to leave, they would still return to the abuser. It is important to ask questions and understand the heart of the person who was in that situation, instead of focusing on why you think they did.

Finally, Held Hostage and Beyond Held Hostage (the parts that are about my life story), are written from my perspective, they record my own views of the events in my life and what my thought processes were. That means that my parents, my siblings, my friends, and even my ex-husband all have their own perspective of events and were going through things individually as well.

I get asked, "Well, how could your family let this happen, and why didn't they stop it?" First, I am an adult, I take responsibility for my own actions, and I don't put my own responsibility and choices on others. Second, I refused to admit I was being abused for a very long time. This is referred to as a 'silent victim,' so I would talk about things but would change the wording to make it positive. An example of this was when my ex-husband would leave for long periods of time; his excuse was wanting to make more money (which never happened), but truthfully it was that he wanted to be away from me. So instead of telling people that I was being abandoned all the time, I would say, "He is working in another state to save up money so we can send it to his family to help them. In his culture it is our responsibility to provide for them." I took the truth, but twisted it to make him look good, so that people wouldn't know that I was being abandoned. Why? Well, why would I want to admit to

---

[3] Michele Rosenthal, "The Science Behind PTSD Symptoms: How Trauma Changes The Brain," Boston Clinical Trials, June 27, 2019. https://www.bostontrials.com/how-trauma-changes-the-brain/#!/

being abandoned, when that would reveal my humiliation that my own husband did not want me or love me? I remained silent about much of what I faced. My family and my friends knew something was going on, but they did not know the details or full extent. Third, how do you know my family and friends weren't doing things to help me and to get me out of the situation? Unless you talk to them directly, you do not know the facts.

So, to sum it up, if you are not the victim, be careful of your heart and thoughts, be on guard against assumptions and judgements, and instead find truth from the individuals actually involved. Get the answers from the source and make sure that you do not become a hindrance to the one hurting. Also, remember that we are to be a light on a hill, ambassadors of God, bringing His love to those who are hurting. Don't give satan room to use you as a tool for destruction but let yourself be used by God as an instrument for healing. If you have been a victim of abuse, betrayal, or trauma, be aware that you may be misunderstood, but don't let it keep you silent and in suffering. It is time for you to be healed and restored. It's time to be brave, to BE BOLD!

To those of you who are about to begin the adventure of Beyond Held Hostage, I pray that God takes you deeper into deliverance, freedom, and restoration.

Week 1: God the Father

"[1] See what great love the Father has lavished on us, that we should be called children of God! And that is what we are! The reason the world does not know us is that it did not know him. [2] Dear friends, now we are children of God, and what we will be has not yet been made known. But we know that when Christ appears, we shall be like him, for we shall see him as he is."
(1 John 3:1-2 NIV)

Day 1: Father

What comes to mind when you think of father? (Write it out.)

For many of us we think of our earthly father. This can bring amazing, warm, and joyful memories and feelings. Yet for others, it can bring sadness, pain, and traumatic feelings and memories. Fathers play an important role in our lives. They are meant to help guide and lead us into becoming the adults God designed us to be. They should be our role models, our encouragers, and supporters. More importantly, they are meant to give us understanding of how Christ loves the church. These are just a few roles that fathers play in our lives. The list goes on and on.

I come from a family that has a father who longs to show us Christ and raise us in Him. He actively seeks God in how to teach us, lead us, and build us up. I have always known a beautiful father's love. It breaks my heart knowing many do not grow up with this.

Fathers have abused their children and wives, abandoned, and ignored them; they have been excessive in their sarcastic putting-down of their children, and corrected them in the flesh and not in Christ. This list goes on and on as well.

This has left children and adults with a broken and almost always tainted, traumatic view of father and fatherhood.

So, what comes to your mind when you hear Father God? (Write it out.)

Many see Him as loving and giving, correcting in love, and our source of life. Yet those two words, "Father God" can also bring shame, guilt, and thoughts of a man who is standing and waiting to bring fault and accusation. Those who have been frightened by mean earthly fathers think of someone they would not willingly share their secrets with.

This week we will be focusing on who God is as a Father, His role as such, the Truth, and the understanding of where our perspectives are flawed. Here are the questions that will be answered this week.

1. What does God as Father mean?
2. What is God's role as a Father?
3. What is the Father's characteristics?
4. How does the Father love us?
5. How does our Father discipline us?
6. How does our Father train us?
7. How does He equip us?
8. What is His heart for us?

Today, we will focus on preparing our hearts and minds to receive the Truth of God the Father and letting go of views flawed by man.

~Prayer~

Today I come before You, God. I acknowledge that there are areas in my heart where my views of You as a Father have been skewed and flawed. Reveal to me now what some of those might be. (Write down what He gives you)

I admit that a part of me is scared to take this step to see who You truly are. (Write down what fears come to mind)

God, I want to see You for who You really are. I do not want to stay stuck in the past, but I long to have a healthy relationship with You. I feel like I have made so many mistakes that keep me from You.

(Write down what mistakes comes to mind)

Forgive me, God, for these. Cleanse me. Help me to overcome by Your blood.

Today I pray for a cleansing of my mind, thoughts, and heart. Prepare me, God, to receive Truth in the coming days. May I understand Your great love for me. I pray that You would heal my view of You as a Father. Search my heart and prepare me for this week.

In Jesus' Name, Amen.

Read Today: Romans 8:15-16, 2 Corinthians 6:18

~My prayer for you today~

Heavenly Father, I come before You. I ask that You cover the child who is diligently longing for more of You. You see their wounds, their brokenness, their fears, and yet, God, You see their boldness in taking this step to dig deeper and draw closer to You. I pray that You would flood them with Your love and peace. Help them to face what they need to face. I bind you, satan, in the name of Jesus. Your lies, your demonic spirits of destruction will not have a hold over this child of God, in the name of Jesus. I plead the blood of Jesus over you right now. You are covered, you are protected, and I proclaim breakthrough, freedom, and healing over you in the name of Jesus. Flood this child with Your love and forgiveness, Father. Take them deeper into You.

In Jesus' Name, Amen.

Day 2: The Father and David

~Prayer~

Heavenly Father, we come before You broken and in need of realignment. Open my ears and eyes to Your truths today. Convict me where my views are flawed. Align my mind to You. I long for Your thoughts and Your ways. Transform my mind today. Renew my spirit. I bind you satan, and your lies that want to Hold me Hostage, in Jesus' name.

Father, I invite You to come into my thoughts and my heart. Pull down every wall that does not align to You. Break off every piece of foundation that is contrary to You. I want to be built with a strong and sure foundation. Who I am to become is who You designed me to be. Meet with me today. I repent for the ways that I was in the flesh today. I repent of responding out of myself instead of in You. I turn from my ways and ask that You would take me deeper in You today.

In Jesus' Name, Amen.

Today and tomorrow, we are going to focus on the Biblical account of David. When I think of King David, I see a lot of my own story. He had so many failures and traumas, and yet he is known as a man after God's heart. It was not until I was going through my time of healing that I began to see an image of the Father God that I had not recognized when it came to His relationship with David.

Here are some big events in David's life:

1. He was left alone to tend the sheep at a very young age. This was a very lonely job, but it was also looked down upon.

2. He had to kill bears and lions with his own hands in the power of God working through Him. However, he still had to be bold.

3. No one in his family thought that he would be king, which is why when the prophet came to pick a king, David's father did not call for him to come.

4. He killed Goliath the giant

5. He had to flee for his life for years

6. His best friend, one whom he considered his brother, was killed

7. His wife Michal betrayed him in her heart

8. He had an affair and killed the woman's husband

9. He did not discipline his children correctly, and because of his lack of leadership, brother betrayed sister, brothers betrayed brothers, and it ended with the loss of his children's lives

10. He worshipped God without fear

11. He fought battle after battle so his children could reign in peace

12. God shared with him how his son would build the temple

13. God made a covenant with David that his children would sit on the throne and that out of his lineage the Messiah would come

Honestly, there is so much to the account of David. I would encourage you to do a Bible study on him.

David, a young boy, alone with his sheep, playing his instruments in worship to God. David was a boy of godly character, who sought the Lord and was led by Him; we can see that because God would not have chosen him to be king if he was not the one for the task. God knew David's heart intimately.

They had fellowship and communication, and the Father gave David boldness to protect what he was over. The Father gave him strength to kill the lion and the bear. I love what 1 Samuel 17:34-36 (RSV) says, "[34] But David said to Saul, "Your servant used to keep sheep for his father; and when there came a lion, or a bear, and took a lamb from the flock, [35] I went after him and smote him and delivered it out of his mouth; and if he arose against me, I caught him by his beard, and smote him and killed him. [36] Your servant has killed both lions and bears; and this uncircumcised Philistine shall be like one of them, seeing he has defied the armies of the living God."

Write verse 37.

David recognized that it was the Father's hand of protection on him. He trusted the Father to provide and take care of Him. By the time we get to 1 Samuel 17, David has already been equipped, trained, and has learned to rely on the Father. Therefore, David could be bold and kill the lion, bear, and Goliath. He knew his Father intimately. He knew that He would bring protection for the Israelites, and he was willing to let God use him as that weapon of protection.

Let me set the stage before we read the account of David and Goliath. King Saul has taken his men into battle against the Philistines. Amongst all the Philistines is a giant who goes by the name Goliath. The Bible says this giant was over nine feet tall and completely decked out in armor. For his weapons he carried a sword, a spear, and a javelin. Every morning and evening Goliath would come and taunt the armies of God, and his menacing words caused fear and trembling to hit Saul's armies. Finally, David arrived on the scene. His father had sent him to check on his brothers, and when David heard the arrogant words the Philistine said against his God, a righteous indignation arose within him. There was no fear, only bold trust in God. Immediately David declared that he would fight against Goliath. King Saul tried to equip him with manmade armor, but David found it too weighty and knew that it was not the right covering he needed. So, he spoke boldly of how God used him to protect the sheep of his father, and that with his bare hands, he had killed both lion and bear. From there he took his slingshot, found five smooth stones, and went to face the giant. (1 Samuel 17)

Read 1 Samuel 17:43-47.
What did Goliath say?

What was David's response?

Goliath the giant charged towards an unwavering David; and David swung his slingshot, aimed for Goliath, and by God's favor, hit Goliath in the only spot that armor did not protect him, which was his forehead. Goliath toppled over, and David followed through with his warning. Using Goliath's own sword, he chopped off the giant's head. The armies of God rallied together and charged toward the shocked Philistines, causing them to run for the lives. Dead Philistines covered the roads, their camp was plundered, and the victory belonged to God. (1 Samuel 17)

Just think, David had been alone and basically abandoned by his family to serve sheep. How many of you have been abandoned and alone? YET, he chose a relationship with the Father that would take him into places he never dreamed. In fact, we find that before David was called upon to protect the kingdom of God, he was first chosen and anointed by the Father for it. In 1 Samuel 16:13 (AMP) says, "[13] Then Samuel took the horn of oil and anointed David in the presence of his brothers; and the Spirit of the LORD came mightily upon David from that day forward. And Samuel arose and went to Ramah."

How many of you right now are facing Goliath's and these giants of hard decisions, trauma, painful memories, and so on?

(Write down things that you are facing at this moment)

~Prayer~

Heavenly Father, we recognize that for us to face the things we need to face, we need You so very desperately. We need You to come alive in us, to refresh our relationship with You, and we need Your Spirit in us. We cannot face these things alone. To understand what You are doing, we need You to help us process, understand, and heal. You are asking us to face very painful things, Father, and we need You. Please fill us with Your Spirit and anoint us so we can accomplish all that we are called to. In Jesus' Name, Amen.

For so many of us, we might have a hard time seeing how the Father was there for us in the midst of complete darkness and betrayal. We struggle to understand how He can be a good Father, when we had to experience so many things in life that caused deep wounds and heartache. When I look back at my own life and think about the times where He did not just come and remove me from the situation, I asked the Father to help me understand what He was doing during those times. Although at the time I wished I had never gone through them, today I would never go back to change it, because who I am today would change if I went back. The me today is able to see the Father in a whole new way, and I am stronger, healthier, and bolder than I have ever been before.

Pick a situation where the term 'Father God' brings negative memories and feelings to you. (Write it down)

~Prayer~

Father, please show me what You were doing in this situation. Show me Your perspective of the situation because I long to see what You were doing through Your eyes and not my own. Speak to me now and show me.

(Write down what God reveals about what He was doing, what His character is in the situation.)

(Write down what you learned about yourself from that situation)

(Write down ways you were equipped and trained)

Apply this step to every memory and situation you remember that has given you a negative and flawed view of the Father. You will need this step not just for today, but until you find complete freedom and healing in these areas.

Read Today: 1 Samuel 16 and 17

~My prayer for you today~

Heavenly Father, I come before You and I ask that You bring Truth to the areas that are holding Your children Hostage in the area of You as their Father. I break off every lie and deception from satan and the ways he would try to keep them stuck, in the name of Jesus. I pray that Truth would flood them, and with it they would be released to let go of the pain, anger, resentment, and negative beliefs about You as Father.

In Jesus' Name, Amen.

Day 3: Train Us and Discipline Us

~Prayer~

Heavenly Father, we come before You today knowing that You are going to reveal even more of Your heart for us. I refuse to let fear, worry, or my past keep me from knowing You as Father. Open my eyes and ears to You today. I surrender my own ideas and ways of doing things, and I hold onto You. Speak to me today.

In Jesus' name, Amen.

Yesterday we learned how David, as a young boy and into a young man, spent quality time with God. He was being equipped and trained and was finally called and anointed by the Father. We are going to jump further ahead in David's life, but before we do let's find out what David had done up to this point.

1. Killed bears and lions by God's grace of protection

2. Killed Goliath

3. Was anointed as king

4. Used his gift of music to do spiritual warfare against the evil spirits that plagued King Saul.

5. He fought many battles and was well-known throughout Israel

6. He had a friend who became a spiritual brother, Jonathan, who would later die in battle

7. He spent years running for his life because Saul did not want to give up his throne to David

8. He was made king

9. He had many wives; one was a betrothal to King Saul's daughter; one was Abigail, who we will learn about later

10. He led his men valiantly in defeating enemies so that there would be peace for when his son would rule.

There are many more things that King David did and experienced, but just from these alone we can see that he was a man of character. He did what was right in the eyes of God and obeyed His leading. But something happened. A choice was made that changed his relationship with God for a time. Instead of being obedient and going with his men to war, he chose to stay back and relax. He gave others the call and authority that was supposed to be on his back. There is more to how David got here, but we are going to focus on what he did, where he went after he did it, and finally what the outcome was because of it. (2 Samuel 11)

Read 2 Samuel 11:1-3.

Who went to war and who remained at home?

Write verse 2.

2 Samuel 11:4-5 (AMP) says, "[4] David sent messengers and took her. When she came to him, he lay with her. And when she was purified from her uncleanness, she returned to her house. [5] The woman conceived; and she sent word and told David, "I am pregnant.""

So, David stayed back in Jerusalem instead of going with his men, and then the perfect circumstance took place where he saw a woman and took her into his bed. When I say, 'perfect circumstance,' I am being sarcastic. I believe that satan had it planned. He knew exactly how he wanted to tempt David and get him off course. Sadly, we find David did not stop, but he allowed it to take him farther away from truth, righteousness, and God.

Read 2 Samuel 11:6-10.
What was David's response to the situation?

What did Uriah do?

2 Samuel 11:11 (NIV) says, "[11] Uriah said to David, "The ark and Israel and Judah are staying in tents, and my commander Joab and my lord's men are camped in the open country. How could I go to my house to eat and drink and make love to my wife? As surely as you live, I will not do such a thing!""

I love Uriah's response, because it shows he is a faithful, responsible, and godly man. However, what happens next shows the ugliness of the sin that David chose to surrender to. David sent a message to Joab saying that, in the midst of the battle, to have Uriah go forward to attack, but when the fighting was at its worst, abandon him there and let the men of the city kill Uriah. Uriah was murdered in that battle; and now, not only did David take a married woman into his bed, but this woman then got pregnant. Instead of stopping there, David goes a step forward to kill her husband. Immediately my mind goes to Bathsheba; what must she have thought when she found out her husband was killed? First, she did not stay faithful to her husband, then she hid it from her husband, and finally lost her husband. Later she went and married the man who murdered her husband. The blood of her husband was on her hands, and she would be reminded of their choices for the rest of her life. There is nothing righteous or pure about this situation. In fact, even writing this causes me to be triggered, but I am pushing through because there is something so powerful here that I want you to grasp hold of.

We then get to 2 Samuel 12 where Nathan the prophet goes and rebukes David in the authority of the Father. Nathan said that there are a couple of consequences that David would now have to face because of his sin. There would be constant battle in his family; someone close to him (his son) would sleep with David's wives and the country would know about it, and the son just born to him through Bathsheba would not live. David repented and Nathan said that he was forgiven, but he still had to bear the consequences of his choices. If you read further on about David's life, we find that his sons constantly fought amongst themselves, and this led to their deaths. We see that a son revolted against David and in daylight slept with David's wives, and the son born to him and to Bathsheba died.

Correction, discipline, and the Father's love was shown. We can look back and ask how, if the Father did not stop the consequences and the correction, could it be love? God gives us freewill to choose Him. He does not force us to obey and love Him. With this freewill, it means that there are consequences to our choices. We do not like to view discipline as loving, but if done in the Father's heart, it is a very loving and beautiful thing. Why? Because the Father wants to get us back onto the right path and relationship with Him. He wants to cleanse us and help us understand why we should never make that same decision again.

Now we are going to get into something that is so powerful, and yet triggers me. We later find out that the Father redeems and restores them and us. Our Father decides that His precious Son Jesus, would come from the line of David. Not only that, but He would use the son Solomon, whose mother was Bathsheba. Right now, I just feel like crying as that hits me. You see, after my ex-husband had his affair and I found out about it the day before our second anniversary, reading this story was extremely hard to do. I thought about the wives of David who were betrayed and then had to accept this woman into their family. They had to love on the children that the mistress bore to their husband.

My heart broke when I read about it; anger surged within me at the unfairness of life, and yet God was about to show me something so powerful. For a year after the affair, this girl would still contact my ex-husband. He refused to let me be around when they talked and would not let me read the messages. Then he left for six months, and I had no way of knowing what was said other than checking the phone logs to know they were talking and messaging. I finally blocked her without my ex-husband knowing, so that I would not have to keep worrying about it. The first couple of months I had a lot of anger towards her, but realized she was a victim too, because (supposedly) she did not know my ex-husband was married. But for a couple years after that I had a lot of pain and unforgiveness that I had to walk through concerning her, because she would not let him go and put me through more pain as I constantly relived the betrayal for a year while they communicated. I finally had to continue to say over and over "I forgive you." Finally, I was able to see that I truly had forgiven her and was even able to pray for a marriage that would be healthy and life-giving for her, that her husband would never betray her and that she would never experience what I had. I kept tabs on her through the years, and one year I saw that God had answered my prayer and she had married someone who made her smile. I was able to see how God answered my prayers for her.

Through the story of David and Bathsheba we glimpse how the Father redeems us. I am sure that Bathsheba's history was known throughout the palace, and I am sure it was talked about in secret. I am sure that the sins of David and the consequences that came from it, brought much pain to those around him. The Father knew that although their pasts were still known, He wanted to reveal that He does not hold our pasts over us. In fact, He takes us out of it, places us back into realignment with His original design for us, and then has us continue to walk forward with purpose and belonging in being fully known and loved by Him. The Father used two people who caused so much pain and hurt to show that He is powerful enough to realign, redeem, restore, and bless us.

Therefore, we cannot allow anger, hatred, and bitterness towards those who have hurt us cling to our hearts. If we allow those things into our hearts we will not be realigned, restored, redeemed, or blessed. Anger, hatred, and bitterness will not affect the person who hurt you and it will not redeem the situation. But they *will* destroy you and your future. Allow forgiveness and the Father's love to flow through you to those individuals (this does not mean you need to have a relationship with them or be around them), so that the Father can realign, restore, and redeem you.

~Prayer~

Heavenly Father, we recognize that You are the Father who redeems, restores, and realigns us. At times we can become angry that You love all of us and want all of us to find redemption, even those who have hurt us and caused us pain. We get so excited when we hear that You will do that for us and our situations, but when it comes to those who have tried their best to destroy us, we begin to question Your love for us. Forgive us for not understanding Your heart for everyone. Forgive us for holding onto anger, bitterness, and hatred towards them instead of releasing them into Your hands. Today I forgive (Write down who you need to forgive)

Today we thank You for loving us. Thank You for removing our past from Your eyes. In Jesus' name, Amen.

Continue to forgive the individuals that come to mind until you have truly forgiven and released them. It is easy to pick those feelings back up, especially when we struggle with nightmares and flashbacks. Remember to think on good things, and when those feelings, nightmares, and flashbacks happen, immediately pray for them and forgive them.

Read Today: 2 Samuel 11, 2 Samuel 12

~My prayer for you today~

Heavenly Father, I come before You and I ask that You bring comfort to Your children who right now are hurting from betrayal and brokenness. I pray that You would wrap Your arms around them and reveal Your great love and forgiveness for them. Reveal to them how You are redeeming them, restoring them, realigning them, and working out their life for a great future.

In Jesus' Name, Amen.

Day 4: His Character and Love

~Prayer~

Heavenly Father, we are ready to go deeper with You. We understand Your heart is much larger, bigger, and more righteous than our own. We understand that Your ways are for the good of everyone, not just us. We bind every work of the enemy and his lies and deception he would use to keep us from truth, in Jesus' name. We come against every demonic spirit that would try to keep its claws digging into us and we say NO, in the name of Jesus. You have no authority or power in our lives, and we command you to flee from us, in the name of Jesus. Today, Father, speak to us about Your character and love. In Jesus' Name, Amen.

Yesterday we discovered the greatness of our Father's love. Today we are going to see what Jesus says about our Father.

2 Corinthians 6:18 (NKJV) says, "[18] "I will be a Father to you, And you shall be My sons and daughters, Says the **LORD** Almighty."

Psalm 103:13 (NLT) says, "[13] The LORD is like a father to his children, tender and compassionate to those who fear him."

So, what does this look like? how is God our Father? In Luke 15, we read a beautiful account of our Father. It is a parable that Jesus told so that we could understand the Father. I think Jesus knew many of us have negative views towards God as a Father, and so He expresses the heart of the Father in such a down-to-earth way that removes the fear. The example is that of a father who had two sons. One son worked hard, was faithful, and continued to help his father. The other son asked for his inheritance, left, and lived in a wild way full of sin. When he had spent all his money, and could barely keep his stomach full, and after working in bad conditions; he chose to return home, not as a son, but as a servant.

Read Luke 15:20-24.

(Write down what you notice about God the Father in how He treats the lost son.)

(**Read Luke 15:25-32** and write down what you notice about how God the Father handles the situation with the son who had remained by His side.)

We see how a son chose to leave his father and live in disgrace and sin. He knew he had gone astray and that he was not worthy of his father's love. I love how it says "loose living;" another version puts it as "wild living" because honestly, how many of us fit in that category when we chose sin? The fact that it is wide open for interpretation and imagination, I believe, was done on purpose, to show that this is the Father's response to every "wild living." Wow! I love reading about the compassion of the Father. In verse 20 it says that the Father saw the son from far away and with great compassion ran, embraced, and kissed His son. How many of us right now are needing the Father of compassion to come running to us, picking us up into His loving embrace, and shower us with kisses? You might be feeling today that you are not valuable, not worth loving, and that what you have done to yourself or what others have done to you, will make it impossible for the Father to respond this way to you. I want to tell you right now, that is a LIE from the enemy, to keep you Held Hostage. You are valuable, you are worth the Father's great love, and I am telling you now the FATHER is REJOICING that you have returned home. He is REJOICING that you long for a deeper relationship with Him. He is REJOICING that He can finally hold you without a fight from you.

~Prayer~

Heavenly Father, I come before You and I pray that Your child who is reading this right now would stop running from You. Father, You are relentlessly running after them, arms outstretched, ready to embrace them. I break off the spirit of fear that would try to make them feel they are unworthy, not valued, and unwanted, in the name of Jesus'. I proclaim over you, child, you are loved, you are wanted; you are more than enough, you're valuable, and the Father loves you with a deep passion that overwhelms His heart. Father, I pray that You would work in their heart right now, open their eyes to You, and their ears to hear Your voice. In Jesus' name, Amen

(Write a prayer of love to the Father and your commitment to not run from Him anymore.)

In Luke 18:2-5 (AMP) says, "[2] saying, "In a certain city there was a judge who did not fear God and had no respect for man. [3] There was a [desperate] widow in that city and she kept coming to him and saying, 'Give me justice and legal protection from my adversary.' [4] For a time he would not; but later he said to himself, 'Even though I do not fear God nor respect man, [5] yet because this widow continues to bother me, I will give her justice and legal protection; otherwise by continually coming she [will be an intolerable annoyance and she] will wear me out.' "

I want us to focus on this parable as well today, because I sense that the Father is asking if you will come and sit on His lap and rest in Him. Not only is He asking if you will, but He also longs for you to share your heart and make requests of Him. How many of you are needing to get out of a situation in your life? How many of you are needing to know that you are forgiven? How many of you are needing to know that He will rescue you? How many of you are needing answers, wisdom, and understanding for a situation? In verse 7 and 8 my heart just melts inside me. I am going to change this up a bit in order for you to understand what the Father is saying in an intimate way. Because I feel that this is a prophetic word, He is giving you. "Will not I, your Father, bring about justice for you, My chosen one, who cries out to Me day and night? Will I keep pushing you away? No, I tell you, I will make sure you see the justice I give you and it will happen quickly."

~Prayer~

Heavenly Father, I come before you and I ask that right now these words from You would penetrate the hearts of Your beloved children. Reveal to them now that they have freedom to ask of You and the assurance that You will answer them quickly. In Jesus' name, Amen.

Take time to rest in the Father's embrace. Get comfortable and just rest for a bit. When you feel released in your spirit, then move on to the next portion.

(Write down your requests to the Father)

Remember the Father's answer can be "YES," "NO," or "WAIT." Make sure that you are open for the answer He gives and not push for what you want as the answer.

Read Today: Luke 15, Luke 18

~My prayer for you today~

Heavenly Father, I come before You and I ask that You reveal how You see Your child. In Your eyes they are more precious than gold, silver, or even diamonds. To You they are Your beloved daughter/son. In Your Word it even says that You sing over us. I pray that today You would sing over Your children.

In Jesus' Name, Amen.

Day 5: Equip Us and His Heart for Us

~Prayer~

Heavenly Father, we come before You and we acknowledge our need for You today. We cannot do this on our own, for the healing that needs to take place in our lives can only be done through You. We understand that because of our past mistakes, sin, traumas, and abuse our views and perspectives of You have become flawed. We also realize that this does not give us the excuse to continue in those flawed ideas. Your Word tells us to renew our minds. So today we ask that You help us to renew our minds. Let Truth sink in and bring freedom where we have been bound and Held Hostage. In Jesus' Name, Amen.

'God our Father.' Do those words carry a different meaning and feeling for you now? If not, by the time we get to week 16, they will. Our Father loves us so much and He continually is revealing Himself to us, but we must be willing to see it. We must stop running and allow Truth to enter our hearts. So many of us have been in denial about our situations to survive, but by being in denial we have allowed those very things to Hold us Hostage. The Father is wanting to break us out and free us from the grave we find ourselves in. I absolutely love what Jesus said about the Father.

Read John 5:19-23.

(Write down all the things the Father does)

I am absolutely amazed at Jesus and what He did and does do for us. We will get more into the Son next week but having His life playing out in my head makes this chapter from John stand out even more. The Son is the reflection of the Father, to show us the Father's heart. All the teachings Jesus gave about how we are to live came from the Father's heart. He did not give us do's and don'ts to take away our joy and desires. He gave them to us for our futures to be blessed and favored. By following the Word from the Father, we will have greater freedom, anointing, authority, and intimate relationship with Him. If we do not let Him equip us and follow His heart, then our lives become full of negative consequences and our futures will be lacking as we are Held Hostage and trapped.

(Find five chapters in the New Testament where the Father speaks through Jesus on equipping us.) Example: Matthew 25:1-13

(Write down the references for the five chapters and paraphrase what the Father is saying to you about the direction He longs to take you in.) Example: Matthew 25:1-13 - Jesus is telling us that we need to be always ready for His return. We are to be wise in how we live each day, and unselfish in our motives. We need to follow through with what the Father has given for us each day, so that when He returns, the Son will find that we have been faithful in what the Father has given us to do.

Read Today: The 5 Chapters you are supposed to find.

~My prayer for you today~

Heavenly Father,

I come before You and I pray for Your child who is right now longing to understand Your plan and purpose for them, and that they realize that You have so much more for them. It can be overwhelming when we cannot clearly see the direction You are leading us into. I pray that You would speak very clearly in the coming weeks about the direction You are leading them in. I pray that they would step out in boldness and in obedience.

In Jesus' Name, Amen.

Day 6: My Story and Testimonies

The Father has really broken my heart and flooded it with a love that cannot even be described. There are so many examples from my personal life of how God is my Father.

The first ones I want to hit on can be the hardest ones. It's when He is warning and correcting us. In Week 11, I will share about the situation I was in while dating my ex-husband, so I will not go into details now. But God gave me a big warning, trying to get me out of a bad situation. I can still remember it like it happened today. It was either a vision or an angel that appeared before me. He came in the image of my earthly dad, but it was not my dad because I later asked him if he had come to my room, and he said no. I remember the words the angel said: "Aubrey, what are you doing?" I responded and said, "Nothing." Again, he spoke to me, "Aubrey, then why were you sleeping in his bed?" I remember being jolted awake, and when I looked around no one was there. I knew I was in sin, but I continued to rebel.

A few months later, I picked up my ex-husband (at that time boyfriend) from the bus station three hours away, because he was visiting for a week. It was harvest season and it was dark out. It was also hunting season. As I was driving, a huge buck with gigantic antlers was laying down in the middle of the road staring straight at me. I quickly swerved and his antlers scratched the side of the car. We went into the ditch, and my ex-husband grabbed the wheel and got us back onto the road. We pulled over and looked, but the buck was nowhere to be seen and the scratch on the car rubbed off. It was another warning that I did not listen to because I feared nobody would ever love me again.

Our Father loves us enough to warn and discipline us, but rarely do we appreciate His love. When it means giving up our own desires and flesh, this causes a battle to break out between our spirit and flesh. Yet now when I look back, I see His great love for me. Even though I did not listen, which caused fifteen years of pain and suffering, He still relentlessly pursued my heart.

The Father loves us enough to discipline us. Sometimes the consequences are natural, and other times they are clearly the Father's hand on us. I chose my marriage, and the natural consequence was the suffering. Other examples: having to restore broken relationships with family and friends because my choices broke down those relationships.

Honestly the list can go on and on, but I think it is time to discuss another example of God as my Father. Through all the pain and suffering, He was always there. I cried out and I know He heard. There are countless times where I should have died or been hurt, but no harm came to me. Although it took Him eleven years to get me back into a relationship with Him and back on the path He has for me, He faithfully pursued me. He did not shame me, or guilt-trip me. He did not force me or condemn me. No; instead, He lovingly pursued me. He lovingly cleansed me and made me whole. Through His redemption I can call Him "Daddy"!

Another aspect of Him as Father is that He asks us to always trust Him even when we do not understand. This occurred right before my ex-husband and I separated and then divorced. He asked me right before my breakthrough if I was willing to step out of the box and boldly claim my calling and ministry. I said, "YES"! God told me that something big was coming, but if I remained in Him, I would remain standing. Even though everything else would be gone. Two weeks later my ex-husband's inappropriate friendship with another woman was exposed. You can read more about this in Held Hostage Chapter 7. I listened and obeyed, which gave me the steps and breakthrough to overcome PTSD (Post-Traumatic Stress Disorder), so it does not control me, and led me to freedom even through my divorce, trauma, and life experiences.

I now see God not as a Father who is trying to destroy me or take away my desires and longings, but a Good Father who gives us the desires of our hearts, protects us, and leads us along His path of righteousness.

Testimonies:

*God has been a Father to me by teaching me how to love other people [see 1 Thessalonians 4:9]. He has rebuked me when my attitudes, words, and behavior were immature, toxic, and destructive in order that I can change, improve, and grow. He doesn't passively allow me to stay the way I am, but He teaches, coaches, equips, and empowers me to change in the way I think and act.

He primarily teaches, rebukes, corrects, and trains me in right relationships through His Word [see 2 Timothy 3:16]. His laws teach me to recognize attitudes like pride, bitterness, fear, shame, guilt, anxiety, strife, complaining, depression, etc. as unhealthy, so that I can turn to Him and remove those things from my life. Only by receiving His love which He demonstrated through Jesus can I be made free from all those mindsets which want to ensnare me, steal my joy, and destroy my health. My Father trains my hands for spiritual warfare as His love teaches me how to love Him with all my heart, soul, mind, and strength and to love my neighbor as I love myself. ~Steve D.

Day 7: Self-Reflection

~Prayer~

Heavenly Father, as we come to the end of Week 1 and learning about Your heart and love for us, I pray that we would continue to see You in a fresh and brand-new way. Help us to continue to be aware of what You are doing and how You want our minds to change. I pray for Your conviction to be alive in us, especially where we have become dull to it by our sin and traumas. Today help us to break free from those areas. I come against any demonic attack sent to take us out today, any demonic spirit that would try to steal our healing in the name of Jesus. Satan, you have no authority or power here. I pray that our ears and our hearts would be open fully to You, Father. In Jesus' Name, Amen.

Today I will be asking hard questions and I want you to write down your answers truthfully and honestly.

What are the areas in my mind that the term Father God has been negative and not based in Truth?

Father, reveal to me the reason behind my thinking, and give me Your perspective on those areas in my life.

What situations have I been in where I judged the Father in the way He handled it and that caused bitterness, resentment, and distrust towards Him?

Father, show me what You were doing in these situations and how the way You handled it was for my good.

Do my views of Father God fall into line with what the Bible says?

How has God renewed my mind on God the Father?

Week 2: Jesus the Son

"[16] For God so loved the world that he gave his one and only Son, that whoever believes in him shall not perish but have eternal life."
(John 3:16 NIV)

Day 1: Jesus

So many of us have gone through experiences in life that have had a lasting effect in how we process, what we believe to be true, and ultimately how we see God the Father, God the Son, and God the Holy Spirit.

What comes to mind when you hear the words 'Jesus the Son?'

How do you view Jesus when it comes to living your life?

When my life began falling apart, I did not understand the Son at all. I could not understand why He did not force my ex-husband to change. I believed that He would not give me more than I could handle, which I found out later was not true, because if we could handle everything in life on our own there is no need for God the Father, God the Son, and God the Holy Spirit. We are not made to handle everything on our own; in fact, we are told over and over to cast our cares upon Him.

Truthfully, I did a lot of blaming of Jesus, and I had anger and bitterness towards Him for not changing my circumstances. However, as I once again drew close to God, and my healing really took off and I began to truly understand the Son's character, I realized my anger and bitterness were wrong.

The truth is that many struggle with their relationship with God when something bad happens, whether through consequences of their actions or just hard times that come for no reason. This could be from sickness, death, financial problems, marriage problems, struggles with children, and the list goes on and on. When anything goes wrong in the world, especially if nature is involved, it is automatically blamed on God, and everyone asks why a loving God could do such a thing. Interesting how the first thing is not, "God, have I sinned in an area that led to this? Is this something that has come from another person's consequence that affects me? What can You do in this situation, because it really hurts and is hard to go through?"

So many churches have become religious and left out relationship. They teach that when you accept Jesus as Lord and Savior of your life, then you will not have hardship, pain, or a hard life. I have seen so many churches in these later years that have back tracked and changed this teaching, because they are seeing the damage it has done. There is not one place that says you won't have problems, persecution, or struggles. In fact, the Bible makes it clear that life will get harder, because what Jesus the Son does, goes against the norm and breaks cultural standards.

This week we will be going deep into who Jesus the Son is, what His life is about, and what He calls us to.

Read Today: Luke 3

~Prayer~

Heavenly Father,

We come to You and we ask that this week You would radically change our views, how we process life situations, and how we respond to it. We ask that our faith in You would explode and that the zeal for our relationship with You would burst forth and change our lives forever. We ask that as we seek You today, You would begin to work within our hearts and prepare us. Thank You for the healing and for what You are doing. Although we might not see it clearly right now, You are doing amazing things in the spiritual realm and laying a strong foundation in us.

In Jesus' name, Amen

Day 2: What Does God Say About the Son?

~Prayer~

Heavenly Father,

We come before You today and we ask that You make Yourself known to us. We break off every lie of the enemy that would say You are to blame for everything that goes wrong, in the name of Jesus. We know that You are good, and in You there is no sin or evil. You love everyone and desire that all would come to know You. Forgive us where we have chosen to blame You, instead of loving You. Forgive us when we failed to acknowledge Your goodness during our hard times. We know we have failed You many times, but You have not failed us. Help us in our unbelief today and help us change our perspectives and minds on who You are. In Jesus' Name, Amen.

Today we are going to read about what the Word (Bible) says about who Jesus is. We are going to answer the question, what does God say about the Son?

John 3:13-15, 17-18 (NKJV) says, "[13] No one has ascended to heaven but He who came down from heaven, that is, the Son of Man who is in heaven. [14] And as Moses lifted up the serpent in the wilderness, even so must the Son of Man be lifted up, [15] that whoever believes in Him should not perish but have eternal life."

"[17] For God did not send His Son into the world to condemn the world, but that the world through Him might be saved. [18] "He who believes in Him is not condemned; but he who does not believe is condemned already, because he has not believed in the name of the only begotten Son of God."

(Write down who Jesus says He is)

In John 3, we see that the reason the Son came was to bring light, healing, and forgiveness. Yet, part of our struggle is that we hide our sin and struggles, which keeps us in darkness and Held Hostage. When we choose not to come into light and repent and change, we are bringing condemnation upon our own heads because of our choices. In other words, we are casting judgement upon ourselves for not coming into the light. So, when we are Held Hostage, the first thing to ask is, 'have I come into the Light of Jesus the Son?' The Son very clearly wants to save us and bring us into a greater future that is so abundantly beyond what we could even think or imagine, but He does not force us into the Light.

Jesus makes it very clear about the full reason of why He came, who He is, and what happens to the man who chooses to ignore Him. I also love how it explains that because of light, darkness must flee. So, our sins that we do in secret are not actually a secret, and they will be exposed, because we need them to be so if we want to be with Jesus. Jesus is so very loving, so much so that He allows His very nature to bring us to repentance, so that we can live in light and not darkness.

Read John 5:26-30. (Write down what these verses say about the Son)

(Write down what the Son has authority over)

In John 5, we see that everlasting life and our time spent in Heaven is based upon believing the Word of the Son and believing in the Father, through whom we receive full forgiveness and pardon. Does the Son want people to suffer and go to Hell? I love what John 5:30 (NKJV) says, "³⁰ I can of Myself do nothing. As I hear, I judge; and My judgment is righteous, because I do not seek My own will but the will of the Father who sent Me." So, does the Father want us to go to Hell? No, the Father longs for us to be with Him, which is why He sent His Son in our place to die our death. But He will not force us to the Light.

~Prayer~

Heavenly Father, I come before You and I ask that today You would reveal to us our flawed hearts. Search us, Father, and reveal to us if we have come into the Light or if we are still in darkness. I pray against every distraction and tormenting voice that would try to keep us from hearing You, that they would be bound and broken off us, in the name of Jesus. Father, reveal to us now the things and ways we are still in darkness.

(Write down what God reveals to you)

Father, I do not want to stay in darkness in these areas. I want freedom, I want healing, and I want to be restored. Help me to be bold and come out of the darkness.

(In your one-on-one, with a counselor, pastoral, or spiritual mentor, share what is keeping you in darkness and come into the Light. Write who you told and the date you stepped into the Light)

I thank You, Father, for the healing we are about to receive by coming out of hiding. Through our bold steps coming out from darkness and into Your light, we are choosing a future that is bright, favored, and blessed. These areas will no longer hold us back. In Jesus' name, Amen

Read Today: John 3, John 5

~My prayer for you today~

Heavenly Father, I come before You and I ask that You bring Light onto our path so we won't sin against You. Let Your Light shine upon us and destroy the darkness that wants to hold us in death. We love You, Father.
In Jesus' Name, Amen.

Day 3: How Did Jesus Live?

~Prayer~

Heavenly Father, we come before You, expectantly knowing that You long to speak to us. Remove from us every distraction that would keep us from digging deep today. Break off every arrow that has been shot at us and has left us worn and tired. Pick us up, Father, and restore to us energy and strength. Be our source of comfort and joy. We rely upon You for all that we need. You are more than enough. We trust in You, we seek You, and we long to be close to You. In Jesus' name, Amen

Today we are going to look at how Jesus lived and continues to live. The first thing I find interesting is WHO came to the world. Yesterday we talked about how Jesus came as the Son to bring light, hope, and everlasting life through His sacrifice. Today I want us to get into John 1:1-28.

Read John 1:1-5.

Read John 1:14.

Read John 1:9-13.

Read John 1:15-18.

What do these verses say about Jesus and who He is?

From these verses alone we understand that the WHO that came is Jesus, WHO is also the WORD that was with God from the very beginning. The Word became flesh, which is Jesus, who is the Son, and through Him we have the right to be called CHILDREN OF GOD! I love how verse 13 says we are born of God, not through natural ways, not through human decisions or will, but born of God. Do you understand your value and worth? The Son, the WORD, HE came to give us the right to become children of God the Father. He is our light, He is our Hope, He is our Joy, and He is more than enough. For in Him, we have family, and because we are part of His family we can stand in complete freedom.

So, what did Jesus do before ascending to Heaven? Matthew 4:23-24 (AMP) says, "[23] And He went throughout all Galilee, teaching in their synagogues and preaching the good news (gospel) of the kingdom, and healing every kind of disease and every kind of sickness among the people [demonstrating and revealing that He was indeed the promised Messiah]. [24] So the news about Him spread throughout all Syria; and they brought to Him all who were sick, those suffering with various diseases and pains, those under the power of demons, and epileptics, paralytics; and He healed them."

(Circle all words that describe what Jesus did here on earth.)

Traveled

Taught

Proclaimed the Kingdom of God

Healed every disease and sickness

Brought freedom to those Held Hostage

Healed those with mental problems

Healed those with physical problems

Healed those with spiritual problems

If you circled every single one, then you understand He came to break us out of darkness and bring us into the Light. So, we see that Jesus traveled everywhere that God told Him to go. He taught the ways we should live. He wanted us to live out the Kingdom of God here in this world. He brought freedom. He healed many. We also see in Matthew 14 that Jesus also cared about the health of those who followed and listened to Him. There are couple times in the New Testament where it is mentioned that Jesus fed a multitude. We also see that in Matthew 14:23 (AMP) says, "[23] After He had dismissed the crowds, He went up on the mountain by Himself to pray. When it was evening, He was there alone."

This means that Jesus spent time alone with the Father in prayer. He took time to pull Himself away from all the distractions and people around Him, to be alone and spend it with the Father. If Jesus modeled this and found it important for His own life, how much so should we be active in this area of pulling away to be alone with the Father?

Read Mark 11:15-18.

What did Jesus do at the Temple?

Write verse 17.

Jesus also rebuked and brought correction to those who were not following the laws of the Father. In fact, we see throughout the New Testament that He brought correction in order to bring realignment to those who heard and obeyed. In Matthew 23, Jesus specifically talks about warning against being a hypocrite and then goes on to verbally condemn the religious leaders of His time.

(**Matthew 23:** Write down the ways that the religious leaders were doing wrong, and then write down all the ways Jesus gave them chances to change.)

Read Today: Matthew 1:1-18, Matthew 23

~My prayer for you today~

Heavenly Father, I come before You and I ask that You reveal to the child reading this how You long for them to be Your hands and feet to the world. You long for them to go where You send them, to teach Your ways, and proclaim the Kingdom of God through action and word, to heal all those who are sick in Your name, to spend alone time with the Father, and to bring correction and truth to those who are in darkness. In Jesus' name, Amen.

Day 4: The Heart of Jesus

~Prayer~

Heavenly Father, we come before You today, amazed at who You are. You are love, You are good, and Your plans go beyond anything we can imagine. So many of us have lost our purpose, our focus, and our desires. Although alive we feel so dead inside. Father, we long to come alive, to have a purpose, and more importantly to understand our identity in You. Today help us see how we can implement a relationship with Jesus today. In Jesus' name, Amen.

To think about how Jesus lived on this earth absolutely melts my heart. He was always giving of Himself to help those in need, to heal those who needed healing, to set free the captive from darkness, and He was all about relationships.

Jesus truly breaks the mold of culture, religious, and even status. During a feast, known as the Passover, we find this lifestyle reflected in what Jesus does. During this time of remembering what God had done in the past, Jesus was fully aware that His time in this world was coming to a close. I can only imagine the sense of pain He felt in His heart when thinking about those whom he loved, because He knew that soon He would love them with His very breath. Sitting at this table with Him was a disciple who had allowed satan room to move in his life and heart, Judas Iscariot. Not only was Jesus feeling the emotions of grief over having to leave His beloved family, but He was also feeling betrayal. Yet, when the meal had finished Jesus does not act out in grief or anger, but instead, He removed His clothes, grabbed a towel and bucket of water, and began to wash the feet of His beloved family. I can only imagine the feelings and emotions that the disciples experienced as the Messiah so very lovingly washed their feet; even the one who would betray Him. (John 13)

In John 13:6-8 (NKJV) says, "[6] Then He came to Simon Peter. And Peter said to Him, "Lord, are You washing my feet?" [7] Jesus answered and said to him, "What I am doing you do not understand now, but you will know after this." [8] Peter said to Him, "You shall never wash my feet!" Jesus answered him, "If I do not wash you, you have no part with Me."

What a beautiful example of the heart of Jesus. The King of Kings, Lord of Lords, the Word that became flesh, God in human form; and instead of ruling with brute strength and authority, we see Him serving and giving of Himself to honor those under Him. He longed for our identities to be established in God the Father. He wanted us to understand our value and worth to Him.

Read John 12:3-8.

What did Mary do?

What was Judas' response?

Write out verses 7 and 8.

I love this image before us. Mary worshiped at Jesus' feet and in raw adoration anointed His feet and wiped them with her hair. Mary clearly understood her identity and longed to honor Jesus, even when it appeared to go against culture and financial gain. She poured out her worship in a deep intimate way, and her love is written for all to read about. Then in chapter 13 we read how Jesus then washed His beloved disciples' feet. Jesus knew what many of them were going to face for believing in Him. Many of them would die horrible deaths, martyred for their relationship with Jesus. They counted the cost and knew that no matter what they would face, they would never give up their relationship with Jesus. They understood their identity, they understood their purpose and calling, and refused to be separated from Jesus.

~Prayer~

Heavenly Father, forgive us for choosing things or people instead of You. Forgive us for the times we turned away from You and chose our own path and desires. We forgot our identities, we forgot our purpose and calling, and we forgot our relationship with You.

(Write down the times you turned from God to your own gain, relationships, and sin)

(Write your own prayer of repentance to God and let Him know you will put your relationship with Him first.)

Read Today: John 12 and 13

~My prayer for you today~

Father, I ask that You help each child here to choose You over their own desires, sin, and relationships, and that they would put You first again and walk in relationship with You. I pray that right now You would go to them, comfort them, and lovingly draw them close, revealing Your heart for them.

In Jesus' Name, Amen.

Day 5: Jesus the Lover

~Prayer~

Heavenly Father,

I come against the spirit of fear in the name of Jesus. The fear that when people say, 'You are coming soon' and we then begin to lose our purpose, because the spirit of giving up and the mindset that says, 'why continue if You are coming back right now,' tries to latch onto us and destroy our callings. You will be coming back, but You still expect us to fulfill Your plan for our lives. Nothing has changed. Your promises will still come to pass, Your calling upon our lives will still take place, and there is purpose in what we are doing here. So, I come against the lie of the enemy that says to just give up, in Jesus' name. I pray that we would never let satan take away our calling and purpose and identity. In Jesus' name, Amen

Right now, I feel like crying. I have such a strong sense of Jesus' love surrounding me as I am writing this, and it's flooding over me in waves. Today we are going to be talking about Jesus as our lover. Jesus came so that we would have life—eternal life—with Him, and that through His sacrifice and resurrection we would be able to have fellowship with the Father. Jesus is coming back for a pure Bride, one without spot or blemish.

(Read Ephesians 5:25-32 and write down what Paul says about Jesus loving the church.)

Too many times I forget that Jesus truly loves us, even more than a husband loves his wife. His love is beyond our imaginations, and yet how many times do I tell Him that He doesn't through my words and actions? My heart feels grieved for how even His very own church has forgotten it, and I pray that His Bride will never forget and repent and turn if they do.

Read Matthew 24:29-31.

Matthew 25:31-33 (AMP) says, "[31] "But when the Son of man comes in His glory and majesty and all the angels with Him, then He will sit on the throne of His glory. [32] All the nations will be gathered before Him [for judgment]; and He will separate them from one another, as a shepherd separates his sheep from the goats; [33] and He will put the sheep on His right [the place of honor], and the goats on His left [the place of rejection]."

Read what Matthew 25:34-36 says about what God says to the sheep.

John 14:1-4 (NKJV) says, "[1] "Let not your heart be troubled; you believe in God, believe also in Me. [2] In My Father's house are many mansions; if it were not so, I would have told you. I go to prepare a place for you. [3] And if I go and prepare a place for you, I will come again and receive you to Myself; that where I am, there you may be also. [4] And where I go you know, and the way you know."

Write John 14:6.

The Bible makes it very clear that Jesus will be returning for us. He clearly describes the signs that we will see in order for us to know the times. He warns of the hard times that we will endure before He returns. And I can see very clearly how He longs for us to be with Him in Heaven. We can see that He has gone on before us to prepare a place for us. This shows me that Jesus longs for me to belong to Him and be with Him. Did anyone notice the warning? If we are longing to be with Him, then we need to be His. I do not want to be rejected by Him and sent to eternal judgment.

Hebrews 7:23-25 (AMP) says, "[23] The [former successive line of] priests, on the one hand, existed in greater numbers because they were each prevented by death from continuing [perpetually in office]; [24] but, on the other hand, Jesus holds His priesthood permanently and without change, because He lives on forever. [25] Therefore He is able also to save forever (completely, perfectly, for eternity) those who come to God through Him, since He always lives to intercede and intervene on their behalf [with God]."

So, while Jesus is also preparing a place for us, He is also interceding and intervening on our behalf before the Father. That means when accusations come against us, He defends us. When satan lies about us or wants to take away our value and purpose, Jesus is standing in the gap proclaiming His truth over us. The problem is that we forget that, and we live like we are weak. We have forgotten how-to live-in power and in authority. As we continue to go through each week of this book the goal at the end is that Your relationship with God will be completely restored, you will be healed and whole, and you will be walking in authority and power.

Read Revelations 19:6-8.

Write verses 7 and 8.

So, until His return, we are to adorn ourselves and prepare ourselves. This is done by living in righteousness and holiness in obedience to the Word and following the leading of the Holy Spirit. It is living in the light and not in darkness. If you have not read the Bible concerning how we are to live, start with the Ten Commandments, and then begin to soak in the New Testament because it gives detail for how we should live each day and what our heart's responses should be.

Read Today: Matthew 24 and 25, Ephesians 5, Hebrews 7, Revelations 19

~My prayer for you today~

Father, I am so excited to prepare myself as a bride. I pray that Your child who is reading this today would also be excited about the processes and journeys You are taking them on to become a pure Bride. I ask that You help them not to fight against it, and that they would surrender to what You are doing in their lives. Open their eyes and ears to understand Your ways and thoughts.

In Jesus' Name, Amen

Day 6: My Story and Testimonies

When I think about Jesus, I see someone who was willing to risk it all for me. I see His love for the Trinity, and His love for me that made Him willing to give up His very life for me. He daily chose to live outside the box that His family, His culture, and His religious leaders put around Him. He continually defied the "rules" and used His everyday life to break the mold.

We are called to be like Jesus. To love so radically that our very lives mean nothing, and we would gladly lay them down for the Father. Jesus is calling us to go deeper. He is telling us to step out of the box, to not be defined by the labels given from family, culture, or religious leaders. He is calling us into a life of bringing the Kingdom of God into the world.

I grew up in a Christian family. My dad is a pastor, and my parents were also missionaries to Kenya. I grew up knowing my need of a savior and I was constantly in fear that I would go to Hell. I had asked Jesus many times to come into my heart, but that fear of "is this enough?" Held me Hostage.

I remember so clearly the day when all that changed. I was thirteen and we went to a youth retreat as a family in Kansas City. Before every service, they would play techno music, and now every time I hear techno it takes me back to that youth retreat. It was during one service when something just clicked. My parents' relationship with God was not mine; instead, I chose a personal relationship with God that belonged to me.

Everything changed that day. God was very real to me. Not long after, God gave me a dream. My sister and I had shared a room up until I was about twelve years old. In the dream we were older but still sharing the same room. I woke up to a noise and looked over to the corner of the room, where a white figure began to glow. The figure was not solid but appeared like fog or clouds. Out from this cloud a hand appeared and beckoned me to come. I reached over to wake up my sister, but the hand motioned for me to stop and again beckoned for me to come. I reached out and grabbed the hand. The next second I was flying into the sky and as I looked around, my family and a great multitude were ascending to Heaven. He never let go of my hand. When I woke up, I knew Jesus had met with me. I no longer feared going to Hell, because I knew Jesus was telling me I would be going to Heaven with Him.

Many of us get to the part in the Bible where He gives the great commission and then leaves to prepare a place for us. We have forgotten that He will be returning for a pure Bride. We live our days for ourselves instead of stepping out of the box and bringing more into the Kingdom. We have forgotten our mission and our callings. We watch those around us become deceived by the culture, people who are dying and going to Hell. We lost our voices and our passion to save and heal. We chose what is comfortable and easy. This is not what the Kingdom of God looks like. This is not the pure Bride that He is returning for.

Jesus is calling out to us to follow His example; to step out of the box, out of deception, and out of what is contrary to the Word (Bible) of God. He longs for us to live in power, in authority, and in authentic love of Him, to remember our callings and mission, and to save and heal the lost and broken.

He will return when the Gospel has been shared, AND when the Kingdom of God has been revealed in every country, tribe, and nation and every 'mountain'.

Testimonies:

*God speaks to me in many ways…yesterday my husband and I were on the other side of town in which we have been living in, where I was born and grew up at. We were in a familiar area near the high school I had gone to, and I had a flashback (a picture of where I had been forty-three years ago). I was twenty-four years of age and a mess. I had a real problem with alcohol and drugs and was living from one high to another and was searching for meaning in my life.

I cried out to God, "Lord, if I don't change something, I will not make it to the age of thirty." He drew me at that moment on a Saturday morning into my old high school. As I was looking over the pictures, of all the previous graduates, I found my picture in the graduates of 1973. A girl approached me and called me by name and said, "What are you doing here?" I didn't recognize her, but she invited me into the "charismatic prayer meeting" that they were having. Our Bishop at that time was born again and Spirit-filled and as I sang songs, I sensed a joy and an atmosphere that filled me with hope.

It was so different from the soulless religious ritual I had been accustomed too. Thus, my journey with Him began. ~Valerie W.

*I found Jesus by talking with my boss and co-worker about Him. I didn't know what to do with my life, so I followed a friend to beauty school. Then I worked five years at one salon, and then one of my customers left and went to another shop.

I followed her there and that is what led me to my friends. I ended up going to a Lowell Lundstrom Crusade and asked Jesus into my heart. God puts us in places where we find Him! ~Nancy C.

*I got saved when I submitted my will and life to Jesus Christ around the age of ten. One night I realized that I would spend eternity separated from God because of the way I lived. However, I also realized that God sent Jesus to die on the cross in my place in order to remove that penalty of hell that my rebellion against Him had earned and deserved. In a moment of honesty with God, I told Him that I did not want to go to hell, and I found myself asking Him to forgive me for all my sin (the selfish attitudes and mean things that I did to others). Finally, I told Him that if He would help me, I would obey whatever He told me to do in my life. ~Steve D.

*I came to the Lord through a youth meeting and the song was saying, 'your life is just like a flower and one day it will fade away.' I was so overwhelmed, I saw how my life was, and I stood up and gave my life to Jesus. I began witnessing on the streets; I remember one time talking to ten guys, another time was in a bus full of people, and I stood up and I sang, 'this could be your last day to receive Jesus.' One of my worst experiences in doing spiritual warfare, though, was rebuking a guy who was seducing me. I said, 'I rebuke you in Jesus' name' and the guy was so puzzled. Thank God, I'm standing by His grace. The Word convicts me of my sins, and I choose not to be overwhelmed. One of my best teachings is moving in the opposite Spirit. I learned that in the DTS and I model that. It's not easy, but by the grace of God I manage. Be angry but don't sin... ~Habona K.

Day 7: Self-Reflection

~Prayer~

Heavenly Father, we take time to thank You for who You are. Thank You for revealing Truth to us and helping us understand that we do not have to fear the process or what You are doing. Instead, we can have great joy knowing that we are becoming a pure and radiant bride. Help us not to give up, but to continue to push forward in this process and take back the direction of where our future is heading. In Jesus' name, Amen.

Today I will be asking hard questions and I want you to write down your answers truthfully and honestly.

Do my views of God the Son (Jesus) fall into line with the Bible?

What are the areas in my mind that the term Jesus the Son has been negative and not based in Truth?

Father, reveal to me the reason behind my thinking, and give me Your perspective on those areas in my life.

What situations have I been in that I have judged Jesus in the way He handled it and it has caused bitterness, resentment, and distrust towards Him?

What are your views about Jesus that you found to be contrary to the Word?

In what ways do you live like Jesus?

In what areas do you need to begin to walk like Jesus?

How are you being prepared to be the Bride?

How has God renewed your mind regarding Jesus the Son?

Week 3: God the Holy Spirit

"[15] "If you love me, keep my commands. [16] And I will ask the Father, and he will give you another advocate to help you and be with you forever— [17] the Spirit of truth. The world cannot accept him, because it neither sees him nor knows him. But you know him, for he lives with you and will be in you."

(John 14:15-17 NIV)

Day 1: Holy Spirit

What comes to mind when you hear God the Holy Spirit?

So many churches do not talk about the Holy Spirit, His function, and His power. They leave Him out of the Sunday services and then turn around and don't understand why their members are struggling and living in bondage and brokenness. They eliminate the gift of tongues, which is our spirit communicating with the Holy Spirit. In fact, I have been to many churches and talked to many individuals who have no understanding of the Holy Spirit and the baptism of the Holy Spirit.

A study done by Arizona Christian University on August 31, 2021; reveals the darkness the church has found itself in. In this study it says that among those who identify as a Christian, 58% believe the Holy Spirit is not real, but just a symbol. 176 million individuals were a part of this study for those who self-identify as a Christian. In fact, when you look at the numbers for all five categories of faith in each category, either more than half or almost half believe that the Holy Spirit is not God, not living, and just a symbol.[4]

My brain has a very hard time understanding this and being able to sympathize with them. I grew up knowing who the Holy Spirit is, how He operates, and the importance of communicating with Him. So, I have a hard time understanding people who do not believe in the Trinity and so forth, because I can sense they are not experiencing freedom in their life. Yet many choose not to listen or to understand what is true.

I am tired of seeing the church broken, battered, and walking in defeat. I am tired of seeing people living under darkness instead of finding true freedom. The truth is, though, that we need the Holy Spirit in us to have freedom and direction. We desperately need Him to work in our lives and keep our spirit in line with Him.

Read John 14:15-17.
If we love God, what should we do?

What is the Father's response?

Write verse 17.

John 14:26-27 (RSV) says, "²⁶ But the Counselor, the Holy Spirit, whom the Father will send in my name, he will teach you all things, and bring to your remembrance all that I have said to you. ²⁷ Peace

---

4 Dr. George Barna, "Release #6: What Does It Mean When People Say They Are "Christian"?" Arizona Christian University, 2021, https://www.arizonachristian.edu/wp-content/uploads/2021/08/CRC_AWVI2021_Release06_Digital_01_20210831.pdf

I leave with you; my peace I give to you; not as the world gives do I give to you. Let not your hearts be troubled, neither let them be afraid."

I want you to take a little time and think about verse 26. God the Father, through His son Jesus, is now declaring who the Holy Spirit is and how very real He is. How beautiful and intimate is our relationship with Jesus, the Father, and the Holy Spirit? The fact that Jesus called his disciples out on their lack of joy over this beautiful gift that is the Holy Spirit should bring conviction upon those of us who claim the Holy Spirit is not real. The Holy Spirit, the Spirit of Truth, our advocate, was sent by the Father. He was sent to us, and yet how many churches push Him away? He was sent to us, but because many cannot comprehend Him, they ignore Him. This week, we are going to focus on who the Holy Spirit is, what He does, and what the baptism of the Holy Spirit is.

Read Today: Luke 14

~Prayer~

Heavenly Father,

We come to You and worship You. We want to sit at Your feet, to fellowship with You, and to be known by You. We desire true intimacy with You and not just a religious experience. This week, help us to understand the Holy Spirit. Help us to connect with the Holy Spirit like never before. I pray that we would experience a greater freedom and healing like never before.

In Jesus' name, Amen

Day 2: God the Holy Spirit

~Prayer~

Heavenly Father, we come before You. We ask that You speak to us very clearly today, that we would understand Your truth and who You are. Take away any doubts, any beliefs, and any ideas that would hinder us from entering into this beautiful relationship with You. We need You, Father. In Jesus' Name, Amen

Today we are going to focus on who God the Holy Spirit is and what the Holy Spirit does.

We get a beautiful glimpse of the Holy Spirit in John 1:31-34 (NLT) says, "[31] I did not recognize him as the Messiah, but I have been baptizing with water so that he might be revealed to Israel." [32] Then John testified, "I saw the Holy Spirit descending like a dove from heaven and resting upon him. [33] I didn't know he was the one, but when God sent me to baptize with water, he told me, 'The one on whom you see the Spirit descend and rest is the one who will baptize with the Holy Spirit.' [34] I saw this happen to Jesus, so I testify that he is the Chosen One of God."

John 1:32 (RSV) says, "[32] And John bore witness, "I saw the Spirit descend as a dove from heaven, and it remained on him."

What a beautiful image of the Holy Spirit coming down in the symbol of the dove and resting upon Jesus. Did you catch where it says the Holy Spirit remained on Him? That means that for the rest of Jesus' ministry here on earth before He ascended into Heaven, the Holy Spirit remained with Him, because I do not see a place in the New Testament where it says the Holy Spirit was removed. What an incredible relationship the Three have as One. It really makes Jesus' life come alive even more. Why? Because He communed not just with the Father here on earth, but also with the Holy Spirit. What a beautiful picture that gives us, that the Trinity was visible and revealed here on earth before the believers experienced it for themselves.

(**Read John 16:1-15** and write down what Jesus said the Holy Spirit would do when He came)

(From **John 16:1-15** also write down what the relationship is between Jesus and the Holy Spirit)

I love reading about the Holy Spirit and His relationship with me. Once I begin to understand who He is, and how He works in my life; I then know how to live my life with Him. The very fact that the Holy Spirit brings glory to Jesus, because of His very nature and His communication with us; gives us an even deeper revelation of the relationship between Jesus and the Holy Spirit. In the beginning of the passage, we read about how Jesus is warning us of what we will face following Him. He does not sugarcoat it or cause us to blindly follow; instead, He tells us how it is and then says, "Pick up your cross and follow Me." Jesus knew that as hard as the path will be, we have the Holy Spirit who will be with us every step. Therefore, He had full confidence in us, because of Him who is in us.

Read Today: John 16, John 1

~My prayer for you today~

Heavenly Father, I come before You and ask that You would come upon Your child who is reading this. I pray that they would grasp and understand You like they never have before. Open their eyes and ears into the 'Spiritual Realm'. I pray that a deep connection would take place with You this week.

In Jesus' Name, Amen.

Day 3: Never Alone

~Prayer~

Heavenly Father,

We ask that today You would reveal Your details in our lives. The Holy Spirit is actively communicating with us, and I pray that we would understand what He is speaking to us. Reveal Your heart for us today. In Jesus' Name, Amen

Before we begin, I want you to **read Romans 8:1-17**. Read it carefully so you can answer the questions below.

What happens when you live according to the flesh?

What happens when you live according to the Spirit?

What does the Holy Spirit give us?

When we ask Jesus to be Lord and Savior of our lives and acknowledge our sin and repent and turn from sin, we receive the Spirit of God. When the Holy Spirit then comes in, it says the Holy Spirit brings our adoption to sonship with God the Father. So how do we know we will go to Heaven? Because the Holy Spirit testifies with our spirit that we belong to God as His child. I love what Romans 8:17 (NIV) says, "[17] Now if we are children, then we are heirs—heirs of God and co-heirs with Christ, if indeed we share in his sufferings in order that we may also share in his glory." The Holy Spirit causes the Fatherhood of God to become a reality, legal, and binding. What a beautiful image that is. Not only are we adopted into His family, but with that we have full rights to use His authority, as His child.

In Luke 11, Jesus was asked an important question: how should we pray and talk to God? We can find Jesus' response in Luke 11:2-8 but I find verses 9-13 especially important.

Read Luke 11:9-13.

(Write down verse 9 and 10)

(Write down verse 13)

I find the connection between prayer and the Holy Spirit very interesting. Jesus goes straight into how to pray, then moves into how good the Father is, how we should ask, knock, and seek, and then finishes with how our Father desires to give the Holy Spirit to us. Our Father is a good, good Father. In verse 13 we clearly see that the Father desires for us to have the Holy Spirit. I can just see (the joy and delight the Father receives) when a child of God asks for the Holy Spirit. And He gladly and willingly gives the Holy Spirit to us. In fact, as we read yesterday, He sends the Holy Spirit to us. We are supposed to live our days with the Holy Spirit. He is to be with us, and He longs to be with us. Why? Because that is why He is sent to us. He is sent to spend the rest of our lives on earth with us, and because of that, we are truly NEVER ALONE!

Read Today: Romans 8, Luke 11

~My prayer for you today~
Heavenly Father, I come before You. I am so blessed that through every trial, through every experience of abuse and trauma that Your child has endured, You were always with them. They have never been alone. Your Holy Spirit was with them, and You were leading them and reminding them of You. Thank You, Father, for never giving up on them. For calling them into a deeper relationship with You.
In Jesus' name, Amen.

Day 4: What Is the Baptism of The Holy Spirit

~Prayer~

Heavenly Father,

We come to you today and we declare that You are holy. There is no one like You. You formed us in our mother's womb, and You have called us into a glorious purpose and ministry. We are to be about Your Kingdom. However, Father, I acknowledge that the church has missed it. We have been walking with a limp and barely making it through our days. Most days, if we are honest, the church probably barely even thinks about You. We want to be different. We want You every single minute of our day. We long for a deep relationship with You, and we desire You above everything else. Today, reveal to us where we are lacking and walking powerless and without authority. Reveal to us where we have limited the Holy Spirit. In Jesus' Name, Amen

Today we are going to talk about the baptism of the Holy Spirit. As we found out yesterday, when we ask Jesus into our heart to be Lord and Savior, acknowledge our sin and need of forgiveness, and repent and turn from our ways, the Bible says that the Holy Spirit then comes and dwells within us. He is in us, and He is working in us. There is another factor in this relationship that many do not go further with. Churches exclude it, and say, 'it's not for now,' and so on. Yet the Bible makes it clear that there is a baptism of the Holy Spirit that is given, and with this is a power and authority given from the Holy Spirit that allows us to have great victory. With this baptism, the gift of tongues is usually also given. We will get into that more in week 6.

In Acts 2:1-4 (NKJV) says, "[1] When the Day of Pentecost had fully come, they were all with one accord in one place. [2] And suddenly there came a sound from heaven, as of a rushing mighty wind, and it filled the whole house where they were sitting. [3] Then there appeared to them divided tongues, as of fire, and one sat upon each of them. [4] And they were all filled with the Holy Spirit and began to speak with other tongues, as the Spirit gave them utterance."

(Circle all that shows what took place that day.)

There was unity

Sounds from heaven

It filled the place they were at

Tongues of fire rested upon them

They were filled with the Holy Spirit

They were given other Tongues

Read Acts 2:17-21.

What will God do in verse 1?

After God pours out His Spirit, what will we do?

What are signs of the Lord's return?

Write verse 21.

For every Christian these verses should bring clear reality to their belief system. If you are going to proclaim yourself a Christian and yet you deny the Holy Spirit is God and deny His power, do you really know the Father and the Son? I do not need to argue my case, and honestly Christians have the choice to believe or not. But when I read the Bible, it is true, and it is the WORD that became Flesh who is JESUS!!! So, I refuse to be swayed by man who is limited in knowledge, power, and understanding. I refuse to come under their authority and lies, and instead I cling to what the WORD says. Plain and simple, no other option.

So that brings us to an important question.

Is the Holy Spirit living in you? _____

Have you been baptized and filled with the power of the Holy Spirit? _____

Are you tired of living life without Him and ready to experience life in His Authority and Power?

_____

(During worship with your group or one-on-one [with the individual you pray and receive counsel from], pray for the baptizing of the Holy Spirit, for Him to come and fill you, and that the gift of tongues would be given.)

(Write the date you were baptized and the date you received your tongues)

_____

Read Today: Acts 2

~My prayer for you today~

Heavenly Father, I come before You and I pray over Your child who is reading this. I pray that they would recognize God the Holy Spirit. I pray that they would be baptized and filled with the Holy Spirit, that You would come upon them like a flood, and that from this day forward they would walk in Your authority and power like never before.

In Jesus' Name, Amen

Day 5: How Does the Holy Spirit and My Spirit Connect?

~Prayer~

Heavenly Father,

We come before You and we are so excited for what You are doing in our lives. You have a plan and a purpose for what we are doing, and learning, and every detail matters to you. We are so thankful for the healing and the truth that is being revealed to us. Remove every lie and demonic spirit that is trying to persuade us from Truth and the WORD, in Jesus' name. We proclaim victory over our minds, victory over our thoughts, victory over our memories, and we proclaim TRUTH be revealed to us today. In Jesus' Name, Amen.

Today, before we get into how the Holy Spirit and our spirit connect, I think it is first important to see a little bit more about what the Bible says about the Holy Spirit. Especially because as we are filled with the Holy Spirit and getting closer to a great movement of God, we need to be aware of what we are getting involved in.

The Bible says there is one unpardonable sin, and Mark 3:28-29 (AMP) says, "[28] "I assure you and most solemnly say to you, all sins will be forgiven the sons of men, and all the abusive and blasphemous things they say; [29] but whoever blasphemes against the Holy Spirit and His power [by attributing the miracles done by Me to Satan] never has forgiveness, but is guilty of an everlasting sin [a sin which is unforgivable in this present age as well as in the age to come]"—"

In this chapter, the religious leaders were saying that Jesus was sent by satan and filled with satan and not the Holy Spirit. Jesus clearly lets them know that, by their hardening of hearts, their vile words against the Holy Spirit, and their disrespect towards the Holy Spirit, they have committed an unpardonable sin. Remember we learned that the Holy Spirit had come during Jesus' water baptism and rested upon Him.

As we get closer to a movement of the Holy Spirit that the earth has never seen before, following yesterday's reading of Acts 2:17-21, it is important to also talk about our response to Him. In Acts 5 we are going to read an account of what not to do.

Read Acts 5:1-11.

Why did they die? (Answer is found in verse 9.)

Write verse 11.

WOW! The power of our words and heart is revealed here. Ananias and Sapphira lied to the Holy Spirit, and because of their heart issue, they dropped dead. God is calling us to walk in a new level of purity with Him. We must be under His anointing and power. If we are lying to the Holy Spirit and then trying to work in the Holy Spirit, we are condemning ourselves. Our hearts matter, our thoughts matter, and we are without excuse. It is time that we begin to live lives that are holy and pleasing to the Father.

The Holy Spirit is in us, and the way He communicates to us is both unique and beautiful to each child. He uses the Bible because that is the WORD. He speaks through our surroundings and in warnings, through His still small voice, whether we hear with our ears or in our spirit. He also reveals things through nature and the people around us, through dreams, visions, and prophesy.

The Holy Spirit and our spirit have a beautiful secret conversation that satan cannot ever understand, and that is through the Holy Spirit and our spirit communicating through tongues. It's a beautiful conversation between us and the Holy Spirit, full of intimacy and vulnerability, and it is powerful. It is through these conversations that the Holy Spirit reveals things to our spirit, which is how when a situation happens and we know right away what God is saying, it is because the Holy Spirit told our spirit. Our spirits have more understanding and awareness of what is going on than our earthly minds do, because our spirits have communion and relationship with the Holy Spirit. Many times, when I run out of words or what is taking place in my heart is so unbearable that words are gone, I begin to pray in tongues and there is a great release that occurs as my spirit communicates with the Holy Spirit. Great breakthrough takes place, and peace floods through me. We will discuss more on tongues and its importance in week 6.

Mark 13:9-11 (AMP) says, "[9] "But be on your guard; they will turn you over to courts, and you will be beaten in synagogues, and you will stand [as accused] before governors and kings for My sake, as a testimony to them. [10] The gospel [that is, the good news regarding the way of salvation] must first be preached to all the [Gentile] nations. [11] When they take you and turn you over [to the court], do not worry beforehand about what to say, but say whatever is given to you [by God] in that hour; for it is not you who speak, but it is the Holy Spirit [who will speak through you]."

(Write down who gives us words in hard and good times.)

Read Today: Mark 3, Acts 5, Mark 13

~My prayer for you today~

Heavenly Father, I come before You and I pray over Your child who is reading this. I come against any fear that would keep them trapped or stuck where they are at. I proclaim freedom and breakthrough over them in the name of Jesus. I come against the spirit of the flesh that would want to place their own wants and desires before truth and righteousness. I plead the blood of Jesus over them, their minds, hearts, and spirits. Make Yourself known to them, Father.

In Jesus' Name, Amen.

Day 6: My Story and Testimonies

The Holy Spirit is a key to us living in full victory and authority, and stepping when we are supposed to step. The Holy Spirit leads us through rough times, through good times, and through painful times, and He is constantly communicating to us.

So many churches have taught that the Holy Spirit is not God. They do not believe in the Trinity and therefore they try to remove His authority. So many have become deceived and stripped of their purpose and calling.

The Trinity, God in one, is God the Father who has been and always will be God the Son, Jesus Christ, who is the Word that became Flesh, and the Holy Spirit, who is our comforter, guide, and the power of God. All three are God, working in Three ways. To me, I look at it as the sun who represents God the Father. The light which represents God the Son, Jesus, and the warmth which represents the Holy Spirit. All three are the sun, just as God is all three in One.

The way the Holy Spirit works in our lives is so very powerful, unique, and beautiful. It is different for each individual and yet the same.

When I was thirteen, I became a born-again believer. It completely changed my life. As I mentioned in week 2, I had a dream of Jesus taking me home, which freed me from fear. A few months after that, we were at one of our church events, where churches from around Sioux Falls would come together on one Sunday night a month to worship and fellowship together. They were called Unity Nights. At this one, we were finished with the sermon and were going to have a time of praying and worship. I was standing by myself, hands raised, when the baptizing of the Holy Spirit took place. (I still remember it so vividly, twenty-two years later.) A strong and heavy warmth went from my fingertips to my toes. There was a great peace and this sense of being known. I did not have to say a word, because I was understood by the Holy Spirit.

That day I began to walk in a greater power and authority. The Holy Spirit was with me and had done a great work in me. The important thing is that He has always been with me, even when I left Him. That night I also received the gift of tongues, as previously mentioned, we will get into that later.

When we are baptized in the Spirit, we carry a new mantle of authority and power that comes straight from the Holy Spirit. Now understand people who have been told the Holy Spirit isn't God and whose authority the church tries to downplay. And the church wonders why there are so many wounded, hurt, and weak believers out there. It's because they have tried to limit the Holy Spirit and put Him in a box. It's time we realize who the Holy Spirit is and take Him out of the religious box.

One of the amazing ways I saw the Holy Spirit work in my life was the night I planned my suicide. As I mentioned in my book Held Hostage, I had cheated on my boyfriend. In week 11, I will go more into how I ended up in that situation, but I want to share more of that particular night today.

It was two weeks after my twenty-first birthday. I had broken up with both boys and I was in deep guilt, shame, and pain. I could not handle it anymore, so I told my parents I needed some time away and I booked two nights at a hotel. The first night was for planning my suicide, and the second night was to follow through with it. I brought three things with me. My boombox (CD player) and dark CD's, my Bible, and my journal. I honestly do not even know why other than I thought I should write down what happened that night so my family would understand why I did what I did.

I turned on the dark rock/scream music and immediately I heard the demons screaming at me. They told me I had no value, no worth, that I was beyond forgiveness, and I would not be able to handle getting out. Their voices were whispers, hoarse, and scratchy. The torment immediately began, and I clawed at my stomach, leaving long scratch marks, and I cried in so much pain. This lasted for six to eight hours.

During that time, I planned that the following night I would take a knife across my stomach and wrists and bleed out. A slow, agonizing death of what I deserved. And then amidst the demonic torment, I heard the Holy Spirit. He quickened to me this: "Aubrey, I know you cannot open your Bible right now, so I want you to open your journal and read everything I have said you are." So, I went and opened my journal from my time at a mission's school up until then, which was two years of words from God. The Holy Spirit began to fight the demons. He boldly would speak what He said over me. As I read, I heard it being spoken to the demons around me.

After a couple of hours, the atmosphere had changed. The demons were gone, and I understood that taking my life would be the easy way out for me, but would bring even more pain to my family. I knew at that moment that the following months would be so hard, but I would not be alone.

I am so thankful for the Holy Spirit and His relationship with me. I would not be here if it was not for Him.

Testimonies:

*Although I received Christ by trusting Him to bring me into a relationship with God around the age of ten (in the year 2000), I still grew up with a lot of struggles. Going into high school, something inside me hated my younger brother; sometimes I would verbally abuse him and then I'd feel great shame, guilt, and self-hatred because of it. Because I started to memorize Jesus' teaching around that time with some friends from church, I began to realize that my hatred was not from God, it was deserving of hell (see Matthew 5:21-23), and I was filled with shame for desiring to follow God and yet making Him look bad through my hypocritical actions.

Finally, at the invitation of a classmate, one evening I attended a meeting of young people at a different church. Something about the singing, worship, message, and delivery was different from what I had been familiar with growing up, as if God's transforming power was somehow more present and real in the hearts of the worshippers and pastors who gave the message (or at least that the difference in style and atmosphere was important for me personally to encounter in my own spiritual journey). Near the end of the meeting, the pastor said to raise your hand if you hadn't thought about the cross within the past two weeks. Then he said to come up to the front if you raised your hand.

Since I found myself raising my hand, I *had to* go up to the front. In the midst of all that was going on, I was imagining Jesus as He was whipped, spat upon, rejected, abandoned, abused, mocked, judged, and crucified. In a fresh way, I sensed how Jesus took upon Himself all the abuse that I both experienced and did to others. In hindsight, I find this Scripture to describe what I was experiencing spiritually: "For even Christ did not please Himself; but as it is written, 'The reproaches of those who reproached You fell on Me.' --Romans 15:3 NASB1995

When I arrived up front at the stage of the church, people gathered around me in a group to pray for me with their hands on me (something that was new to me then). Someone asked God to "take away his heart of stone and give him a heart of flesh" (see Ezekiel 11:19; 36:26). Afterwards, the pastor encouraged us to speak in tongues for the first time, opening our mouths to speak in an unlearned language. The pastors and people around me did the same, and I sought to try imitating them with a desperate longing to do so and to be filled with God's love and power. As I did so, I also experienced something like a warm wave of love come over me and it removed all the hatred that was inside me, filling me with joy and peace instead.

I experienced what reminds me of this verse: "and hope does not disappoint, because the love of God has been poured out within our hearts through the Holy Spirit who was given to us." (Romans 5:5 NASB1995). Since that time, my speech impediment with "r" sounds went away, I no longer hated my brother, and I would interact more freely with high school peers (no matter their background) without the fear of rejection holding me back the way it did before. ~Steve D.

Day 7: Self-Reflection

~Prayer~

Heavenly Father,

We come before You today and we ask that You search our hearts and make our ways and thoughts known to us, Father. Give us clear understanding for where we are at and areas we need to grow and get freedom in. In Jesus' Name, Amen.

Today I will be asking hard questions and I want you to write down your answers truthfully and honestly.

What are the areas in your mind where the term 'God the Holy Spirit' has been negative and not based in Truth?

Father, reveal to me the reason behind my thinking, and give me Your perspective on those areas in my life.

Do your views of God the Holy Spirit fall into line with the Bible?

Do you believe that the Holy Spirit is God?

Have you been filled or baptized in the Holy Spirit?

How has your mind been renewed in this area?

Week 4: Covenant Relationship

"^{20} In the same way, after the supper he took the cup, saying, "This cup is the new covenant in my blood, which is poured out for you."
(Luke 22:20 NIV)

Day 1: Covenant Relationship

I find it very interesting that many Christians have limited understanding on our relationship with the Father and with the Trinity. In fact, I find it very interesting that the study I mentioned in week 3 also showed that many "Christians" do not hold the Bible as absolute Truth and that there is no true "right" for everyone. They believe that many religions can get you to Heaven, and that Jesus did not really die and rise again, nor will He come again. It really gave me the understanding that the Bride Christ is coming back for is not as large as we believe. So many who proclaim to be Christians fall into many different categories that we read about in Revelations.

1. Church of Ephesus- Forsaken your first love
2. Church of Smyrna- they are persecuted because of Jesus
3. Church of Pergamos- they are compromising
4. Church of Thyatira- they are corrupt
5. Church of Sardis- they are dead
6. Church of Philadelphia- they are faithful
7. Church of Laodiceans- they are lukewarm

Sadly, many who proclaim to be a Christian will find out that they are a goat and not a sheep.

This week we are going to be talking about the Old Testament Covenant with the Father and then the New Testament Covenant that changed with Jesus. After getting to understand what the covenant is about, we will then understand how this covenant relationship should be affecting our everyday life.

The truth is that many Believers do not understand the important role the covenant plays in our relationship with God, and how we apply power and truth to our daily lives. There is so much important information that a week is not going to be enough, honestly. I will also give you a list of individuals that you can look up who have amazing understanding and wisdom in this area, because they have spent years researching and understanding our history. Many believers have removed the Jewish understanding and relevance because we deem it as unimportant to our Gentile faith. But God never once said it didn't apply to us. Instead, He said that new understanding concerning the laws and regulations are given to us. So it's time we get back to our roots and understand how the covenant applies to us and how we can walk it out.

Read Today: Revelations 2, Revelations 3

~Prayer~

Heavenly Father,

We come to You and worship You. We want to sit at Your feet, to fellowship with You, and to be known by You. We desire true intimacy with You, not just a religious experience. This week, help us to understand covenant relationship and what that means for us today. There is a powerful relationship that many of us are not even aware of. Open our eyes and ears to You today.

In Jesus' name, Amen.

Day 2: Old Testament Covenant

~Prayer~

Heavenly Father,

We come before You with a clear understanding that covenant relationships have not been at the front of our relationships, nor taught in church. Most of the time we do not understand what You are doing or what covenant means to You. I pray that as we go through this week, our eyes and ears would be open to the importance of covenant relationship with You. In Jesus' Name, Amen.

Today we are going to understand what the Old Testament Covenant with God is all about.

There are many covenants between God and man found in the Old Testament of the WORD, but there are four that most covenants fall under.

1. Noahic Covenant
2. Abrahamic Covenant
3. Mosaic Covenant
4. Davidic Covenant

Genesis 9:11-13 (NLT) says, "[11] Yes, I am confirming my covenant with you. Never again will floodwaters kill all living creatures; never again will a flood destroy the earth." [12] Then God said, "I am giving you a sign of my covenant with you and with all living creatures, for all generations to come. [13] I have placed my rainbow in the clouds. It is the sign of my covenant with you and with all the earth."

(Write down what the covenant is.)

(Write down the sign that goes with this covenant.)

In verses 14-17, God confirms over and over His covenant. Finally, He says that the rainbow is the sign that He will always recognize this everlasting covenant. The Noahic Covenant is about when God said that He would never flood the whole earth as He did in the times of Noah. The world has taken the rainbow and tried to create a false symbol from it and the church has allowed it. It's time we take back our symbol and stand in the covenant it represents. The rainbow is an everlasting covenant.

The Abrahamic Covenant has many parts to the promises. The first one we see is found in Genesis 12:1-3 (RSV) says, "[1] Now the LORD said to Abram, "Go from your country and your kindred and your father's house to the land that I will show you. [2] And I will make of you a great nation, and I will bless you, and make your name great, so that you will be a blessing. [3] I will bless those who bless you, and him who curses you I will curse; and by you all the families of the earth shall bless themselves."

The Abrahamic Covenant found here has to do with physical land that would be given to Abram and his children. On top of the land, the nation that would come from Abram would be a great nation full of blessing, and nations that would come against them would heap curses on themselves.

Read Genesis 13:16-17.
Write down what the Abrahamic Covenant is.

The Abrahamic Covenant found here speaks more to the land that was promised. It would forever be their land in God's eyes. God then declares the number of offspring that would be within this nation, and then He tells Abram to walk throughout the land as a way of claiming the promises of God. In verse 18, Abram builds an altar to the Lord.

Read Genesis 15:4-5.
What is part of the Abrahamic Covenant found in these verses?

The Abrahamic Covenant found here speaks about a promised son. Abram had been childless and here God prophesied a son would be given, and through this son a multitude of people would come, creating a nation like no other.

Read Genesis 17:4-7.
What is the Abrahamic Covenant given here?

Through these verses we see that the Abrahamic Covenant is about favor, blessing, offspring, and land. There is also the promise that God will be their God forever, a continued relationship that will last for eternity. However, God the Father does not stop there. All these promises come down to one very key promise, and that is that through the line of Abraham the Messiah would come.

The Mosaic Covenant is the covenant given by the Father to Israel after they left Egypt free and no longer slaves. Exodus 19:5-6 (AMP) says, "[5] Now therefore, if you will in fact obey My voice and keep My covenant (agreement), then you shall be My own special possession and treasure from among all peoples [of the world], for all the earth is Mine; [6] and you shall be to Me a kingdom of priests and a holy nation [set apart for My purpose].' These are the words that you shall speak to the Israelites."

The covenant made with Abraham was now given to Israel. This covenant is about being a treasure, set apart, a holy people, and having fellowship with Him. God makes it very clear that His people would receive these blessings and favor IF they kept His covenant. If they stayed obedient to Him, then He would pour down favor upon them, but if they failed to, it would lead to their destruction.

The Davidic Covenant is a beautiful covenant that reveals the final detail to our Old Testament covenants, and that is the Messiah. In 2 Samuel 7:7-11, God tells David that He knows David's heart, his longing to create a house for God, and that God has been with him. He shared how He had blessed him and His nation, and then He shared how He would plant His people and give them a place of safety and peace, and that through David a special kingdom would come, over which Jesus would reign over.

2 Samuel 7:15-16 (NKJV) says, "[15] But My mercy shall not depart from him, as I took it from Saul, whom I removed from before you. [16] And your house and your kingdom shall be established forever before you. Your throne shall be established forever." ' "

Out of the four Old Testament Covenants three of them are unconditional and one is conditional. The Noahic, Abrahamic, and the Davidic Covenants are all unconditional and nothing anyone does changes the decision God made concerning these promises. However, the Mosaic Covenant is conditional, and it requires obedience to God. Failure to obey means that certain promises will be unattainable until there is obedience.

Many of us might look at these and say, 'well what does that have to do with me?' I look forward to day 5 and 6, where we can take a deeper look at how this applies to us.

Read Today: Genesis 12, Genesis 13, Genesis 15, Genesis 17

~My prayer for you today~

Heavenly Father, I come before You and I lift up Your child who is right now understanding that they have been adopted into these covenants with You. This is their heritage and the family we belong to. They have been adopted into Your family, You are their Father, and You desire covenant relationship with them.

In Jesus' Name, Amen.

Day 3: New Testament Covenant

~Prayer~

Heavenly Father,

We come before You and we are excited to see how You changed the Old Testament Covenant into the New Testament Covenant through Your son Jesus. Today we get to see how Your Word and Promises came to pass through the Son. May Your truth fall onto good ground today, Father, and let all the weeds and lies be plucked from our soil. Give us the right mind, and may we walk in Your Spirit today. In Jesus' Name, Amen.

Today we get to dive deep into the New Testament Covenant. Jeremiah 31:33-34 (NKJV) says, "[33] But this is the covenant that I will make with the house of Israel after those days, says the LORD: I will put My law in their minds, and write it on their hearts; and I will be their God, and they shall be My people. [34] No more shall every man teach his neighbor, and every man his brother, saying, 'Know the LORD,' for they all shall know Me, from the least of them to the greatest of them, says the LORD. For I will forgive their iniquity, and their sin I will remember no more."

A new covenant, one that is different from the past, one that will lead the nation of Israel and the people of God into new territory and favor. The law of God would be upon their minds and hearts, and their walk between God and them would forever change. Once this new covenant took place, there would be no going back to the past. It would be impossible to go back because God Himself would tear the veil separating His glory from them, and forever He would have a personal relationship with them without anything separating them.

Read Ezekiel 36:22-30 for full covenant description.
What do these verses show about the New Covenant?

In these verses we see that God is telling Israel beforehand what would take place when He sends Jesus and the Holy Spirit. This prophecy is found in the Old Testament and yet when you read through the account of Jesus and then the early church, we see that this prophecy is fulfilled. Jesus came and when He ascended into heaven, then the Holy Spirit came. I absolutely love seeing that from the very beginning God had a redemptive plan in place, and that He never intended for the world to remain in darkness.

Hebrews 7:22 (NIV) says, "[22] Because of this oath, Jesus has become the guarantor of a better covenant."

Hebrews 9:14-15 (NIV) says, "[14] How much more, then, will the blood of Christ, who through the eternal Spirit offered himself unblemished to God, cleanse our consciences from acts that lead to death, so that we may serve the living God! [15] For this reason Christ is the mediator of a new covenant, that those who are called may receive the promised eternal inheritance—now that he has died as a ransom to set them free from the sins committed under the first covenant."

Up to this point, it has been assumed that you who are reading this, have already become a believer. However, after learning more about what Christians today believe, I felt strongly led by God to bring up some important truths. Because if you do not believe these truths and your faith is not grounded in them, then, even with every week after this, you will not reach full healing and breakthrough.

As we found in week 2, Jesus is the Son of God, who was the Word that was there in the Beginning with God the Father. In Luke 2 you can read about His birth to a virgin named Mary. In Luke 22 we read about how one of Jesus closest friends, a disciple, betrays Him. From there we see how He was beaten, bruised, and whipped in our place. Finally, in Luke 23, He was led to His brutal death on the cross. If we leave His life there, then there is no answer and fulfillment to the Father's promise to us and to Israel. But in Luke 24, the good news is shared; He rose again, conquering death, Hell, and the grave. He then ascended to Heaven where He is preparing our home and waiting for the Father to say it is time to come get His Bride. If you have not asked Jesus to come into your life as Lord and Savior, if you have not repented of your sin and then changed your ways, and if you realize that you truly need Him, then today is the day for you to come to know the Son.

~Prayer~

Heavenly Father, I come before You, and I lift up this child who realized their need of You. They understand that because of their sin, You came and took their place. They understand that in order for them to have a relationship with You and be able to stand in Your presence, the Son had to come and take their place in death. He is the bridge between them, so that they can boldly enter Your throne room.

(If you are ready to receive the Son and the Holy Spirit, please pray the following.)

Father, I realize that even what I consider good about myself cannot stand in Your presence. My sin (Write down your sin)

is keeping me from You. It's holding me in bondage, and I cannot clean myself. Jesus, please forgive me of my sins. Cleanse me from them and help me walk through the consequences of those sins covered in Your grace. I turn from my sin and my selfish ways. I choose you, Jesus. Jesus, I believe that You died on the cross for Your blood to cover me. I believe You rose again, so that on a day coming soon You will return for me, Your Bride. Holy Spirit, please come and dwell in my heart. I need You and I don't want to spend another minute separated from You. Jesus, today I make You Lord and Savior of my life. You take the lead, and I will follow You. Thank You for forgiving me, for making me new, for death of my flesh, and that I am now a new creation. The old me is gone, and the new me, my spirit, is fully alive in You. Help me to be obedient to You because I long to live according to Your heart for me. I want to reach my full purpose and I long for a deep relationship with You, because only You can satisfy my soul.

In Jesus' Name, Amen
(Write down the date you became a Believer.)

_____

Read Today: Luke 22, Luke 23, Luke 24

~My prayer for you today~

Heavenly Father, it is said that when a child comes home to You, repents, and turns from their ways and follows You, that all of Heaven rejoices. Today Heaven is rejoicing because Your child came home to You. Your heart is overflowing with love and joy over this child of Yours who is now adopted into Your family. I pray protection over you, child of God. I pray that every lie of the enemy would be exposed, and I pray that every demonic agenda, spirit, and sin that has held you hostage would be bound, broken off, and destroyed in the name of Jesus. Today is a new day, it is a new beginning, and it's time to walk in freedom, healing, and authority. In Jesus' Name, Amen.

Day 4: How Covenant Relationship Works

~Prayer~

Heavenly Father,

We come before You today, and we desire to have true fellowship with You. Forgive us, Father, where we have lost You as our first love. I pray that we would find You again. Forgive us, Father, where we have compromised and chosen to say that the Bible is not all fact and truth. We compromised and said that sin was good, and what You claim as good is sin. Forgive us, Father, for where we have become deceived and no longer have been walking in truth and righteousness or according to Your Truth. We have been led astray and yet we acknowledge that we are choosing to come back to You. Forgive us where we have become dead and lukewarm to You. We long to be the pure Bride who obeys the Bible, stands in truth, and does not cave to the cultures around us. We choose to be obedient to You, and to glorify You, even if it means persecution, because we also know that where there is persecution there is blessing and favor. We want to be found faithful to You and not the world. In Jesus' Name, Amen.

To understand how covenant relationship works, it would be good for us to understand how covenants are treated today. A covenant is a binding contract that will not become void or left unfulfilled. It is a contract that is witnessed by many and if failed to keep brings disgrace and shame upon the one who did not stay faithful to their word.

Marriages used to be a covenant relationship before the world got ahold of it and turned it into a relationship without meaning. Divorce has been a very hard topic to discuss in churches because many believe that it is wrong to divorce. The Bible gives many different reasons where divorce would be legal and appropriate. Affairs and abuse are some of the common ones that people understand to be okay. Part of the problem though, especially in the Western World, is that divorce has become a way of doing what one wants without keeping your word. Divorce has become a way of having who you want when you want them.

I have gotten a divorce due to my ex's affairs and the abuse he inflicted on me. However, divorce is not something I run to or believe that a person should do just because they don't love someone anymore. There is now a demonic spirit attached to divorce for those who get married with the idea of, well if it doesn't work out, we can just get a divorce and meet someone better. The Western Culture has diluted marriage and turned it into something to be mocked.

Covenant marriage was about being with someone through thick and thin, sickness and health, and supporting each other through the best and worst of times. It was that you would be faithful and remain true to the one you married, that you would keep the marriage bed pure and holy and not defile it by being with anyone else. It's about not taking the easy way out and going through life together knowing that you have each other's back, always. It is about having love and honor. The Bible makes it very clear what a husband and wife should be in a marriage. I love what **Ephesians 5:21-28 (RSV)** puts it.

What should wives do?

What should husbands do?

What does Christ do for the church?

What a beautiful way to describe the relationship of a husband and wife in marriage. So why am I bringing up God's view of covenant in marriage instead of focusing on His covenant with us? How many of you have a broken view of covenant because of the marriage you experienced? Or maybe it's a parent's, friend's, or relatives' marriage you witnessed that destroyed your view of a covenant? The truth is that many of us do not understand covenant because we were hurt by a relationship that was supposed to be covenant-based. So to understand the covenant with God we need to get back to basic truth about true covenant.

~Prayer~
Heavenly Father, please reveal to me where I have lost the true Biblical view of covenant. Show me how those views destroyed my trust and changed how I view relationships with others and you.
(Write down what God reveals to you.)

I pray that You would redeem this area of covenant relationship. Once again, purify my thoughts and mind. Heal me in covenant relationship. Forgive me in the part I played in destroying this covenant relationship. Help me to walk in true covenant relationship with You and others. In Jesus' Name, Amen.

The Father is all about true covenant relationship. Now remember the Father, the Son, and the Holy Spirit are good. There is no evil in Them, They do not lie, deceive, or break Their promises. They fulfill and remain faithful even when we do not.

Yesterday, if you received Jesus into Your heart and have allowed Him to become your Lord and Savior, the Holy Spirit is now within you, and He is a sign of adoption into the Family of God. That means that the Old Testament Covenants belong to us, and the New Testament Covenant belongs to us too, because we are now a part of His family.

This is God's covenant with us.
1. He will not destroy the world with a flood.
2. Favor, blessing, offspring, and land

3. Treasure, set apart, a holy people, and fellowship with Him.

4. The Messiah would come

5. Forgiveness of Sin, Heaven, and eternal life

Honestly, there is so much more to these covenants that you should really do a study on them, but for now I will only include a few. When you look at the covenant and the promises, do you see them being lived out in your life? If your answer is no, then you are not walking in covenant relationship with God. You are not claiming your identity in His family. Maybe you see a few of these promises being shown in your life, but because you are Held Hostage, you have not walked in covenant relationship with God to claim them all.

So why do these covenants still stand today, and why are they still meant to be walked through in our own lives? I have not found a place in the Bible where it says that God no longer cares about His covenants. I have not found a place in the Bible where it says the covenants have been completely fulfilled so therefore, they no longer matter. Did anyone catch that? Even the New Testament Covenant has not been fully completed yet, because Jesus has not yet returned to reign and bring us back to Heaven. We are still waiting for this last step to be taken. Until then the covenants remain in full activation. Truth is, even when we get to Heaven, these covenants will remain because we will be holy people, clothed in white, in fellowship with the Father, and a Bride ready for her groom. The covenant will be on full display for all to see. The question then becomes, how do we walk in covenant here on earth? Tomorrow, this will be our focus.

Read Today: Ephesians 5

~My prayer for you today~
Heavenly Father,
I pray for the child who is reading this. So many of them have been hurt by a false view of covenant relationship, and they are in need of healing. They need fresh eyes to see that You are faithful and do not change. You will not remove Your love from them, nor destroy them. Help them to understand Your character and heart.
In Jesus' Name, Amen.

Day 5: How Covenant Relationship Works in Our Prayers and Situations

~Prayer~

Heavenly Father,

Thank You for revealing more of Yourself to us this week. We are so thankful for truth and for the understanding You are giving us. We are blessed and favored by You. You call out to us, and You do not let us remain in darkness. Today, make Yourself known to us. We love You. In Jesus' Name, Amen.

I love how at each different time God made a covenant, there was a symbol or action that He gave after it. We have the rainbow, and then for the Old Testament ones we see that they built altars and worshiped God. Gen. 12:7-8, Gen. 13:18 Then in the New Testament Jesus gave His life and rose again to activate the New Testament Covenant.

So, what is the response of covenant relationship in our daily lives and prayer lives, and what does it look like? (1 Samuel 30) David and his men are returning back to Ziklag; when they get there, they found that the Amalekites had taken all of their belongs along with their wives and children. There was great weeping and in 1 Samuel 30:6-8 (NLT) we find it says, "[6] David was now in great danger because all his men were very bitter about losing their sons and daughters, and they began to talk of stoning him. But David found strength in the LORD his God. [7] Then he said to Abiathar the priest, "Bring me the ephod!" So Abiathar brought it. [8] Then David asked the LORD, "Should I chase after this band of raiders? Will I catch them?" And the LORD told him, "Yes, go after them. You will surely recover everything that was taken from you!"

I love David's response. He knew the God of covenant relationship. So immediately when faced with a situation that broke him, he went straight to the Father. It says in verse 6 that David found strength in God. He understood the relationship between himself and God. If we look at a Christian today and their relationship with God, would it be like one found written in the Bible? Regarding the relationship you have with God, would He write about it in the Bible, or is your "relationship" in name only, without covenant or fellowship? Who is the first one you go to in hard times? Is it God? Who do you get your direction and leading from? Is it God? David went straight to God and no one else. He knew who he should depend on, who to trust, and who is faithful. He did not second guess or waver, but boldly went to God.

Another event that took place where a man claimed his covenant is Bartimaeus. He was a beggar and while sitting on the side of the road, he heard that Jesus was coming. Mark 10:47, 51-52 (RSV) says, "[47] And when he heard that it was Jesus of Nazareth, he began to cry out and say, "Jesus, Son of David, have mercy on me!"

"[51] And Jesus said to him, "What do you want me to do for you?" And the blind man said to him, "Master, let me receive my sight." [52] And Jesus said to him, "Go your way; your faith has made you well." And immediately he received his sight and followed him on the way."

In verse 47 we get a clear understanding that Bartimaeus knew who Jesus was. "…**Jesus, *Son of David,*** have mercy on me!" Jesus, and then Son of David…why is that important? Bartimaeus understood that Jesus came from the line of David, he understood the covenant relationship and reminded Jesus about it as he cried out to Him. "Jesus, Son of David! Jesus, Son of David! Jesus, Son of David!" How many times when you are in a deep need do you call out to Jesus, "Jesus, Son of David!"? Do you recognize your covenant relationship with Him and do you understand when you pray in covenant mindset it changes how Jesus then talks to us?

In verse 51 we read Jesus' response. "What do you want me to do for you?" WOW! What do you want Me to do for you? So, when we come to Jesus in covenant relationship, His response to us is, "what do you want Me to do for you?"

So, what is the difference between coming to God in covenant relationship and coming to God of ourselves? When we come to God through covenant relationship, it is through relationship. It is out of a deep love and desire to be with Him. It is longing for Him to be glorified in our lives, it is desiring that we are in the path He has for us. It is about our relationship with Him, and not about ourselves. When we come to God out of ourselves you will find the prayers and requests are selfish, prideful, and have nothing really to do with Him. So, the answer to this question comes down to what is in our hearts and the motive behind our heart action? Hank Kunneman from Lord of Hosts Church had an excellent example for this. Using Bartimaeus as an example of the right heart and faith, versus the mother of Zebedee's sons.

This event is found in Matthew 20:20-22 (AMP) says, "[20] Then [Salome] the mother of Zebedee's children [James and John] came up to Jesus with her sons and, kneeling down [in respect], asked a favor of Him. [21] And He said to her, "What do you wish?" She answered Him, "Command that in Your kingdom these two sons of mine may sit [in positions of honor and authority] one on Your right and one on Your left." [22] But Jesus replied, "You do not realize what you are asking. Are you able to drink the cup [of suffering] that I am about to drink?" They answered, "We are able."

Jesus knew immediately the heart behind the mother and sons' actions. He knew they were not coming in relationship, but for their own gain and purpose. It was for their own glory excluding Him. In verse 20 it says they came and asked for a favor. In verse 21 we see Jesus' response, "What is your wish?" another version puts it this way, "What is it you want?" Do you see the difference? What is it you want compared to What do you want Me to do for you? I want Jesus to say to me, "What do you want Me to do for you?" In verse 21 the mother's request is that her sons sit on the throne with Jesus. Ummm…. does anyone else see the heart motive screaming out clearly here? I love how Hank Kunneman brings this home even further by revealing the setting around this event. He shares how before we get to verse 20, something extremely important happened in Matthew 20:17-19 (NIV) says, "[17] Now Jesus was going up to Jerusalem. On the way, he took the Twelve aside and said to them, [18] "We are going up to Jerusalem, and the Son of Man will be delivered over to the chief priests and the teachers of the law. They will condemn him to death [19] and will hand him over to the Gentiles to be mocked and flogged and crucified. On the third day he will be raised to life!"

Jesus was just sharing about the great trial and suffering He would endure for mankind. He just shared about the darkest moment in His life that He was about to face. And what does the mother and His disciples do? They ask for a favor to sit next to Him on the throne. Talk about heart motives. I wonder if Jesus' heart broke in that moment. I wonder if satan tried to spiritually attack Him by saying His disciples do not actually love Him because they do not even care about what He just shared with them.

So, when you go to pray, is it through relationship with the Father, or is it out of yourself? If you are going to Him through covenant relationship with the right heart and motive your life will become radically shifted and blessed. If it is out of yourself and selfishness and pride, your life will be limited, and you will not experience all that God has for you.

Read Today: 1 Samuel 30, Mark 10, Matthew 20

~My prayer for you today~
Heavenly Father,
I pray for the child who is reading this. I pray that as they begin to go forward throughout the weeks that they would be mindful if they are coming to You through relationship or through selfish means. I pray for the conviction of the Holy Spirit to be activated in their life and keep their hearts steadfast in You. Continue to lead, guide, direct, and change them.
In Jesus' Name, Amen.

Day 6: My Story

Covenant Relationship is such a beautiful relationship. There are truly no words to describe it because all fall short of defining it. Through my process of healing, I learned quickly that my view of covenant had been shattered. The one I thought would protect me and love me was instead the one who purposely hurt me. The years of being abandoned, betrayed, and abused revealed to me that he did not love me. Not in the way the Word said he was supposed to. I understood that through those ten years of marriage, I was unloved, unwanted, and found to be unvalued, not treasured.

Through my time of healing, I saw that I was transferring those feelings and emotions given to me through my ex-husband onto God. I realized that I had a hard time believing that God truly wanted to provide for me because my ex had not wanted to provide for me. I did not believe that God truly loved, wanted, and treasured me, because my earthly husband had not wanted, loved, or treasured me. Although I knew the facts and believed the Bible to be true, fear caused me to transfer those beliefs about myself and my identity onto the Father.

It was during this time that Paula White-Cain preached an amazing couple of months of sermons dedicated to covenant relationship. I began to understand what covenant meant, and in the midst of that began to understand my identity in Christ. I understood that the enemy and demonic agenda was targeting me in worth and value. The Father began to show me that to Him, I was valuable and wanted. At the beginning of the year, before my ex-husband was revealed to be acting like a single man, before our separation and divorce, the Father gave me a chapter in Psalms that changed my life. I mention more about that time in later weeks, as well as in my book Held Hostage.

Read Psalms 91.

During my healing and times of understanding that my true identity was not unloved and unwanted, the Father would take me back to this chapter. I understood that I needed to dwell in His arms and have covenant relationship with Him, that when I do that, all the rest of the verses will be applied to my life. Why? Because in Psalms 91:14-16 (NIV) says, "[14] "Because he loves me," says the LORD, "I will rescue him; I will protect him, for he acknowledges my name. [15] He will call on me, and I will answer him; I will be with him in trouble, I will deliver him and honor him. [16] With long life I will satisfy him and show him my salvation."

This is relationship, true relationship. A couple of songs that I listened to during this time of healing deeply impacted me and my relationship with God and have completely ruined me for the ordinary. One of the lyrics goes "I am seen, I'm known, I am loved by my Father." When we realize that we are seen, known, and loved by our Father, everything changes and shifts. Because no matter what the world does to us, we have confidence in our Father and in His love.

I became a broken mess through my healing process, but that mess was so beautiful. The experience, as horrible and hard as it was, has left a beautiful memory of my Lover, Jesus, pursuing me. Never once did He leave me during that time, and in fact He went even further to reveal that He had purposefully made a way for me to escape a marriage that had become my grave. He revealed that the pain, hurt, memories, and PTSD I suffered from would not keep His love from me. In fact, it was during those times I felt His presence in a way that I had not experienced in almost twenty years.

Deuteronomy 7:6 (NIV) says, "[6] For you are a people holy to the LORD your God. The LORD your God has chosen you out of all the peoples on the face of the earth to be his people, his treasured possession."

Deuteronomy 7:6 (NKJV) says, "[6] "For you are a holy people to the LORD your God; the LORD your God has chosen you to be a people for Himself, a special treasure above all the peoples on the face of the earth."

Once I began to recognize my identity in Christ, that I am adopted into the family of God and that God is now my Father, I began to walk in a new authority and understanding. In fact, I began to walk as royalty, set apart, a warrior ready for battle. Why? Because I am the daughter of the King. Jesus died for me, and I now understand my value and worth to God. This idea of being treasured by God was something spoken over me sixteen years ago from today. During my time of schooling for ministry, the Lord used people to speak on how God viewed me. He once again brought me back to that time. Sermons would mention that we are peculiar treasure; books I would read, such as the Katie Weldon Series by Robin Jones Gunn, and worship songs all spoke the same thing over and over. I am a peculiar treasure, set apart, loved, wanted; and I am known by my Father.

As I began to understand my own identity and the character of God (which we discussed in weeks 1-3), my understanding of God's covenant began to grow. I realized that He would not abandon me, He would be faithful to me, He would not lie, nor deceive me, and every day He longs for me. The Father, the Son, and the Holy Spirit will not break covenant with me.

It is also during this time of coming into a covenant relationship with God, that He revealed He also had set times and seasons where He would move in my life and heart like never before. These set divine encounters are found in the Jewish festivals in the Bible. In fact, Israel still holds that during these holidays, there is the understanding that God will reveal Himself at those specific times. Paula White-Cain also has sermons dedicated to these topics and let me tell you, they are powerful. (Sermons are from around September 2021.)

Here are a few of the holidays or feasts: (Write down what God's response is during this time and what the peoples are supposed to do as well.). Example: Purim—a Day of celebration to remember how God saved them in the times of Esther. They were to give food to others and remember God's faithfulness.

Purim: Esther 9

The Sabbath: Leviticus 23:3

Passover: Deuteronomy 16:1-9; Leviticus 23:4-8

First Fruits: Leviticus 23:9-14

The Festival of Weeks: Deuteronomy 16:9-12; Leviticus 23:15-22

Feast of Trumpets or Rosh Hashanah: Leviticus 23:23-25

Yom Kippur or Day of Atonement: Leviticus 23:26-32

The Festival of Tabernacles or Booths: Deuteronomy 16:13-17; Leviticus 23:33-44

Shavuot/Pentecost (also Festival of Weeks because Pentecost took place on this Festival): Acts 2

As I am writing this Beyond Held Hostage it has been over a year since I began walking in covenant relationship and understanding seasons and times. I find it very interesting how a lot of really big things that have been revealed to me concerning my future line up with these festivals and really show the importance that there is still order and details in my relationship with God that were put in place a long time ago.

God does that with us; He has set times and seasons where divine encounters with Him will take place, but the question then becomes, "Am I awake to see it, read it, and discern it?"

Day 7: Self-Reflection

~Prayer~

Heavenly Father,

We come before You and we ask that You search our hearts. Reveal to us where our past has been pushed onto You. We acknowledge that our pasts have caused us to doubt You, unable to recognize that You love us. Yet the very fact that You died for us is the glaring truth of Your deep love and relationship towards us. Today, help us to go deeper so that we can have a true covenant relationship with You. In Jesus' Name, Amen.

Today I will be asking hard questions and I want you to write down your answers truthfully and honestly.

Do your views of Covenant Relationship fall in line with the Bible?

Where have you pushed your past feelings, emotions, and treatments upon God?

Write down what the Bible says about your identity.

Write down what the Bible says about the character of God the Father, Son, and Holy Spirit.

How has God shown you His Covenant Relationship?

~Prayer~

Heavenly Father,

I come before You and I acknowledge that I have not understood my identity or walked in it. I acknowledge that my past (write down your sin, trauma, etc.)

has been pushed onto You and that I have not held onto the Truth of Your character and love. Forgive me, Father. I pray that You would come and help me to renew my mind. I pray that my thoughts, my understandings about myself and about You, would be aligned with the Word of God and not with emotions and feelings that lie to me. I pray that today I would begin to walk in covenant relationship with You, that every minute of every day, every week, and every year would be spent in fellowship with You, that I would not forget to spend time every day with You, and that I would have You be a part of my life completely, not just on Sunday at church. In Jesus' Name, Amen.

Week 5: Hearing God's Voice

"[16] I have other sheep that are not of this sheep pen. I must bring them also. They too will listen to my voice, and there shall be one flock and one shepherd."
(John 10:16 NIV)

Day 1: Hearing God's Voice

One of the biggest shocks I experienced in the last few years is the realization that many believers or Christians do not believe that God talks to us. They are taught that the only way that He speaks to us is through the Bible alone.

I honestly have such a hard time understanding how pastors have gotten away with preaching and teaching things that are completely contrary to the Word of God. I get angry when I think about the sheep, (the Christians in the church), not even checking to see if the pastor's words line up with the Bible. It really shows how the western Christian's relationship with God is just a way to identify oneself but lacks true intimacy. Again, the Bride of Christ right now is not very large, but I believe that as more Christians truly begin to walk in relationship with God, that will change, and the Bride of Christ will begin to grow.

This week we are going to tear down every lie that anyone has said about how God speaks to us. We are going to understand the importance of why He speaks to us, how He speaks to us, how to get our hearts into position to hear, how He spoke during the Bible times, and how He speaks today.

Before we begin to go through it this week, I want to make something very clear. In the Old Testament it is apparent when God speaks, and in the New Testament there are so many examples of God speaking. The truth is that God recognizes the importance of speaking to us and having open communication with us. We see Him speaking countless times to the new church in the New Testament. He knew they needed to hear from Him, because many would be laying down their lives for Him. In fact, many Christians (up until now) are being killed and martyred for their faith in Jesus Christ. So, let me ask this question, as we get closer to Jesus' return where persecution and hatred towards us will increase as is written in Revelations, is it important for God to speak to us?

If the early church, who was faced with persecution and death, were given opportunities to hear God, would not we, the Bride He is returning for, also be given opportunities to hear His voice? The truth is that the Bride in Revelation will need that connection even more because what is to come will be like nothing ever seen before, for it will be done at a greater level than it had ever been seen. We are talking about all Christians throughout the WORLD, not just one country. In fact, I believe that before it gets to the extreme levels, the true believers now will be taken away. But my heart breaks for those who will be left, and as they realize that to become faithful to God, they will have to face the worst of the worst of what is to come. That is why it is important to have true covenant relationship with God and hear His voice now. A great book that talks about the last days and helps one learn without fear being attached to it is, "The Book of Signs" by Dr. David Jeremiah.

Read Today: John 10:1-6

~Prayer~
Heavenly Father,
We come to You and worship You. We want to sit at Your feet, to fellowship with You, and to be known by You. We desire true intimacy with You and not just a religious experience. This week, help us to understand why You long to talk with us, how You do talk to us, and to recognize what our response to You should be.
In Jesus' name, Amen.

Day 2: Why Should We Hear God's Voice?

~Prayer~

Heavenly Father,

We come before You today, and we ask that this week we would clearly hear Your voice. That we would see how You are talking to us and be able to discern exactly what Your meaning is. Help us to be observant and aware of You this week. We pray that we would seek You and that we would find You. In Jesus' Name, Amen.

Today we are going to begin our understanding of why we should hear God's voice. Yesterday we read John 10, but I want us to take a closer look at it.

Read John 10:1-6.

(Fill in the blanks with your name.)

The doorkeeper opens to Jesus, and _____ hears his voice; and Jesus calls to me, _____ and leads me out. When Jesus brings me out, He goes before me, and I follow him, for I know His voice.

Isaiah 30:21 (RSV) says, "[21] And your ears shall hear a word behind you, saying, "This is the way, walk in it," when you turn to the right or when you turn to the left."

John 16:13 (RSV) says, "[13] When the Spirit of truth comes, he will guide you into all the truth; for he will not speak on his own authority, but whatever he hears he will speak, and he will declare to you the things that are to come."

So why should we hear God's voice? The answer is very simple: to know Him. How can one communicate and have relationship with God if we do not hear Him? Jesus says that His sheep will know His voice. He says that when He speaks it will be to give us direction and will also reveal what is to come. My friend, who is like a sister, and I have called this prophetic reveal as 'the deep down knowing.' It is when our spirits know something is coming without knowing the details; when something does come it is having the answer and peace right away without having to pause and pray. This 'deep down knowing' comes when the Holy Spirit communicates with our spirits during our times of praying in tongues, through prophetic words spoken, and visions and dreams. The list goes on and on.

For us to understand our pasts, our pain, our bondage, and what Holds us Hostage, we need to be able to hear from God for it to be revealed. Proverbs 25:2 (RSV) says, "[2] It is the glory of God to conceal things, but the glory of kings is to search things out."

For us to have complete healing and freedom, we need to search out what God is saying. It is His truth and He alone that brings what our hearts, minds, and souls need. He brings us into realignment, restoration, redemption, and gets us to a place where our pasts are as if they never happened at all. You might think I am crazy for saying that, but even today when I think about the last fourteen years of abuse and trauma, those memories have no power over me and it's like I am reading about someone else's life and not my own. I am telling you, there is power in the blood of Christ. He is our restorer and redeemer, and He alone keeps us alive. But to know how to heal, what to do, and how to live, I MUST HEAR HIS VOICE! Tomorrow we will begin to go into how we should position our hearts to hear Him.

Read Today: John 10

~My prayer for you today~
Heavenly Father,
I come before You, and I lift the child who is longing to hear Your voice. I pray that during this week their ears and eyes would be opened, in the name of Jesus. I pray against every demonic spirit, agenda, and lie that would try to keep their ears and eyes closed. Let it be broken off them, in the name of Jesus. Be open in the name of Jesus.
In Jesus' Name, Amen.

Day 3: How to Position Our Hearts

~Prayer~

Heavenly Father,

We come before You today, and we are excited to hear from You. We look forward to hearing Your voice and drawing close to You. We long to be closer to You. We long to have a deeper relationship than just church on Sunday. We desire for more of You and less of us. So today, help us understand what You are doing and what You are saying to us. In Jesus' Name, Amen.

One of the biggest reasons that we fail to hear, understand, and discern God's voice is because of the position of our own hearts. So many times, we fail because our own desires and longings get in the way. Other times our fears hold us back from trusting that we can hear from Him.

Today I am going to share with you some steps that I learned to take to make sure my heart is positioned accurately. These steps I will be sharing come from Joy Dawson, but I have changed them up a bit to how I feel the Holy Spirit leading.[5]

Step 1: Usually, the first thing that I do is go before God and ask Him to reveal if there is anything that I need to forgive someone for or apologize for myself. I first want to deal with sin, whether towards God or man, and then second, deal with my heart issue towards others who hurt me and forgive them. This is not always easy to do, but if we hold onto our sin, we will be separated from the Father. If we hold onto our unforgiveness, our Father will not forgive us.

2 Chronicles 7:14 (NIV) says, "[14] if my people, who are called by my name, will humble themselves and pray and seek my face and turn from their wicked ways, then I will hear from heaven, and I will forgive their sin and will heal their land."

Mark 11:25-26 (NKJV) says, "[25] "And whenever you stand praying, if you have anything against anyone, forgive him, that your Father in heaven may also forgive you your trespasses. [26] But if you do not forgive, neither will your Father in heaven forgive your trespasses."

Once the Father has revealed to me what I need forgiveness for and what I need to forgive others for, I immediately begin to repent to God and to the person I hurt, and then I forgive those who I need to forgive, and I release them into the Father's hands. If I can talk to that person then I do, and I make it right. Sometimes that person does not care, in the case of my ex-husband, so then it was between God and me, and I released him to the Father. Sometimes talking to someone to tell them you forgive them will place some of you in very dangerous situations. That is why I say then that it is between you and God, and you forgive that person even though they might not ever know or care.

Step 2: I then go into a time of just worshipping and praising God for all that He is, all He has done, and for who I am in Him. I also begin to thank Him for how He also wants to meet with me and speak to me. I love how Revised Standard Version (RSV) words these verses, it shows that our thankfulness should be done out of affection, love, and gratitude, and that by doing this we can let our requests be known to God from the right heart motive.

Psalms 100:4 (RSV) says, "[4] Enter his gates with thanksgiving, and his courts with praise! Give

---

[5] Dawson, Joy. Intercession: Thrilling and Fulfilling. Seattle, Washington. YWAM Publishing, 1997.

thanks to him, bless his name!"

Philippians 4:6-7 (RSV) says, "⁶ Have no anxiety about anything, but in everything by prayer and supplication with thanksgiving let your requests be made known to God. ⁷ And the peace of God, which passes all understanding, will keep your hearts and your minds in Christ Jesus."

Step 3: I begin to pray that the Holy Spirit would lead my time of prayer, that He would direct the relationship, and I then begin to deal with the spiritual realm and test the spirits. I begin to speak in tongues, and as God leads, to pray against the enemy. I then come against the demonic spirits and agendas in the name of Jesus Christ. I can usually sense what spirit and demonic agenda is trying to attack me, but when I first started it was a more generalized covering. Example of prayer, but not one you need to follow word for word: "I command every demonic spirit and agenda that is trying to come against me, deceive me, or take the promises that God has given me away from me, to be bound and broken off me, in the name of Jesus. I command you to flee from this room, this house, and away from my mind, in the name of Jesus. Holy Spirit come and dwell in this room with me. Cover me and this room so that the enemy's arrows will not hit their target. In the Name of Jesus, Amen." From there I submit myself to the Holy Spirit and I release all that I think, desire, and what I feel I should pray about over to the Holy Spirit. I verbally tell Him that I want to hear what He has to say and not what I want to hear.

Read Romans 8:26-27 (RSV).
Read James 4:7-10 (RSV).
Also read Isaiah 55:8-11.

Who helps us pray? _____

Who searches us? _____

Who pleads before God for us? _____

Who do we surrender to? _____

Write James 4:7-8.

Step 4: I begin to pray in tongues and let Him lead what I should pray about. When I feel released from praying His heart, I then wait before God, expectantly waiting to hear His voice. For some people, they immediately speak out what God gives, and for others they write it down. Either which way, the point is to do it in obedience and faith, believing what God is saying. I personally write down what God is saying to me, but if I am in a group then I will verbally speak it forth. I also keep my Bible close at hand if there is any Scripture He wants me to go to. I want to also mention that there are times when what God is speaking is not meant to be shared with everyone or at that particular time. So be sensitive to the Holy Spirit's leading in this area. There have been many things that God spoke to me, and I had to guard who I shared with, because there are people out there who will let satan use them to try to destroy that Word and your faith. So be sensitive to the Holy Spirit. When God has finished talking with me, I then thank Him and praise Him for the beautiful time we had together.

Read Habakkuk 2:2-3 (NIV).
Read Psalm 27:14 (RSV).
Also read Psalm 119:105.
What are we to do with the revelation?

Write Psalm 27:14.

Today set aside time to walk through these steps and see how the Holy Spirit leads you to apply them. It might not be easy at first to hear God, and you might question yourself and wonder if you really hear Him, but continue forth. Do not stop or let fear hold you back. Trust in God and trust that if you do make a mistake, He will reveal it and continue to lead you. Right now, you are in a season of training and equipping. Therefore, He isn't going to go about punishing you if you hear wrong or miss something or share something when you were to wait. He will let you know where you went wrong, how to correct it, and then you continue. He is going to help you practice until one day you realize that you know His voice very clearly.

Read Today: Matthew 6

~My prayer for you today~
Heavenly Father,
I come before You, and I lift up the child who is longing to hear Your voice. I pray that as they begin to apply these steps to their own lives, You would show up in great and powerful ways. I come against the spirit of fear that would try to stop them from hearing from You, and I pray that You would cover them. Protect them, Father, and let Your love flood them.
In Jesus' Name, Amen.

Day 4: How Can We Hear God's Voice?

~Prayer~

Heavenly Father, we come before You and today we are so excited to see the ways that You speak to us. The Bible says that You are the same yesterday, today, and tomorrow. You will not change, and You forever will be. We are excited and ready for our lives to be radically changed and shifted in such a powerful way as we begin to hear You clearly. Be with us here and open our ears and eyes.

In Jesus' Name, Amen.

Yesterday I shared with you some steps from Joy Dawson that I have applied in my own time with the Father. However, through my healing process I realized that God is always talking, not just in my quiet times. He showed me that I needed to continually be in His presence and aware of what He was always saying. I cannot even begin to share the countless times He spoke to me outside of my quiet time.

So today we are going to look at the some of the ways that God has spoken to individuals and how He can still do the same today.

Read 1 Kings 19:11-12.

How did God speak?

Read Exodus 3:1-5.

How did God speak?

Read Numbers 22:28-31.

How did God speak?

Read Romans 1:18-20.

How did God speak?

Here we see that God spoke through a whisper, through a bush, through a donkey, and the deep down knowing, and He has revealed Himself through all the ages. Therefore, no excuse can stand against this truth because it is our choice to ignore or be deceived. The truth is that God has probably talked to many of us, but we have failed to recognize or submit to Him. We miss the mark and fail to recognize our Shepherd's voice.

So, these verses show that God uses creation to speak to us, and that has not changed. God is forever the same yesterday, today, and in the future. What He used in the past, He will also use now, but in the way He so chooses to. There are times I would love if God just opened the mouth of a pet and let it warn me, but I have loved learning to hear His voice, because it allowed our relationship to become intimate. In order for me to know His voice, it required close contact or a connecting of our hearts.

Genesis 3:8 (NKJV) says, "[8] And they heard the sound of the LORD God walking in the garden in the cool of the day, and Adam and his wife hid themselves from the presence of the LORD God among the trees of the garden."

Judges 13:3 (NKJV) says, "[3] And the Angel of the LORD appeared to the woman and said to her, "Indeed now, you are barren and have borne no children, but you shall conceive and bear a son.""

1 Kings 3:4-5 (NKJV) says, "[4] Now the king went to Gibeon to sacrifice there, for that was the great high place: Solomon offered a thousand burnt offerings on that altar. [5] At Gibeon the LORD appeared to Solomon in a dream by night; and God said, "Ask! What shall I give you?""

(Write down the ways He spoke to His people.)

Just think; the very presence of God brings conviction to our lives. God's very presence speaks to us, we can hear Him around us, we can see Him moving, and through it He speaks to us. God also uses angels to speak to us and give us messages from God. I have heard countless stories where missionaries in countries where their lives could be taken for Christ were able to continue living and ministering because angels appeared and helped them with direction from God. The Western church has a hard time understanding that, but this is very real, and angels are not some mythical beings in a fairytale. God also speaks to us through dreams. Solomon is not the only one in the Bible who experienced this, but this is just one example to show that we also can be given dreams from God, today.

We have not even gotten through all the ways that God has spoken. Tomorrow we will go through even more, but for now I want you to consider in prayer if God has spoken to you in any of these ways before.

(Write down when and how He did.)

Read Today: Pick one of the verses above and read the full chapter.

~My prayer for you today~
Heavenly Father,
I come before You, and I lift up the child who is longing to hear Your voice. I pray that today You would reveal to them how You have been speaking to them and bring revelation to them. Remove the blinders off their eyes that they may clearly see.
In Jesus' Name, Amen.

Day 5: Ways God Speaks

~Heavenly Father~

We thank You for who You are and that You do not change. Just as You talked with Your people in the Old Testament and New Testament, You are also talking to us. We come against any lie or falsehood that we heard and claimed that comes against our ability to hear You. We say no to that assignment in the Name of Jesus, and today we recognize that we can hear You. In Jesus' Name, Amen.

As I mentioned in my book Held Hostage, one of the forms of abuse that my ex-husband took on was coming against my spiritual gifts, but also speaking over me the lie that I could not hear God. I have lost count through the fifteen years how many times he told me that I could not hear God's voice. After so many years, I began to truly believe that I could not. That lie led to the almost spiritual death of my relationship with God. I am so very thankful that God proved my ex wrong.

Today we are going to look even further into how God spoke to His people. We will get to see how He spoke through prophets, through images or pictures, through life experience (Hosea), Word of God (Bible).

Read 1 Samuel 3:19-21.

Israel understood that Samuel was a prophet and when Samuel spoke, they needed to listen. Prophets are still around today, but not everyone heeds their words. As I get into later it is important that in these last days, we recognize true prophets and weigh their words before God, so we are not led astray. But to ignore even God's prophets who are doing what is right is wrong on our part.

Read Jeremiah 1:11-13.

Here we see that not only was God's voice audible, but Jeremiah was also given pictures and images, which God then expounded on for him to share with the rest of Israel.

Read Hosea 1:2-3.

God used Hosea's life to speak to the people of Israel. Through Hosea's actions and obedience, Israel was given a physical representation of their sin and God's response to them, as well as His future response.

Read Hebrews 4:12-13.

The Word of God, the Bible, is a very big way that God speaks to us. In fact, we should daily be soaking in the Bible and letting the words penetrate our souls, our thoughts, our longings, our sins, and our obedience. We should allow the Word of God to have full access to ourselves and then listen very intently for what the Word is saying to us.

Read Proverbs 19:20-21.
(Write down from all the Scripture references, the ways God speaks.)

God has people that He has positioned into our lives to speak to us; but it is very important that when picking out those you seek counsel from, you are being led by the Holy Spirit. It is very evident in our world today that people have become deceived. Therefore, make sure that who you choose is God's best. The Word says that we will be led forth by peace. If you do not have a peace, then make sure you are seeking God if they are the right person. Also, even if they are the right person, everything they share should be taken back to God, and then you follow through with what He says, no matter what others say. Even though we can be used for wise counsel there are times we will miss it. We should always allow God to have the final say and direction.

Read Today: Pick one of the Scripture references from today and read the full chapter.

~My prayer for you today~
Heavenly Father,
I come before You, and I lift up the child who is longing to hear Your voice. I am so excited for Your child who is growing in You and refusing to stay a baby. Instead, they are applying truth to their lives no matter how hard. Bless them today and reveal Yourself to them in a way they have never experienced before.
In Jesus' Name, Amen.

Day 6: My Story and Testimonies

Getting to the place where you can hear God's voice over all the chatter and noise from the demonic agenda is key to living in freedom. As we have learned this week, there are so many ways that God speaks to us. There is through the Bible, visions, dreams, through others, details, things He reveals in the world around us, and through His audible voice.

I have been able to experience His voice in all these ways. Each one was for a reason and purpose. It was specifically done for His glory and for where I was at. God is such a loving Father, and He knows where we are at and what we need.

I have shared the visions and dreams that He has given me in week 1 and 2, but there are a few more that I haven't shared. The purpose at this time is not to be revealed. But once that release is given, I can share more. I shared about God speaking with His audible voice in week 3. An example of God using things around me to speak happened before I moved to Utah in 2009.

My family took a trip to the Black Hills; my brother flew from Kenya to come with us, and while there we decided to go horseback riding like we normally do. It was a time in my life where I was drawing close to God, hearing Him speak, and receiving prophetic words for my future (that I didn't clearly understand, but I will get into that in week 6), and yet was going my own way. It mainly came down to what I wanted, and so everything I got I saw through my own eyes and went in that direction, instead of asking God what He meant.

So, we go horseback riding and I should have known right away that something was up when they said the horse's name was "Howdy." It was a smaller horse who was stubborn as all could be. The guide who took us out kept commenting on my patience. I felt anything but patient. I felt embarrassed. What was supposed to be a 45-minute trail ride took over an hour all because of HOWDY!

At one point he decided we did not need to follow the path that the others had taken, OH NO, he thought we should take this narrow path between TWO pine trees with LOW limbs. No matter what I did (I am not new to riding, I have been horseback riding many times) he would not budge from his path. Immediately when we reached the trees, I had to lay completely on my back legs up by his head to make it in between and under the pines.

Finally, I got him back on the right path and was praised for the way I handled it. Meantime, I was like, "God, are you saying I am being stubborn in my own will right now?" Sadly, even though I knew that was what He was saying, I still wanted my way. I ended up moving to Utah, which led to more and more choices that would lead further to a marriage of torment and death. The heart behind my choice to still go my way had to do with my perspective. I will talk about that in week 11.

The year my life truly changed was in 2021, when my healing and breakthrough came. God gave me Psalm 91, as I shared in week 4. He gave me this chapter for myself and my brothers (I share more about them in week 7). Friends would reach out and tell me God had said they were to give me Ps. 91, which turned out what I was exactly needing because it was a rough day. I remember one rough day in particular; I looked up and Ps. 91 was on the license plate in front of me. I cried because it was a reminder. Even key words that God has spoken over me, "Stand firm, be courageous, be bold, etc." would pop up through friends, media apps, bible apps, prophetic words, and pastors.

Right after my divorce, during a time of fasting and praying, the Lord revealed that the number three had significance for that time in my life. The biblical meaning is that of completeness, but not to the degree that seven represents. Things that had felt left unfinished began to be completed during that time. That day He showed me the importance of three and then there were a couple ways it was spoken to me. I ended up being in three states that day; at lunch time the restaurant accidentally gave us triple the amount of food; and when reading my journal entries from 2008, God revealed that at that time it had been three years of long-distance relationship with my boyfriend (who would become my ex-husband). A couple weeks later I was driving with my niece, who was only two years and four months old, when she looked at the light pole and said, "Auntie, there is a number three." I looked at her and I knew God was reminding me again. In fact, God has used my niece many times to confirm things He had spoken to me. There is no way for her to know about it, especially because during those times she was one and half years old, to even now where she is only three years and three months old, and God is still using her to speak and confirm things to me.

I began to see God in all the details He revealed, I began to see that He was right by my side, leading and speaking. I was not alone. I was cherished. I was wanted. I was loved, and He was right there with me.

I have found that God talks to us all the time, but are we listening? Are we surrendered to Him, seeking Him, and clearly understanding what He is giving us? Are we giving Him time to speak to us or are we busy? Are we willing to slow down and seek His Face? Are we willing to face the darkness in order to overcome in obedience what He gives us to do?

Testimonies:

*One day I made plans to play tennis with the pastor of our church; we both like to play, and it was good fellowship too. I had some time in the morning before we were to meet at the courts. As I began to pray in the Spirit and to sense God's presence, I got quiet and I heard God's voice say, "Pastor Mike is going to call and say he's not able to play tennis today, that something came up."

Well, being I really enjoyed tennis and having fellowship, I believe the Lord was just preparing me so I wouldn't be disappointed in not going. Within five minutes the Pastor called me and postponed our tennis appointment just as the Lord said. Because of the Lord's love and compassion, preparing me, it didn't faze me at all. He really is a good, good Father. ~Douglas W.

* I could write pages about that question. Many times, for me, it is just a sense or a thought that comes to mind when I am still long enough to listen. One time, it was a stack of Irish Spring brand soap that God used to confirm to me I'd be in Ireland for Spring. (I moved to Ireland in March of the following year and have enjoyed several "Irish Springs" since then.) Just this past weekend, a shirt I wore prompted two different people in my church to give me encouraging words from God.

I think one of the biggest things I've learned about hearing God's voice is that He always has stuff to say, but it can be easy to miss it if we get caught thinking that He only speaks in one way. Many times, He will speak through His written word to confirm what He is saying, and nothing He says will ever contradict His Word. But He can speak in so many ways that we can miss them if we aren't opened to hearing Him. One of the hardest things for me about hearing God when I'm needing a word from Him is being still and quiet long enough to listen. (That doesn't mean just sitting and twiddling your thumbs while listening either. It's about having a quiet enough heart to hear His voice even in the middle of a busy day. He just might break into your day with a word that can change your life.) ~Stephanie H.

Day 7: Self-Reflection

~Prayer~

Heavenly Father,

We come before You and we take time today to hear Your voice. Please direct this time of fellowship with You. Reveal to us what You are wanting to say and direct us. In Jesus' Name, Amen.

Today I will be asking hard questions and I want you to write down your answers truthfully and honestly.

Have your fears and the lies spoken about hearing Him been broken off you?

Do you feel confident that you can hear Him?

How have you heard God's voice?

Following the steps on day 3, write down what God is speaking to You.

~My prayer for you today~

Heavenly Father,

I come into agreement with the Words You are speaking to Your child right now. I pray that these visions, these promises, these directions, and these truths would continue to grow and be fulfilled.

Lead and direct them, and I say "Yes, and AMEN!" to all that You have for them.

In Jesus' Name, Amen.

Week 6: Gifts of The Spirit

"[8] To one there is given through the Spirit a message of wisdom, to another a message of knowledge by means of the same Spirit, [9] to another faith by the same Spirit, to another gifts of healing by that one Spirit, [10] to another miraculous powers, to another prophecy, to another distinguishing between spirits, to another speaking in different kinds of tongues, and to still another the interpretation of tongues."
(1 Corinthians 12:8-10 NIV)

Day 1: Gifts of The Spirit

I am amazed at how many individuals are completely clueless as to what the gifts of the Spirit are and how many churches remove these gifts from their pulpits. In fact, some churches go to the extreme to say that if you do some of these, you are in error and in sin. Why? Because they are teaching that God no longer wants these in operation after the New Testament era.

The truth is, nowhere in the Bible does it say that to be true. In fact, in Revelation, the last book of the Bible, it is very clear that the gifts of the spirit will be in full operation by the Bride of Christ. Again, I see how so many Christians are walking wounded, broken, and dead. The pastors are making their congregation sick, keeping them dependent on the pastors themselves, instead of the Lord.

Read 1 Corinthians 12:7-11.

Another interesting note I want to make is that churches are also doing the same thing towards the 5-fold ministry spoken of in Ephesians 4:11-13 (RSV) says, "[11] And his gifts were that some should be apostles, some prophets, some evangelists, some pastors and teachers, [12] to equip the saints for the work of ministry, for building up the body of Christ, [13] until we all attain to the unity of the faith and of the knowledge of the Son of God, to mature manhood, to the measure of the stature of the fulness of Christ."

Many churches are now only teaching that pastors, teachers, and apostles are needed, but the rest, evangelists and prophets, are no longer at work. I'm sorry, but who in the world would call Christians today "united in faith and in knowledge of the Son of God," and how many are truly mature and have brought the Kingdom of God to the world around them??? How long will Christians believe the lies and give power to satan?

Have you ever wondered why the world does not desire what a normal Christian has to offer? In all my traveling overseas, I began to get glimpses and understanding of the reason. To the world, a person who calls themself a Christian, yet looks and operates exactly like the world, has become a laughingstock and the world does not believe what they say. When I went to the Middle East to teach English and my adult students found out I was an American, it took me a month to prove my character, my morals, and my beliefs, before I earned their respect. To them, they view Christians as what is portrayed in movies and music industry in America. After a month they realized that what they had seen in the movies and music did not represent me and how I lived life.

Before coming back to the states, I had the opportunity to go to Israel, and while there I was sadly ashamed of westerners who were showing that the movie and music from the west is how they are and how they live. I distanced myself from them and went around to the Jews and Arabs because the Christians from the West were not showing Jesus. They were not being His ambassadors, and instead they delighted in showing off their worldly selves.

So many Christians today are living for themselves and their beliefs, and they no longer hold to truth. Many of them are weak and young in the Lord, unable to stand against the schemes of the enemy. I am ready because the Remnant, the Bride, which I am a part of, has taken up their mantle. They stand firm and are bringing the Kingdom of God to the earth. I am ready to see the weak and deceived Christians become alive and restored as they once again get right with God, follow Him, and become the Bride of Christ. Right now, the Remnant, the Bride, is small, but I believe a great harvest is going to come in and the Remnant and Bride will grow.

This week we are going to look at what exactly the gifts of the Spirit are, and in week 9 we will talk more about 5-fold ministry.

Read Today: 1 Corinthians 12, Ephesians 4

~Prayer~

Heavenly Father,

We come to You, and we desire to be fully living our lives for You. We do not desire to be like the world, but set apart for Your purpose and glory. We long to make You known throughout the world.

We hold fast to truth, to Your WORD, and we say, have Your way with us, Lord.

In Jesus' name, Amen.

Day 2: Wisdom and knowledge

~Prayer~

Heavenly Father, we come before You and we understand that we have not understood what the gifts of the Spirit are. In fact, our church might not even believe them to be true. Yet we want to live our lives according to Your Word, and so we let go of what man says and we cling to what You say. In Jesus' Name, Amen.

Today we will be looking at two gifts of the Spirit called wisdom and knowledge. These gifts go beyond just human wisdom and knowledge. Instead, these gifts bring in God's wisdom and knowledge to a situation. These gifts allow for great freedom and direction and reveal steps to take no matter the situation.

Proverbs 19:8 (RSV) says, "[8] He who gets wisdom loves himself; he who keeps understanding will prosper."

How many of us love wisdom and actively search for it? God says to learn it because wisdom brings favor and blessing. It opens doors that foolishness keeps shut.

Proverbs 4:5-7 (RSV) says, "...[5] do not forget, and do not turn away from the words of my mouth. Get wisdom; get insight. [6] Do not forsake her, and she will keep you; love her, and she will guard you. [7] The beginning of wisdom is this: Get wisdom, and whatever you get, get insight."

How many of us try to solve life problems from our own wisdom and understanding? The truth is that our own wisdom and knowledge is faulty and full of errors because we only see from our eyes and miss what is taking place through other people's eyes.

Psalms 111:10 (RSV) says, "[10] The fear of the LORD is the beginning of wisdom; a good understanding have all those who practice it. His praise endures for ever!"

I love how this clearly shows that wisdom is found in the fear of God. This fear of God is not a terrifying or dreadful fear that grips you and makes you paralyzed to live. No, the fear it talks about is a deep reverence and awe of God. It is understanding that He is pure and holy, and that He is also our judge. This fear moves us to live our lives in obedience to His Word.

Read James 1:5-8 and write out verses 5-6.

Wisdom according to the definition of the Merriam Webster dictionary means, "ability to discern inner qualities and relationships, insight, good sense, judgement, and a wise attitude, belief, or course of action."[6] The definition for knowledge is, "the fact or condition of knowing something with familiarity gained through experience or association, acquaintance with or understanding of a science, art, or technique, the fact or condition of being aware of something, and the range of one's information or understanding answered to the best of my knowledge."[7]

---

[6] "Wisdom," Merriam Webster Dictionary. 2023. https://www.merriam-webster.com/dictionary/wisdom
[7] "Knowledge" Marriam Webster Dictionary. 2023. https://www.merriam-webster.com/dictionary/knowledge

When looking at the difference between wisdom and knowledge, it becomes very clear that one can be knowledgeable, but to have true knowledge they first need wisdom. The truth is that one can have knowledge but not be wise. I am currently learning how to use a handgun, because I want to know how to protect myself and others. So, I am gaining knowledge on how to use one, and becoming experienced through practice in how it works and, in my aim, to hit the target. Wisdom is knowing when to use a gun and when to keep it holstered.

2 Peter 1:3-4 (NIV) says, "[3] His divine power has given us everything we need for a godly life through our knowledge of him who called us by his own glory and goodness. [4] Through these he has given us his very great and precious promises, so that through them you may participate in the divine nature, having escaped the corruption in the world caused by evil desires."

Read 1 Peter 1:5-8 and write out what we need to add to our lives, so we are effective in our knowledge of Jesus.

Remember how we talked about 'it is the honor of kings to search for truth'? God is telling us that His divine power has given us everything we need in order for us to search and understanding this truth. That as we add to ourselves goodness, knowledge, self-control, perseverance, godliness, kindness, and love; we will then be effective and productive in our knowledge of Jesus. So, what happens if we don't follow wisdom and instead follow our flesh? Well verses 9-11 puts it this way; you will be blind, constantly forgetting what God has done for you. God longs for us to diligently stand in our calling and who we are in in Him. If we stand in truth, then we will receive a beautiful welcome into heaven.

Read Colossians 3:1-4 and write verse 10.

Knowledge comes from our experiences, what we have gone through, studying the Word (Bible), and researching what is truth. Wisdom is given by God, and it reveals how to apply knowledge. How many of you are searching out knowledge in God? Do you know how to study the Bible? And have you been asking God to give you wisdom? Verses 5-9 tells us to put to death our earthly nature because it is full of sin, and before we came to Christ we walked in that sin, but now we are to live in Christ. Some of the sins described are: Sexual immorality, impurity, lust, evil desires and greed, and idolatry.

King Solomon known as the wisest man, shows us exactly how to honor God.

Read 1 Kings 3:7-12.
What was Solomon praying, and what did he ask for?

How did God respond?

God blessed Solomon with wisdom and knowledge, which led to a blessed and favored life. How many of us are applying wisdom and knowledge in our own lives? When I look back at the past fifteen years, to all the decisions I made that put me through horrible experiences, I realize how foolish I was. It is so important that we ask of God for wisdom and knowledge and then apply it every day. The days will eventually turn very dark, and if we have not learned how-to walk-in wisdom and understanding, our days will be shortened, and hope will be hard to cling to. In verses 13-14, God tells Solomon that even though it was not asked, He was going to bring such a great amount of blessing and favor, wealth, honor, and that there will be no one like him in all the earth. He commanded Solomon to walk with Him every day and not to forget His laws.

Read Today: Psalm 111, 1 Kings 3

~My prayer for you today~
Heavenly Father,
I come before You, and I pray for Your child reading this. I ask that they begin to pray and ask for wisdom and knowledge from You, and that they would be able to learn from their pasts and cling to Your truth. Fill them with Your wisdom and knowledge, Father.
In Jesus' Name, Amen.

Day 3: Faith and Healing

~Prayer~

Heavenly Father, we come before You today, and we are excited to learn more today. We want to grow in belief, in our faith, and in our relationship with You. So today, reveal to us the deep and hidden things, and take us further out of the box.

In Jesus Name, Amen.

Today we will be talking about two gifts of the Spirit called faith and healing. You would think with the amount of time that pastors talk about faith and having faith, more people would be walking in said faith. So many times, through the past fifteen years, I truly did not have a full amount of faith. The abuse was doing everything it could to destroy the faith that I had. Yet, the Bible makes it so clear as to why we need faith, and how to use it.

Read Hebrews 11:1-3.

_____ is the assurance of _____.

By _____ we _____ the _____ was _____ by the word of God.

Read Hebrews 11: 6.

Without _____ we will not be able to please God. In order to get close, we must _____ that _____ is real and that he _____ those who look for him.

Read Ephesians 2:8-10.

How are we saved?

Read Matthew 15:22, 26-28 (RSV).

Write verse 28.

Matthew 17 talks about a man who came and humble knelt at Jesus feet. He asked for the healing of his son because the disciples could not heal him.

Read Matthew 17:18-20.

(Count how many times the word FAITH is in each verse from Scripture references above.)

Faith is a must when it comes to living our lives for Christ. If we want freedom, healing, and breakthrough in our lives, we must have FAITH. There are many individuals in the Bible who show great faith, but when I think about faith my mind goes straight to Paul. His life, his story, and what he went through are all reasons that I find his faith so encouraging. As someone who has been abused, betrayed, and abandoned, I have a hard time just taking anyone's word about faith. Sometimes, even though they have good hearts behind (it) their words, they still have made me feel judged and misunderstood. Most of the time it stems from the fact that they haven't experienced what I have experienced and so they do not know the right things to say and do. Words like "it will be ok," "God will turn it into something beautiful," and even "perfect love casts out fear," made me feel worse. Although those things are true, sometimes when they are said, and the way they are said, can give the reverse effect people are wanting. Yet when people who I know have experienced abuse, betrayal, and abandonment and they would declare it, it came across so very differently. They would listen without judgement, they would pray with me, and then finally they would declare the truth over me.

So, Paul is someone that screams, "be encouraged and strengthened." Paul applied faith until he was martyred for it. He went from killing Christians to being an amazing missionary to the Gentiles. He had great faith and today his life is still an example for all of us.

I have heard many preach on the word 'faith,' but when I left their message it seemed that more power was given to the word itself that to whom the word applies to. Faith is meaningless unless that faith is grounded in trust in Jesus. Any other kind of faith leads to disappointments and misunderstandings. Faith is trust in Jesus, which then gives us hope to see what has not yet taken place. Faith is believing in Jesus. Faith is a gift; it is not something that man makes happen. It is God who makes it happen, and our faith rests in Him. I have seen faith misused in order for believers to get what they want and if they don't get it, they feel condemned because they must not have had enough faith. We are to ask in faith, but we are also called to have the right motives. In Matthew 17:21 some versions say that the only way the demon could be removed is if the disciples fasted and prayed. I think many believers need to partake in active fasting and praying.

James 5:13-16 and vs. 20 (NLT) says, "[13] Are any of you suffering hardships? You should pray. Are any of you happy? You should sing praises. [14] Are any of you sick? You should call for the elders of the church to come and pray over you, anointing you with oil in the name of the Lord. [15] Such a prayer offered in faith will heal the sick, and the Lord will make you well. And if you have committed any sins, you will be forgiven. [16] Confess your sins to each other and pray for each other so that you may be healed. The earnest prayer of a righteous person has great power and produces wonderful results."

"[20] you can be sure that whoever brings the sinner back from wondering will save that person from death and bring about their forgiveness of many sins."

There are so many powerful truths in these verses. How many of you are in trouble? If you are, God says pray. If you are full of joy, let it come out of your mouth in song. Are you sick? Pray for healing. If you are remaining in sin, confess and change. Our prayers are so very powerful, but so many times we remove the power when we are stuck in sin and living in unrighteousness. I also love how verse 20 talks about what we are here for: it is saving sinners from hell and revealing grace to them. How many of us need grace for ourselves but fail to give grace to others? We need to be living in righteousness so when we apply faith, things will begin to change, lives will change, and healings will take place.

Luke 9:1-2 (NLT) says, "[1] One day Jesus called together his twelve disciples and gave them power and authority to cast out all demons and to heal all diseases. [2] Then he sent them out to tell everyone about the Kingdom of God and to heal the sick."

Our power does not come from our own strength, but it comes directly from Jesus, and who do we have living inside of us? The Holy Spirit. God wants us to bring the kingdom of God into this world. He desires to heal and make people new. I find it interesting that when the twelve were sent out, Jesus told them to take nothing with them, but to rely on individuals who will be placed along their journeys. Yet, He gave permission that if those individuals refused, then the disciples could 'shake the dust off their feet' and it would be a sign against those individuals. I find it interesting that people actually lost out on their answered prayers because they refused to believe and accept those God used to answer that prayer. So be careful not to judge, but be aware of whether the person you are bothered by is an answer to your prayer.

1 Corinthians 1:7-9 (NLT) says, "[7] Now you have every spiritual gift you need as you eagerly wait for the return of our Lord Jesus Christ. [8] He will keep you strong to the end so that you will be free from all blame on the day when our Lord Jesus Christ returns. [9] God will do this, for he is faithful to do what he says, and he has invited you into partnership with his Son, Jesus Christ our Lord."

(Highlight 1 Corinthians 1:7-8)

In the Old Testament and in the New Testament, there are so many examples of healing taking place. The purpose of healing is for God to be glorified and to be a sign that the Gospel is true. So many churches believe that healing is no longer functioning today. In fact, when I was researching for this day, I could not believe the lies and words spoken by believers concerning "healing." I am not going to argue or debate what is true concerning healing; instead, I want you to read out loud 1 Corinthians 1:7-9. The term "the day of our Lord Jesus Christ" is referring to the great day where Christ will return to earth. The spiritual gifts will not be lacking, and will remain as we wait for His return.

Read Today: Hebrews 11, 1 Corinthians 1

~My prayer for you today~

Heavenly Father,

I come before You, and I pray for Your child reading this. Father, understanding faith and healing and believing that it is still relevant requires them to go against everything they might have been taught and against the fear of man. There are stories from around the world that show You are still healing. Help them to grasp hold of truth and to understand that You are still moving, and You have not changed. You healed in the Old Testament, You healed in the New Testament, and if You remain the same yesterday, today, and tomorrow, then You will also be healing now.

In Jesus' Name. Amen.

Day 4: Miraculous Power and Prophecy

~Prayer~

Heavenly Father, we come before You and we understand that our freedom and breakthroughs are limited when done in our own strength. We long to be free from our past mistakes, wounds, and traumas. Today we recognize that for us to receive our full healing and breakthrough it requires Your miraculous power working in us. So today, let Your Words penetrate our souls and bring deliverance.

In Jesus' Name, Amen.

Today we will be focusing on miraculous power and prophecy. We will focus on miraculous power first. When I think of miraculous power, an image of a strong muscular person comes to mind. While it's not that God won't cause us to become physically strong, it has more to do with the strengthening of our spirits. Considering the things that I have faced; it has been His power working in me that has given me the strength to endure and face it head on. When you think about it, it's also a physical power because I was able to endure and still make a difference in other people's lives, while being destroyed by others. Another way that God defines it is miracles. Miraculous power is also miracles.

When I think about where God has taken me and what He has done in my life since my divorce, it is miraculous. It can only be a miracle for me to be able to look back and live as though my past never even happened.

Read Romans 15:17-19.

Acts 19 we find that there are men who using Jesus names to cast out demons; but they have no relationship with Jesus, and so things went differently than they expected. Acts 19:15-16 (AMP) says, "[15] But the evil spirit retorted, "I know and recognize and acknowledge Jesus, and I know about Paul, but as for you, who are you?" [16] Then the man, in whom was the evil spirit, leaped on them and subdued all of them and overpowered them, so that they ran out of that house [in terror, stripped] naked and wounded."

Read Mark 16:15-19.

Miraculous power, or "miracles" that transform lives are meant to reveal the glory of God. When I think about the world we live in, the world does not see the glory of God. In fact, many "Christians" do not see the glory of God. Many pastors feel that miracles are irrelevant now because the church has been established, but the church is extremely flawed, and God is about to do something new. He is going to take the church out of the old wineskin and take us into the new wineskin. Too many churches today are dead, too many are conforming to the world and compromising to sin; they have become unfaithful, deceived, corrupt, and finally, lukewarm. God is about to move and reveal His glory through His spiritual gifts.

The world needs to see action with our words. If we are declaring the gospel, talking about how Jesus wants them to be healed, healthy, and thriving, then it makes complete sense why God then gives miraculous power. Power to overcome, power to succeed, power to heal, and it all comes down to Jesus, and for His glory. Jesus will use us just like He used Paul. But just like Acts 19 says, it is with the name of Jesus, and it is through relationship with Jesus. The demons only fear us if Jesus is in us. If the Holy Spirit is living in us, then the demons must flee. So, if we expect things to change without having that relationship with God, well, we are going to be put into situations where fear will grip us, and we realize our error of being away from Him.

Prophecy is another spiritual gift that the church has turned its back on. Many churches claim this gift is no longer in operation and call prophets horrible names. Yet so many prophets today are having the Words God has given them come to pass. So, what does God say about prophecy?

1 Corinthians 14:1-5 (NIV) says, "[1] Follow the way of love and eagerly desire gifts of the Spirit, especially prophecy. [2] For anyone who speaks in a tongue does not speak to people but to God. Indeed, no one understands them; they utter mysteries by the Spirit. [3] But the one who prophesies speaks to people for their strengthening, encouraging and comfort. [4] Anyone who speaks in a tongue edifies themselves, but the one who prophesies edifies the church. [5] I would like every one of you to speak in tongues, but I would rather have you prophecy. The one who prophesies is greater than one who speaks in tongues, unless someone interprets, so that the church may be edified."

Also read 1 Corinthians 14:22-25 and Acts 2:17-21.

We have not yet reached the very last days yet. Therefore, prophecy is important for right now. We need that direction and leading from God. I cannot imagine not having prophecy, and then expecting to make it through the last days. No, prophecy is very important so we can be aware of the times and the direction that God is leading us in. Tongues is important because it allows our spirit to connect to the Holy Spirit, but then prophecy needs to come into play in order to know the directions that God is leading us to. Prophecy cannot be ignored in these last days. There is much evil and dark intent directed towards believers, and if we want to be fully in God's will, then we need prophecy in our lives.

(Write down Acts 2:17)

Read 2 Peter 1:16-21.
Write out verses 20-21.

Today, prophecy is needed for the church to be able to discern the times and the directions we are to take. It is meant for the body of Believers. I love how Tongues is for others to know we belong to

God, and prophecy is meant for us. The Bible also makes it very clear that prophecy comes from the Holy Spirit. It is not from man, but directly from God. Has there been a time that you mocked a prophet, only to see their words that God gave them come to pass? You were mocking God. Take time to repent and then ask God to reveal to you how to test a prophet, in order not to be led astray by a false prophet.

Read Today: Acts 2, Acts 19

~My prayer for you today~
Heavenly Father,
I come before You and I pray for Your child reading this. Make this Word relevant to them. Open their eyes and ears to understand how these spiritual gifts are meant for today, not just yesterday. They desperately need direction, miracles, and breakthrough in their lives. I break off every lie that satan has spoken concerning the gifts of the Spirit, in the name of Jesus. Today I pray, Father, that You would bring forth truth and tear down the lies.
In Jesus' name, Amen.

Day 5: Discerning Spirits, Tongues, and Interpretation

~Prayer~

Heavenly Father,

We come before You and we are ready to be renewed and changed. We are ready for You to move in our lives and break us free from the box we have placed You and ourselves in. We no longer want to live dead and weak, but strong in You. So today, open our eyes and ears. In Jesus' Name, Amen.

Today we will be talking about three gifts of the Spirit: discerning spirits, tongues, and interpretation of tongues. Let's dig in right away.

Read 1 John 4:1-6.
Write verse 3.

I find these verses so very powerful. In the Western culture we are finding a new level of the antichrist movement than ever before. The world's viewpoint is being pushed down our throats, taught to our children in school and universities, and any contradiction to these viewpoints results in persecution. This persecution is nothing compared to what we see overseas, but if Christians do not wake up soon, we will see persecution unlike anything we have seen before. As Christians, we are to remain standing firm in our faith and unwavering in our relationship with God, and failure to do so results in a country filled with the antichrist spirit. There are many false prophets within the western world, and throughout the world as well. So, I love what verse three says because it clearly states how to find out the spirit of that individual.

Read 1 Corinthians 12:1-3 and write out vs. 3.

Again, we see it so very clearly that demons and satan cannot say Jesus is Lord, so when you are testing out people and looking at what they say about Him, we can understand the spirit they are moving in by what the claim about Jesus. In America, it seems we are teaching the younger generations to listen to everyone, respect everyone's opinions, and tolerate and condone what they say and do. Yet, how many in America are speaking in the Spirit of God? We need to stop teaching our children to listen to lies and condone it, but instead teach that what Jesus says is the only thing we live by. Everything that is contrary to the Word of God (Bible) is to be brought before God and dealt with through spiritual warfare. Our physical action is then to stand in the Truth of God's Word and not pattern our lives to the culture of the antichrist spirit.

So why do we need to be able to discern when someone is speaking and moving in God and when they are not? Why do we need to know what spirit is working amongst us whether from God or satan?

Read 1 Corinthians 6:1-11. (I personally love how AMP version says it.)

So why do we want to be able to discern the spirit behind every man? Because we do not want to become deceived. Once we move into being deceived, walking in that spirit, and once again become like the world, we have turned our back on Jesus and truth. Sin separates us from God, and our turning away from Him signifies where we will end up when we die. Verses 9 and 10 gives us a clear understanding of those who will not inherit the kingdom of God and will have no share in it. Now would be a good time to give yourself a spiritual check to see if any of these apply to you. If they do, now is the time to repent and turn back to God and away from sin. If one of these areas holds you hostage, then repent and continue to apply to your life everything you are learning through these weeks. By dealing with the issue, the heart issue, and then lining up your mind and actions with God; you will find that at week 16 you have already begun to change. So do not become discouraged or shamed but press into the Father's love and forgiveness. Hold fast to Him, and take His hand to be pulled out of the deceiving spirit you have invited in and be delivered from.

Revelations 13 talks about a second beast that comes out of the earth. He is able to do amazing things, even being brought back to life, which allows him to deceive people.

Read Revelation 13:15-17.

Just reading these chapters alone gives clear understanding and wisdom that we need the Gifts of the Spirit in full operation so that we can remain true to the end. I do not want to become deceived and led away from God. I want to remain in Him, stay faithful to Him, and stand as His Bride. Revelations reveals what happens to those who are not in relationship with God, remaining free from deception. It also reveals the importance of our relationship with God, because we will need Him to stand against the persecution that we will receive in those days. I have heard both sides, concerning whether believers will have already been taken in the second coming before this time of persecution, but regardless; if we are taken or if we remain, we need to be prepared and ready. Also, we need to teach these things, because if an unbeliever becomes a believer during these times, they need this relationship with God, as many of them will be martyred for their faith. They will be desperately clinging to God during these times.

I absolutely love hearing pastors speak on tongues. God has given them amazing understanding concerning it and they have studied the Word, history, and other records, in order to share understanding and knowledge with us. I then go over what they share and line it back up to the Word and I am telling you, it is powerful. Paula White-Cain and Hank Kunneman are a few pastors that have amazing teachings on tongues. (Some sermons are in April and May of 2022.)

Mark 16:17 (AMP) says, "[17] These signs will accompany those who have believed: in My name they will cast out demons, they will speak in new tongues;"

Not only should believers be actively casting out demons in Jesus' name, but we should also be speaking in new tongues. I have mentioned before the power of tongues, and the coming verses reveal what should accompany tongues when they are used in different situations.

1 Corinthians 14:26-28 (NLT) says, "[26] Well, my brothers and sisters, let's summarize. When you meet together, one will sing, another will teach, another will tell some special revelation God has given, one will speak in tongues, and another will interpret what is said. But everything that is done must strengthen all of you. [27] No more than two or three should speak in tongues. They must speak one at a time, and someone must interpret what they say. [28] But if no one is present who can interpret, they must be silent in your church meeting and speak in tongues to God privately."

I find this very interesting, because in most churches you have singers and teachers, but very rarely do you see prophesy, tongues, and interpretation. Yet, Paul says we should be seeing these in our meetings, but if no one there has the gift to interpret the tongues, then those tongues should be kept private. Remember, tongues is so men know we belong to God, but prophesy is for edifying the church. Tongues is communication between our spirit and the Holy Spirit. I also want to make note that during a church service, when everyone is praying, speaking in tongues is good and right to do. These verses are specifically towards the structured or programed parts of the service. So, when you have prayer time and the Spirit takes over, there should be freedom for believers to pray not only with their normal language, but also their tongues (language).

Read Jude 1:20-23.
What are we supposed to do?

I love how these verses explain in great detail what we are supposed to do. We are to be daily building ourselves up in our faith, our relationship with God; we should not settle and maintain but continue to grow in our relationship. We are to be praying in the Holy Spirit, which is through tongues, and then listen to what the Holy Spirit reveals to us. We are also to keep ourselves in God's love, why? So that we can be that love to others, showing mercy while others boldly snatching them from hell. Therefore, tolerance is not love, and conforming (accepting) to the world is not love; by doing those things we help them into hell instead of saving them. Many Christians have a very limited view; they are so focused on life right now that they forget their mission is for eternity and where the souls around them will end up. By speaking in tongues and hearing our orders, the blueprints for our futures, from the Holy Spirit, we are then able to act upon the love of God in a way that will change the future of millions.

Acts 19:4-6 (AMP) says, "[4] Paul said, "John performed a baptism of repentance, continually telling the people to believe in Him who was coming after him, that is, [to confidently accept and joyfully believe] in Jesus [the Messiah and Savior]." [5] After hearing this, they were baptized [again, this time] in the name of the Lord Jesus. [6] And when Paul laid his hands on them, the Holy Spirit came on them, and they began speaking in [unknown] tongues (languages) and prophesying."

The tongues are for our spirit to communicate with the Holy Spirit. It is a beautiful and intimate connection. With the tongues there should be interpretation of what we are speaking. Usually in my personal time, once I have prayed in tongues, God then gives me direction on what to pray about, or He gives me a prophetic word. I love how the previous verses state that first they began speaking in tongues and then from their words of prophesy came. It shows the beautiful relationship between the two gifts and how they work together.

As we come to an end of studying about the Gifts of the Spirit, I want you to begin to pray about what God is wanting to show and reveal to You. What truths He is longing to reveal to you, and how He wants to open your eyes and ears. Begin now so when you get to Day 7 you will be ready for the questions.

Read Today: Revelations 13, 1 Corinthians 14

~My prayer for you today~
Heavenly Father,
I come before You, and I pray for Your child reading this. I pray that You would guard their minds so that they would not become deceived. So many have fallen away from You and from truth, I pray that they would not be one of them. I pray that they would hold fast to You and Your Word, and that they would begin to discern in the Spirit and move in You. Reveal Yourself to them today.
In Jesus' Name, Amen.

Day 6: My Story and Testimonies

As I mentioned in previous days, 1 Corinthians 12 gives a list of gifts that come from the Holy Spirit. They are wisdom, knowledge, faith, healing, miraculous power, prophecy, discernment of spirits, tongues, and interpretation of tongues.

These gifts catapult us into living lives out of the box and in His Spirit. When we allow these gifts to be used in our lives, we become a powerful weapon to stop the demonic agenda. We will get into that more in week 14.

Some of us have a few, while God has given others many of these gifts. However, I believe that many of us should have more than what we do, but because we put ourselves in a box, we do not reach our full potential in Christ. We limit what He can give us, or we end up not receiving the gifts He gave us.

I have mentioned before how I received my native language, which is tongues, in week 3. For me, I was baptized in the Spirit and in the next moment speaking in tongues. I opened my mouth, and my language was there. I love having a language that my spirit can automatically connect to the Holy Spirit in such a deep and intimate way. There are many times where I do not know what to pray, so I will begin to pray in tongues and then understanding, interpretation, and leading of what to pray for comes. Other times a release takes place in my spirit and a weight comes off. I do not always know why, but my spirit does.

I want to take time to share how some of these gifts have been used in my life, how there were times I used them wisely, but also times I failed miserably.

The year 2008 was when I went through my time of depression and then return to God. Towards the end of 2008 I reconnected with my ex, (who is now my ex-husband), and we became an official couple around October. From then and through 2009 we dated. God was speaking to me all the time and I was excited for the future. However, once you get to week 11, you will see I was not in a healthy, good, or even Christlike relationship. I was in sin and addicted to sexual desire. So, what does that have to do with prophecy?

All the prophetic words about my future husband were, in my mind, related to the man who would become my ex-husband. After our divorce I went back through my 2008-2009 journal, and I could see very clearly when the shift, of who the prophecy concerned, changed. Well, what does that mean? The promises and words God gave me are true and will come to pass, but the one who (the person it is with) has changed. This goes back to God giving us free will. We choose if we will be obedient to Him. I talk more about that in Chapter 10 in Held Hostage.

So, in other words, my ex was refusing to obey God and change, which led to God saying, "These promises and words will come to pass, but I am going to bring another who loves Me and will love you." Because of my choices, I failed to ask God what the promises and prophecies meant to Him. It led to my miserable failing, and I stubbornly clung to a man I should have let go of. This led to ten years of marriage filled with abuse, betrayal, and abandonment.

I failed to discern the times and the shift. Now I can see very clearly how none of the prophecy applied to my ex but actually has to do with my future spouse God is going to bring to me.

When God speaks to us prophetically it is very important not to put our own thoughts on it, but to seek Him and let Him reveal the meaning.

Now that I shared an example of my failure in the gift of prophecy, I want to share an example of how I used it properly. In 2020, I began to draw close to God, and came to a place of admitting I was being abused. The beginning of January 2021, I reached the place where I was able to clearly see the shift and reality that was surrounding me. In a moment of deeply admitting this in prayer, this hit my spirit. My relationship with my ex was going to experience something big. Two weeks later God spoke so very clearly and prophetically about what was going to take place. "There is a shaking that will be taking place. Your husband will be rebuked and challenged. You will be protected during this time; I will bring family to help you. During this time, if you stay pressed into Me, you will stay standing amidst the shaking. Everything will change."

Less than two weeks later, the shaking took place. I had no idea what to expect, but I trusted God. I knew that the outcome would end in divorce. So, when the shaking came and my ex crossed lines with an acquaintance, I had peace. I had been warned and knew to be prepared. It did not take me out like his affair eight years before had. I remained in Christ, and so I was planted on a firm foundation.

God has given us all gifts, and He asks that we use them wisely and spiritually so that it will build the Kingdom of God on earth.

Testimonies:

* Regarding my gifting, I've always had discernment, even though I didn't realize it until I was older. God would allow me to know things before they happened; I have always been very sensitive to what's going on in the spiritual realm too, as well as other people's emotions and struggles. As I have grown closer to the Lord, He has been showing me how He has also gifted me in prophecy. When I was in high school, a guest speaker came to my home church. I no longer remember what he preached on, but he invited any who wanted to be baptized in the Holy Spirit to the front, and I immediately went. The entire time beforehand, I felt strange and sick to my stomach. When the speaker touched my forehead, an invisible wall of heat surrounded me; it seemed that I could see it, and in that moment, I was filled with the Spirit. But not understanding why it physically affected me so strongly, I turned to run out of terror. I did not speak in tongues then, and for quite a few years I thought I had not been filled with the Spirit because I didn't speak in tongues. Then, just a few months ago, a friend told me about a sermon she'd heard online, encouraging me to listen. In it, the preacher spoke of how he learned to speak in tongues. He did not receive that gift immediately when he was filled with the Spirit, but instead he had to practice and learned it over time. As I listened to this sermon, I immediately sensed that this was what I had to do as well, that the gift of tongues was within me, but that God wanted to teach me. Despite my embarrassment and fear of being disrespectful, I began to simply make noises and practice. I now can speak in tongues fluently, though it is changing and growing as I continue to speak it. It has brought me to a new depth in my relationship with the Lord, and I am so thankful for the way He continues to teach me. ~Krystle V.

Day 7: Self-Reflection

~Prayer~

Heavenly Father,

We come before You and we take time today to hear Your voice. Please direct this time of fellowship with You. Reveal to us what You are wanting to say and direct us. In Jesus' Name, Amen.

Today I will be asking hard questions and I want you to write down your answers of what God truthfully and honestly has revealed to you.

Concerning the Gifts of Spirit, where have you believed the lies?

What has God revealed to you concerning how He wants you to use the Gifts of the Spirit?

Look up five miracles that took place in the New Testament and write the reference and a summary of the miracle.

Look up three examples where people were filled with the Holy Spirit and spoke in tongues. Write the reference and summary.

Look up five examples of prophecy in the New Testament and write the reference and summary of each.

Look up three examples of faith and give the reference and summary.

Look up five examples of discerning spirits, wisdom, and knowledge. Write the reference and summary.

Find one example of each of the Gifts of the Spirit in today's world, write down what country, who it was involved with, and what God has done with it.

~My prayer for you today~
Heavenly Father,
I am so excited to see what things your child learns as they study the Bible for themselves, as they discern the spirits and see how these gifts are being used in today's world. Open their eyes and ears.
In Jesus' Name, Amen.

Week 7: Spiritual Support System (Tribe)

"[44] All the believers were together and had everything in common. [45] They sold property and possessions to give to anyone who had need. [46] Every day they continued to meet together in the temple courts. They broke bread in their homes and ate together with glad and sincere hearts, [47] praising God and enjoying the favor of all the people. And the Lord added to their number daily those who were being saved."

(Acts 2:44-47 NIV)

Day 1: Tribe

When I think about everything that I have been through, I praise God for the people He brought into my life that encouraged, prayed, and held me up when I would have fallen. The truth is that many do not have the support system or what I call the tribe.

The 'tribe' has been a new term that has been popping up in prophetic words lately and I truly believe that we are about to see a major shift in our way of living. A tribe could be a church you belong to, it could be the people who you can talk and pray with, and it could be something that you have not obtained yet.

For many people the word 'tribe' is going to be foreign, but I believe that after this week is over you will have better understanding and wisdom on how to go about having a tribe.

We will start our week by learning about the tribes in the Old Testament; we will then move to learning about the tribe (Church) in the New Testament, what to look for in a tribe, and then begin to see what God is wanting to do now with tribes.

For many who are reading this, you might have experienced your trauma, abuse, or even greatest betrayals in the church. Sadly, what the Church has become today is never what it was supposed to be like. The church has two extreme realms that it can fall into. You have those who judge, segregate, and gossip about others. And then you have those who allow anything and say that you do not need to change because God accepts you how you are. The flaws these two pendulums bring have caused many wounds and hurts and have also kept people hostage to sin and death.

The old wineskin, the old appearance, and the way the church has been done is in the past. God is doing a new thing, and we are now putting on a new wineskin. We are getting back to our original design, and back to our roots in Christ.

Read Today: Acts 2

~Prayer~

Heavenly Father, we come before You, and we cry out to You. Jesus, Son of David, have mercy on us. Help us to understand why the old is not working anymore, and how You are wanting to do a new thing. We get the opportunity and the privilege to be a part of the new that You are doing. We get to be empowered to bring Your Kingdom here to the world. Help us today to understand what You are wanting to reveal to us. We break off every distraction, disappointment, and lie from the enemy, in Jesus' name. We speak freedom and healing over our minds, hearts, and souls. Open our eyes and ears today. In Jesus' Name, Amen.

Day 2: What is a Tribe?

~Prayer~

Heavenly Father, we come before You and we are so excited to get a glimpse of Old Testament tribes, because we understand that there are parts of the tribe of the Old Testament that should be active in our tribes today. So, speak to us, and reveal to us Your truth. In Jesus' Name, Amen.

Today I pose the question: what is a Tribe?
(Write down what you think a tribe is.)

For many, this is a foreign concept they have never experienced before. Therefore, to give a statement of what a tribe is would be hard for many. I never really thought about the tribes of the Old Testament or their function before. In fact, it was not until my divorce proceedings had been started that tribes began to stand out to me. It was during this time of healing that I decided to read the whole Bible in one year, which I did; there have been some books of the Bible that I will read, but not a lot necessarily stands out, such as Leviticus and Numbers.

Yet when I reached these books, I began to understand something very clearly. First, God cares about the details, and He has an order to everything (even when it looks chaotic). Second, everything He did and told His people to do was for specific reasons and purposes and was not in vain. And third, we get a better understanding of tribes and how they work.

So, the twelve tribes are mentioned in Genesis 49, because Jacob is about to bless his twelve sons, and these twelve sons birth their own tribes. We then find these tribes living in Egypt, prosperous and fruitful, and then hated because of their wealth and favor, so they were forced into slavery. It is then that Moses comes forth and is used by God to deliver the people. Miracles upon miracles, deliverance, and freedom were gained through hardship and trial of faith.

We then get to Leviticus, which talks about what offerings need to be made and how they are to be made, the laws for health and cleanliness, and the ways people should be treated. We then get into Numbers, which should tell you what it's about. Right away in Chapter 1 it talks about how many individuals are in each tribe. I find it very interesting that every tribe was counted except for the tribe that served God in the Tabernacle: the Levites. Instead, they were left uncounted; their whole purpose was to take care of all the equipment and the items used in the tabernacle, as well as the Ark of the Covenant, which God rested upon in the Holy of Holies. This shows me that the number is not what matters in a tribe. Then we get into how each tribe was supposed to travel as they wandered in the wilderness. There was an order and a direction given from God for this.

(**Read Numbers 2** and fill out the information about where each tribe was to camp.)
What is in the middle of the tribes? _____

Judah _____

Issachar _____

Zebulun _____

Reuben _____

Simeon _____

Gad _____

Ephraim/Manasseh (tribe of Joseph) _____

Benjamin _____

Dan _____

Asher _____

Naphtali _____

I love what Numbers 2:34 (NIV) says, "[34] So the Israelites did everything the LORD commanded Moses; that is the way they encamped under their standards, and that is the way they set out, each of them with their clan and family."

We see throughout Numbers that when the tribes were being obedient and living according to the will of God they prospered and were blessed. We also see how when they sinned or made wrong decisions it would affect their families, and often the entire tribe. Sometimes their sin affected all the tribes. Numbers 12, 13, 14, 16, 20, and 21 are just a few of the examples given for this.

I love how each tribe had a function and something that they were personally called for. Some were meant to follow, others to lead; some were known for their battle skills, some were called into a greater sense of ministry, and others struggled to find their place because of wrong connections and sin, and it took them time to get back into alignment.

I would encourage you to go through and read Leviticus, Numbers, and Deuteronomy in the following months. The reason being that as you read it, you begin to see how detail-orientated God is. As I read them the question that came to my mind was, "How often have I failed to see God's details in my life?" Because God has not changed, and if He was detail-orientated in the Old Testament, then that remains true for my own life. Not only that, but you will begin to understand the important of having right connections and relationships, and how our choices affect others, not just ourselves.

It is very interesting to me how all the tribes worked together.

Read Joshua 1:12-15.

Although two and a half tribes had already received their promised land, they stayed to fight the battles with their brethren from another tribe. Together they fought against the enemy and took the ground that God said to take. I just love their hearts being revealed here because they understood what being a tribe meant. Not only that, but they submitted to authority, and came up with their own consequences if they failed to obey. (**Read Joshua 1:16-18**, anyone notice how important they took this, the consequence they chose was DEATH!) They encouraged one another on. I can only imagine the rest of the tribe's relief and encouragement, knowing that these two and a half tribes would continue to go on with them and help them with their own land that needed to be conquered.

Another examples of tribes in the Old Testament that I want to hit on is in the story of David. In 1

Samuel 21 we find David alone, on the run from Saul, and he is traveling from place to place. I find it interesting that it is in this moment of being alone that David was given the weapon that had once belonged to his greatest triumph: the killing of Goliath. How many of us who have been alone have found that when we have passed through that season, we have become equipped with great weapons to tear down what once Held us Hostage?

In 1 Samuel 22:1-2 (NLT) says, "[1] So David left Gath and escaped to the cave of Adullam. Soon his brothers and all his other relatives joined him there. [2] Then others began coming—men who were in trouble or in debt or who were just discontented—until David was the captain of about 400 men."

In the following chapters more and more men come to be with David. And finally, the country makes him their king. There are times that we must be alone to grow, learn, and depend on God. But we are not meant to be alone forever. David had men from his own tribe that came and supported him, but eventually he had men from every tribe following him. There was unity amongst them.

Read Today: Numbers 12, 13, 14, 16, 20, and 21

~My prayer for you today~
Heavenly Father,
I come before You, and I pray for Your child reading this. I have a sensing that Your child is seeing the power of the tribe, working together for the Kingdom and to advance You throughout the world, but also seeing how their own choices have led to areas of weakness within the tribe. I pray that as these are revealed, they would repent and turn from these areas. I pray that they would begin to look at their connections and see who should remain and who needs to be let go. I also understand that sometimes letting go means having stronger boundaries and not necessarily the complete removal from their life. So please give them wisdom and understanding to discern what You are saying about each of their connections and relationships.
In Jesus' Name, Amen.

Day 3: New Testament Tribe (Church)

~Prayer~

Heavenly Father,

We come before You and we are ready to see the church through Your eyes. Our own understanding of church and its function has become flawed by those who used it as a weapon and a tool for the enemy. We thank You for those who remained faithful and true to You, and we ask for conviction upon those who lost their way. We long for them to return to You, just as we have. In Jesus' Name, Amen.

Today we will be looking at the church, which is a tribe. I think it is important for us to understand that what God intends for the church is not what we see today. To understand our future, it is important to understand our roots and beginning.

(**Read Acts 2:42-47** and answer these questions and fill in the blanks.)

How often did they meet together? _____

What did they devote themselves to? _____

They would break _____ and _____.

_____ and _____ were performed by the apostles.

_____ were together and had _____ in common.

They sold _____ and _____ to give to those in need.

They would meet in the _____ courts, broke bread in their

_____ and ate together with _____ and

_____ hearts.

_____ God and _____ the

_____ of all, the people.

Who added to their number daily those who were being saved? _____

Acts 4:32-35 (NLT) says, "[32] All the believers were united in heart and mind. And they felt that what they owned was not their own, so they shared everything they had. [33] The apostles testified powerfully to the resurrection of the Lord Jesus, and God's great blessing was upon them all. [34] There were no needy people among them, because those who owned land or houses would sell them [35] and bring the money to the apostles to give to those in need."

Amazing! The church oversaw helping those in need. Not the government, not non-believers, but the church. Although we do see this in action, the truth is that it is becoming less and less and more believers are expecting the government to help. Yet, we clearly see that the tribe of believers understood their responsibility and what God was asking of them. But, in today's church, we do not see the evidence of this tribe. I'm excited for when this tribe comes back in full display for the world to see.

Read Acts 11:27-30.

Again and again, we see that the tribe was of one heart and mind. They took care of each other, praying for one another and standing together as one. I find it interesting to note that even during the New Testament days, there were many churches who were babies in the Lord and did not become mature. Not only that, but they were forsaking their first love, judging others, and over and over they were corrected for that. Paul desired for the church to return to what it truly means to be a follower of Jesus.

So many churches today are babies in the Lord. So many are judgmental and live in legalism instead of grace. So many have become lukewarm, and people go to church out of habit with no relationship involved. So many churches preach what is contrary to the Word of God and twist the Bible into allowing sin to be called good. So many churches have lost their way and are dragging believers to hell with them.

It is time we get back to be the tribe we were meant to be. Tomorrow we will look at what we should be looking for in a tribe.

Read Today: Acts 2, Acts 4, Acts 11

~My prayer for you today~
Heavenly Father,
I come before You, and I pray for Your child reading this. So many of Your children have been hurt by the church. They have been judged, condemned, and gossiped about. Your children have been affected by the decisions of those who are called to steward Your people, but who failed. Today, I pray that You would begin to heal their hearts, minds, and souls. Bring truth to them. Father, if any of them have played a part in hurting other believers, I pray that they would take this time to repent and make things right with those they hurt. Redeem these situations and reveal to them how You are going to bring good things out of painful things.
In Jesus' Name, Amen.

Day 4: What to Look for In a Tribe?

~Prayer~

Heavenly Father,

We come before You and we ask that You give us wisdom, knowledge, and understanding on how to connect with the right tribe. We understand that the connections we make right now will affect our future and our promises. We understand that our tribe has a great importance to our own roles. So today we ask that You reveal truth to us and help us to break off connections that should not be a part of our tribe. In Jesus' Name, Amen.

Today we will be answering the question of what to look for in a tribe. For many of us it will require us to let go of where we are at right now. It will also require us to form healthy boundaries in relationships with those both inside and outside of our tribe.

(Answer the questions and sentences.)

Read Galatians 6:1-7.

How should one be restored? _____

What are we to carry? _____

I love the way the church is to be restoration to other believers. It must be done in the Holy Spirit, with gentleness. I find it interesting that right away a connection is made to the believers restoring, and how they could fall into temptation or sin themselves. Ever wonder how pastors can fall, how church elders and leaders can fall? The Bible makes it clear that if our actions are not done in the Spirit we could be tempted. Pride also goes before a fall. We can become so full of ourselves and claim the healing was done in our own strength and we take away the glory and honor meant for God and instead become prideful. This removes us from under God's protection. Pride is sin. It is very important that we remain in Christ, restoring the Bride, staying away from deception and pride, and owning up to our own mistakes and choices in order to receive complete healing and restoration.

Read Matthew 18:15-17.

If a brother or sister sins, what are we supposed to do?

What do we do if they do not listen the first time?

What do we do if they do not listen the second time?

Finally, what do we do if they do not listen the third time?

How many of you see this one acted out among believers today? Truthfully, not many of us see this being lived out in the church. Instead, we see gossip, malice, and the murdering of fellow believers' characters, and God is not in that. Jesus makes it very clear how we are to be interacting with one another, and yet how many times do our leaders fail to lead by example? How many times do grownup believers fail to lead by example? And then we have new believers following the example set by the adult believers and now we can see why the church has become what it is. This principle also applies to work life (Christian businesses), family life, and it's called to be something that believers live by.

Read 1 Corinthians 5:1-5 and 9-13.
Are we allowed to pass judgement on a brother or sister?

_____

Now people might find this very extreme, and I can already sense that some will be full of anger over these verses because of their own pain when power was misused to judge. If a person is in sin, first we follow what Matthew 18:15-17 says. If there is no repentance and change then the consequence of removal is needed. Instead, we have seen the church validate the sinner and say that there is no need to change because Christ accepts us for who we are. Yes, Jesus died for us while we were still sinners, He loves us and accepts us, but if we remain in sin we really do not belong to Him and His family. So, the church has become a tool of satan to allow sin to remain.

But then you have the other extreme, where a person who sinned repented and changed from that sin, but they are still judged, shamed, ignored, and cast out from the tribe. We must understand the person's heart by the leading of the Spirit. If they remain in sin, consequence. If they repent and turn from their ways, then gentleness. I also find it very interesting that we are to judge believers, but not non-believers. That judgement needs to be done in the Holy Spirit and is done so that the individual will return to God, away from the gates of hell.

Titus 3:10-11 (NLT) says, "[10] If people are causing divisions among you, give a first and second warning. After that, have nothing more to do with them. [11] For people like that have turned away from the truth, and their own sins condemn them."

How many warnings should be given? _____

Division is not from God, gossip and malic should not be a part of our speech. If people handle the situation correctly there should be no reason for gossip because they have handled the situation and shared their heart on the matter with that individual. If the individual does not change, then you move on and have nothing to do with them. Yet, more and more we see the church becoming divided and offended over things that mean nothing compared to heaven and hell.

2 Thessalonians 3:14-15 (RSV) says, "[14] If any one refuses to obey what we say in this letter, note that man, and have nothing to do with him, that he may be ashamed. [15] Do not look on him as an

enemy, but warn him as a brother."

How are we to warn them? _____

How many situations have we seen where individuals are treated as an enemy instead of a brother or sister? This has led to many damaged relationships in the church and has also led to brothers and sisters leaving God and headed back to hell's door. As a tribe we should be walking as brothers and sisters, and we really need the Holy Spirit leading us in how to respond accurately to situations, making sure that it is done in the right spirit, attitude, and tone. Our heart should be for the return to God, not helping satan out.

James 5:19-20 (RSV) says, "[19] My brethren, if any one among you wanders from the truth and some one brings him back, [20] let him know that whoever brings back a sinner from the error of his way will save his soul from death and will cover a multitude of sins."

If a brother or sister turns away from sin, what should the tribe do?

What a beautiful image of the tribe. A group of individuals who are not only bringing non-believers to God, but also helping those who once believed come back to God.

Luke 17: 3-4 (NLT) says, "[3] So watch yourselves! "If another believer sins, rebuke that person; then if there is repentance, forgive. [4] Even if that person wrongs you seven times a day and each time turns again and asks forgiveness, you must forgive."

What should we do if they repent?

How many times do we forgive?

(I want to point out that it says, 'the individual repents.' We should always forgive regardless of if they repent, but we should have boundaries in place as well. Do not give people the power to continue to hurt you, especially when abuse is involved. Forgive, but that does not mean keep them in your life.)

Read Colossians 3:12-17.
What are we to clothe ourselves in?

What should rule our hearts?

Write out vs 16 and 17.

We need to remember that sin is sin, but the consequences for each is different. As believers, we are all learning and growing in our relationship with God, and our habits and responses are being challenged and molded into a response that reflects the Father. A believer who is wanting to grow, learn, repent, and change is different from a [believer] who is walking in sin and wants to remain in sin, abusing Jesus' grace. What God is calling us into is going to require us to walk with God in a way that we never have before. We need to be in His presence every minute of every day, flowing in the Holy Spirit, ready to give an account of our own lives.

Read Ephesians 4:29-32.
What should not come out of our mouths?

What should come out of our mouths?

What should we get rid of?

Write out vs 32.

Verse 30 really pulls at my heart. We should not bring sorrow to God's Spirit. WOW! How many times have my words and actions done exactly that? It really makes you step back and reflect on yourself. I do not want to bring sorrow; I want to bring joy to my Father's Spirit. I want Him to feel honored and glorified when He looks at my words and actions. Too many times I have brought sorrow and used the excuse of, 'well so and so did this to me, so I responded with this,' like it gives me the freedom to bring sorrow to His Spirit. This was an area that God really dealt with me in during times when the mental abuse was going on by my ex. I realized that God did not want me to respond in anger, harsh words, etc.; but instead, He wanted me to respond out of the Holy Spirit. I needed to keep my heart right with Him, and not allow in weeds that would destroy my life and my character forever.

Read Hebrews 5:11-14.
What does it mean to be an infant in Christ?

What does it mean to be mature in Christ?

One of my goals is that by the end of week 16, you will have become stronger and mature in the

Lord. That you would crave meat, crave being challenged, crave growing, and crave distinguishing good from evil. I long to see you reaching your full potential instead of being limited by satan. My heart's cry is that you will become part of the tribe, ready for battle, and ready for the promises of God to be fulfilled in your life.

1 Corinthians 1:10 (NIV) says, "[10] I appeal to you, brothers and sisters, in the name of our Lord Jesus Christ, that all of you agree with one another in what you say and that there be no divisions among you, but that you be perfectly united in mind and thought."

What are we to agree on?

What are we to be united in?

United, unified, of one mind. I am pretty sure that those words right now are a dream you would also like to see be brought into reality. How powerful the tribe would be if we all functioned under the power of the Holy Spirit, and in unity with God. There would be no limit to what God could use us for because we would be at a place that is mature and ready.

1 Corinthians 12:12-14 (NIV) says, "[12] Just as a body, though one, has many parts, but all its many parts form one body, so it is with Christ. [13] For we were all baptized by one Spirit so as to form one body—whether Jews or Gentiles, slave or free—and we were all given the one Spirit to drink. [14] Even so the body is not made up of one part but of many."

What are we baptized by? _____

What were we given to drink? _____

Write vs 14.

All of us have been filled by one (ONE) Spirit, although we each have a different calling, ministry, and function in the body of Christ; we are also to be one. I long to see the day where the Bride acts as one instead of many. No wonder the world looks at us and does not long for the relationship we have with God. They are longing to see the true relationship with God that has yet to be revealed through the Bride.

Read Romans 15:1-6.
Those who are strong should do what for the weak?

Who should we build up?

Write out vs 4-6.

Why should we accept one another?

To summarize, our tribes should be people who live for God, love God, and who are of one mind. They should have unity, live free from sin, and be open for correction. There should be vulnerability, love, gentleness, and yet correction too. The gifts of the Spirit should be in operation, we should be serving one another instead of focusing on our own wants, desires, and needs. And ultimately, God should be glorified within the tribe. The tribe is the body of Christ, and we should be bringing the Kingdom of God to the world.

Read Today: Acts 2

~My prayer for you today~
Heavenly Father,
I come before You, and I pray for Your child reading this. I pray that You would help them understand who the people of their tribe should be. It should be those who are following You, longing for You, and passionate about You. It should be those who will correct and yet forgive. It should be those who are mature in the Lord, and if they are infants, they should be striving to become mature and not remain as such. It should be people who are trustworthy, faithful, and have no evil talk coming from their mouths. It should be individuals who desire Your kingdom and are walking examples of You. So today, I pray that Your child would begin to look at those around them and choose wise support systems.
In Jesus' Name, Amen.

Day 5: What is the Remnant (Tribe) Supposed to Become?

~Prayer~

Heavenly Father,

We come before You today and we are so excited for what You have in store for us. You are calling us into a new, and the past is being taken away. We are ready, Father. We are ready to take the step. The waiting has been so hard, being alone has been so hard, and yet, God, we sense the new is almost here. The new is the next steps that we are about to take. They are not distant, and they are not far away. No, the new is now. In Jesus' Name, Amen.

God is about to do something completely new in the coming days and years. It will break down every illusion that the church has tried so hard to build. The church today is a shell of what it is supposed to be and what its function could be. God is going to be doing something new and we get the opportunity to step into the new with Him.

In Acts 2:44-47 (NKJV) says, "[44] Now all who believed were together, and had all things in common, [45] and sold their possessions and goods, and divided them among all, as anyone had need. [46] So continuing daily with one accord in the temple, and breaking bread from house to house, they ate their food with gladness and simplicity of heart, [47] praising God and having favor with all the people. And the Lord added to the church daily those who were being saved."

We are about to see churches that are dead become an afterthought. We are going to see tribes rise up who devote themselves to the teachings of the Bible without the culture changing or influencing them. We will see fellowship taking place throughout the week in gatherings, eating meals together, fellowshipping together, prophesying together, and providing for all those in need. The tribe will not look to the government to help those around them; instead, they will become the driving force in helping them.

We are about to see the harvest coming in. We are about to see a great shift take place as the Bride of Christ comes into unity. What I love is that Israel was made up of twelve tribes and yet they were also one tribe. We are going to see smaller tribes working together with other smaller tribes, all for the glory of God. Instead of denominations and churches who are separated, ignored, or purposefully rejected, we are going to see tribes working together for the Kingdom of God.

God is about to bring connections between different ministries and different organizations, and although they will function separately, there will also be a coming together to help one another in each of their own ministries. Pastors helping pastors, congregations helping congregations, nations helping nations, because the tribes will all be working together for the Kingdom of God.

We are about to see tribes functioning in the Gifts of the Spirit like never before. Those who have promises and callings will be ushered into them, because the tribe will be supporting and speaking forth their futures. The tribe will lay the foundation for one another, build each other up, and encourage one another to be strong and courageous.

We are about to see things shift, and the church as we know it today will be gone. Some churches will try to stay in the old and will not want to change or allow the Holy Spirit room to move within their programs. But the tribes will throw the programs away and allow the Holy Spirit full access to move how He so desires. We will see churches who reject the Holy Spirit begin to fall and be removed. We will begin to see their power and control be taken away.

We will begin to see the tribe take back the ground that the enemy stole. We will bring the Kingdom of God to every area in the world. The Kingdom of God will be brought to the government, education, family, religion, media, entertainment, and business. We will see the Kingdom of God take the lead in music, arts, movies, business, family, education, and government, and the one God uses will be the Tribe, His BRIDE! He is calling us to live for Him not just on Sundays, but every day. It is time for the bride to walk out her relationship with God in fear and trembling. We are about to see God in a new way, and because the anointing and glory around us is greater, we will be held to a higher accountability. We do not want to be like those in the Old Testament who did not honor God the Father, God the Son, and God the Holy Spirit who, because of their lack of honor, integrity, and obedience, lost their lives in supernatural ways.

Right now, we are stepping into a new thing. If we hold onto the past ways of doing things, the past ways of thinking, and the past ways of church, we will miss what God is doing. Two years ago on November of 2020, I sensed a shift taking place in the spiritual realm. We will begin to see this shift manifested into the physical realm in the coming years. Every November since 2020, a new shift has taken place that is bringing the tribe closer and closer. It is almost here. Every day I can sense it, and I can feel in my spirit how it is about to collide into us. Are you READY???????? Have you positioned yourself to be ready for what God is doing right now? Are you willing to be BOLD? In week 8 we will talk about being bold, because what God is doing right now will require it of us. Boldness to face our pasts, to stand in our presents, and to grasp our futures that He has called us to.

Read Today: 1 Corinthians 12

~My prayer for you today~
Heavenly Father,
I come before You, and I pray for Your child reading this. I pray that You would begin to reveal to them their place in Your tribe, that they would begin to walk in unity and understand that every day You are wanting Your kingdom to be brought into what they are doing. Not only that but You are wanting them to take back the ground the enemy has stolen from them. Today, I pray that they would become bold.
In Jesus' Name, Amen.

Day 6: My Story and Testimonies

Many of us have been traveling life alone, fighting the good fight alone, but we were not meant to be that way. I have been fortunate to have experienced what it is like to live in a community of believers that function as a tribe and a family. Although it was short, it ruined me for the normal western Church.

The way that church is in America is not an accurate reflection of the church in Acts. We do not do community, we do not act like a family (because families in America are broken and under attack right now), and we do not have fellowship. Too many churches have cliques or only see each other for a couple hours and then no more the rest of the week. As we have learned the importance of having a tribe, I find it very encouraging that many prophets are sharing how God has placed it on their hearts that He is bringing tribes back, and we will not be alone anymore.

Even as I write this, I am praying for my full tribe to be brought together. We need each other because we are an answer to our prayers for each other.

Some may still be wondering why we really need a tribe. So, in answer, I am going to take us way back into my past. I grew up in my family as a middle child. My parents are pastors, but also have been missionaries, and know about community and tribe. I was taught that my siblings will always be my best friends and that we are to protect each other. I have been given spiritual gifts that were relevant even at a young age. I had common sense, wisdom, and understanding about things beyond my age. This led to my siblings turning to me for help or understanding of a situation.

It also led to my taking over the spiritual role of an older sibling. It's a role that I have carried for twenty-five some years. I became the strong one in my family, under my dad. Our family is very thankful for my father and his role in our family. He has carried the responsibilities of his family in a beautiful example of Father God. In fact, every single one of my friends, from when I was a child to now, has said that they wished they had my parents because of their hearts, the anointing on them, and how they are to us. I am very blessed to have them.

Through the years I saw clearly what the rest of the family was able to handle, and I took on the role of standing strong for my family no matter what I personally faced. Very rarely would I show my own weaknesses, and even if I was broken and at the end of my own strength, I would still stand strong for them.

As I look back, I see the mistakes I made. My protection meant I shielded them from consequences that would have helped them in the future. It means they struggled later to stand on their own without support. Although I did a lot right, I also did a lot wrong. It is an area I repented to my siblings about and asked for their forgiveness. Thankfully, God was with them and able to overcome the mistakes I made in their lives.

Coming back to being the oldest role, the strong one, this role also brought hardships. As I mentioned in week 3 about how I cheated on my boyfriend which led to planning my death, that then led to depression. In week 11, I will share more about my perspective during that time, but today I want to share about the situation that came from this and how it shifted my view of myself that I finally am overcoming.

As I mentioned, I cheated, and although we did not have sex, I went further sexually than I should have. A few months after my suicide bought, I decided I wanted to be tested on some things and see if the doctor had any concerns about my depression or if it seemed better. I was not taking anything for my depression but handling it through some steps I share later in week 13. I was struggling and I really did not want to be alone at this doctor visit. I asked someone if they would go with me, but was told, "You made these choices and you need to face these consequences alone." So, brokenly, I faced it. I remember I met with my spiritual mom after the doctor visit, and I cried. I felt ashamed and alone, and I believed the lies that satan was speaking over me. Now when I look back, I realize that my spiritual mother was there for me, and I was not alone. Also, my parents were praying for me, checking on me daily, even throughout the night, and were willing to listen to me. They were my support team throughout those rough months. Even my brother decided that he wanted to take a trip that summer with me, and together we traveled to Colorado, and got lost in the Garden of the Gods for five hours. Each one of my family was doing things for me, but I didn't see it clearly until God began to take me through the healing process thirteen years later.

Sadly, because I believed the lie, I quit asking for help, I quit sharing about my life in detail with full disclosure, and I began to stand alone. Not only with my family, but also friends. For the next thirteen years I stood alone. I would share different things that were happening, but not everyone would know all the details. In fact, I told my family and friends limited information so they would not experience anxiety, pain, or have to shoulder everything I was experiencing. Another huge factor was that I did not want to admit to the marriage I had. I refused to admit I was being abused and would come up with excuses in my mind for why I was being treated the way I was. I felt that if I admitted I was being abused, it meant all the lies were true, even though I had already been believing the lies for far too long.

It was not until after my separation and divorce that my family and handful of friends knew everything. I told them all the details, the excuses I came up with to make my ex look good and what was really going on behind the scenes, and opened myself up to them to see how my heart was strong and yet shattered. I shared with them all the red flags I saw now but was blinded to in the beginning of the relationship. During those thirteen years, my siblings were going through their own challenges at the same time, and I knew they would be unable to handle mine, so I shouldered theirs and my own. I found ways to share a little bit of what I was facing with my siblings, but I really watered it down. The goal was to keep them from seeing any red flags and that I was struggling. Truthfully, they knew something was off, and all they could do was pray for me, and love me the way they could. Many days my sister would show up with a coffee drink, wanting to let me know that I was not alone and she was thinking and praying for me. My family found ways to show me they loved me and were a great support system. In 2019, God brought a sister in Christ into my life. We would meet once a week and I would encourage her in what God was doing in her life, and although I did not share the details about my life I was comforted. Then as God began to move and speak to me in the later 2020, I began to open up more to her about what God was saying to me, and then opened up about the abuse. Then right away in 2021 everything happened, and each week we would meet and talk about what God was teaching us, speaking to us, and what He was leading us towards. There were times when we didn't know what to say, but as we kept our focus on God we were encouraged and strengthened together. It has been three years and we still meet once a week and talk about what God is doing and speaking to us.

My dad knew more than the rest (in fact, God had told him about many things in prayer, because of his giftings, and so we would pray over what God revealed to him), he was there for me when my ex had his first affair. I would cry all the time and nights were extremely rough. My dad would check on me and we would sit and pray together, and he would hold me while I broke. During the times of the abuse, I would water things down and just say, 'my ex is in one of his moods,' and yet towards the end of the marriage I began to get braver about the things my ex would say, and my dad would then speak truth and life over me. My mom was doing what she could for my siblings, and she was also concerned for me during the different situations she knew about, and I chose to help hold the weight with her for my siblings. When my ex had his affair, she was concerned I might fall into depression so she took away all medicine and anything sharp that could destroy my life. (My depression that time did not lead to suicidal thoughts like before.) I chose to stand alone and stand strong for my family, because I wanted them to be happy even if I wasn't. I wanted them to live in favor, blessing, and unburdened by my choices of who I chose as a husband.

I was able to see my family come together to help during times of challenges, hardships, joys, and consequences. Although I was not able to experience that towards my own marriage and the abuse I was hiding, I was able to experience it in other situations in life. I once had a conversation with some friends, and I explained that even though I had an amazing family and friends who were constantly supporting me and speaking life to me, it didn't make up for what was lacking in my marriage. They cannot and are not supposed to fulfill the role my ex-husband was to fulfill. I am thankful I was able to be there for my family and that they were there for me, sadly I wish I could have seen it at the time, instead, of looking at life through victim eyes.

It is very tiring, being the one to stand alone. Many ask how I was able to make it through everything without sharing all the details, and the truth is it's all GOD! I should not be here. It makes no sense after going through all I went through that I am where I am, but by the grace of God, here I am. I see how He was with me, and the individuals He used even if they had no idea what I was facing or had limited knowledge about it. He is a good, good Father.

I am ready for a tribe, though. To function at a greater level with others who are called into the same field. I am thankful for my family and friends and how this last year brought us closer, but there are still more members to the tribe that need to be added.

When God told me I would be writing Held Hostage, I struggled with the vulnerability it would require. People would know the details and I would not be able to hide. But God gave me confidence and the assurance of His heart. Two weeks after I finished Held Hostage, God told me I would be writing a second book to go with it. Two and a half months later, before I started writing it, God told me I would have to share even more and become completely vulnerable. I said, "Yes!" And then I asked God, "Why? Why me?" His answer was, "The world needs vulnerability, and you are one who will say yes." One of the reasons we see people stuck in sin, Held Hostage in certain situations, and unable to live in authority and favor is because we choose to hide instead of being open and vulnerable.

Silence is destroying us. Our tribes will be a place to be open and vulnerable, where we will be filled in order to be sent out to the Harvest. We need our tribes for what the years ahead will bring. We are not meant to walk alone.

In 2020, God placed a group of boys who I have never met on my heart. He told me that I was to be their spiritual sister and that I needed to pray for them daily. This was before my relationship with God became fully restored. I began in October and by the end of November my relationship with God was stronger than it had ever been. He began to give me His vision, His heart, and His calling for the boys, and told me I needed to pray it into being, that I was laying their spiritual foundation. If you looked at the natural world, you would think I am crazy. But I have learned not to look at the natural world, but the spiritual world.

In December, before God told me that things would shake with my ex-husband, my ex came against the boys with speech that should never come out of a believer's mouth. In that moment my spirit rose up, and I proclaimed, "I will not let you steal this ministry, my calling, and my tribe." God has given me so many words for this group of boys, and several of them are already being answered in the physical realm. I still have never met them, but God knows them.

Tribes matter! We need to be praying for each other, we need to be open and honest. We need a place of safety, we need community, and we need each other for our futures.

Testimonies:

*The Lord has blessed me with many good friends in my life, as well as a family that seeks Him and raised me to know Him. But for the past couple of years since I moved out, ventured out on my own, and grew in my relationship with God, I couldn't seem to find a church that I could call home, a place to put roots down. I am so grateful for the friendships that He gave me, but these friends were from different places, different churches, and—though I didn't know it at that time—what I was waiting for was a community, a group of people that could be my support. My family. What it took was what I call 'the great emptying.' The Lord began to lead me to let go of friendships that I had relied on, friends I had been close with, for many years. I didn't understand it and though it was painful, I knew God was leading me to let go and step back from them for a reason, even if I didn't know what that reason was.

Finally, God released me from a friendship that I had poured everything I had into. My heart, my love, everything that I understood about loyalty and caring for someone, I put into that friendship. It was one of the most painful things I have ever experienced.

Then, only three days after this release, the Lord showed me that He has brought me into connection with many, many people, and churches, far more than I realized, and it was because He was wanting to do a new thing in the church. I am still waiting for a home church, but I understand now that what I think a home church or tribe should look like will not be what it is. It will look different; it will be new. He is still showing me the connections I am to make, the people I am to be close with, and I know that there are more to come. So, I trust Him, and I am excited to see how He brings His church together. ~Krystle V.

*My tribe started with my family finding Jesus and being around people from a church group. We have stayed friends and now belong to a Bible study with them. We need to be around other Christians for prayer and support. ~Nancy C.

Day 7: Self-Reflection

~Prayer~

Heavenly Father,

We come before You and we take time today to hear Your voice. Please direct this time of fellowship with You. Reveal to us what You are wanting to say and direct us. Speak to us very clearly and reveal to us what we need to know.

In Jesus' Name, Amen.

Today I will be asking hard questions and I want you to write down your answers of what God truthfully and honestly has revealed to you.

How has the idea of your support system changed?

Why is it important to choose wisely who speaks into your life?

Who has the final say?

Has God given you a tribe?

Has your tribe stepped into the new or is it stuck in the old?

Take time to praise God for your tribe.
Are you still waiting for your tribe?

Take time to pray for your tribe to come.
Who are individuals God is telling you to let go of or create boundaries with?

Have you been the one to hurt believers? If so, have you gone and asked for forgiveness and made it right? (Email, letter, phone call, or in person)

What is God revealing to you about the tribe?

~My prayer for you today~
Heavenly Father,
We thank You for revealing Your heart to us and what You are longing for us to be. Help us to be obedient to Your word and to be the tribe You have called us to be. We long to see Your kingdom revealed throughout the world, and we say yes to You. In Jesus' Name, Amen.

Week 8: Be Bold

"[9] Have I not commanded you? Be strong and courageous. Do not be afraid; do not be discouraged, for the LORD your God will be with you wherever you go."
(Joshua 1:9 NIV)

Day 1: Be Bold

'Be bold' is what we will be focusing on this week. There is something so very powerful about the words 'be bold,' 'be strong,' and 'be courageous.' So many times, I thought that it was God who gives us the boldness and courage, but I began to understand that God does not force us to be bold. No, our boldness and courage are an action on our end; it is our response to God.

For us to understand why we need to be bold, we first need to understand what that means. As we talked about in week 4, David's wives and children were taken, and he went straight to God for help. There is a verse that I want to show here. 1 Samuel 30:6 (KJV) says, "[6] And David was greatly distressed; for the people spake of stoning him, because the soul of all the people was grieved, every man for his sons and for his daughters: but David encouraged himself in the LORD his God."

1 Samuel 30:6 (NIV) says it this way, "[6] David was greatly distressed because the men were talking of stoning him; each one was bitter in spirit because of his sons and daughters. But David found strength in the LORD his God."

(Answer the questions.)

Who encouraged himself? _____

Who strengthened himself? _____

I love how these two versions put it. David encouraged himself in the Lord; David strengthened himself with trust in God. David's response to the situation was to dig down deep, to plant himself in what he knew to be true. His action of going straight to God led the way to his victory.

Boldness and courage do not mean the absence of fear; they mean that even if you are experiencing fear, it does not hold you back, and you take the necessary steps forward that God leads you into. The Bible says that perfect love, "God's love," casts out fear, and because of our understanding of this truth we can laugh in the face of fear and push forward.

Read 2 Timothy 3:10-17.
Why do we need to be bold? Write out vs 12.

A part of being brave is about our faithfulness to God. In the coming days and years, we will need to be brave and bold like never before. Out of our desire to be faithful to our God and not become deceived. The scripture teaches us what is right so we can stand firm and bold. We do not become swayed, but instead we are equipped for everything that we will face in the past, present, and future. Paul reminds Timothy of his character and heart because he wanted to remind Timothy of who he was trained by. We need to be fully aware of who we let train us and make sure that they are in the right spirit. Paul was persecuted on many occasions and yet his boldness for Christ is loud and clear. There is no misunderstanding his relationship with God.

Read 2 Timothy 4:1-8.
Write out vs. 2.

Verses 3 and 4 tell us why boldness is required. It's because there will be many around us who will not listen to truth; instead, they will twist the truth so that it has no conviction. They will believe in lies so that they can continue to live in sin. I find it interesting how it talks about how believers will search for pastors (teachers) who will speak what makes their flesh happy and carry no conviction of the Holy Spirit. If we were to look at ourselves, look at the church, we would clearly see this situation happening. But I believe that the bold Bride is rising up and will once again allow the Holy Spirit to bring His convicting love into the church services. Again, the word 'faithful' stands out. We are to boldly preach the Gospel, patiently rebuke, and teach sound and wholesome teaching, or sound doctrine. How many churches are teaching sound doctrine, though?

Read 1 Peter 3:8-22.
Why be bold? Write vs 8-9.

Write vs. 15-16

Boldness, standing firm in God, and courage are required for living out our walk with God. We need boldness to go where He tells us to go, and when it's time for Revelations to be fulfilled we will need it, so we do not run away and hide. Remember that boldness, standing firm, and courage is our response to our action. It is remembering who God is, what He has done, and what He said He will do. It is having faith and believing He is faithful and will fulfill all that He has said. Then it is taking that faith and putting it into action by stepping forward in obedience to what God is saying to do.

Another important factor to being bold is facing our pasts. You will need to be bold to face your past sins, your past mistakes, your past abuse, your past trauma, and whatever else has Held you Hostage. You need to be bold. You cannot hide from it, you cannot run away from it; no, you need to face it. When God told me that something was going to take place with my ex-husband, He was warning me so that I would be bold when it came. During the months of healing that started from the day everything came to light, to separation and then divorce, I had to boldly face it all. I faced all the memories, the pain, the abuse, the sin, and the trauma. Why? So that my future would be a thriving one, my past would no longer have a hold over me, and my faith in God would be my action instead of post-traumatic stress disorder (PTSD).

To move forward into the weeks remaining in this study book, you will need boldness. You will need to face reality and go straight to God. It is not the time to be faint of heart, it is not the time to forget what God has done and what He has said He will do, and it is not the time to give satan even more ground. No, now is the time to get freedom and breakthrough, now is the time to reclaim your future, and now is the time to step forward into what God has for you.

In the coming days, we are going to investigate people in the Bible and read about their testimonies and why boldness mattered to the outcome their lives have.

Read Today: Joshua 1

~Prayer~

Heavenly Father, we come before You, and we recognize that we need to be bold. You are asking us to face things that have Held us Hostage. You are asking us to move out of the past, and step into a present that will forever change our future. You are moving us into new things that will take us out of our comfort zone, and we will need to trust You. We will need to encourage ourselves in You, and we need You so very desperately.

In Jesus' Name, Amen.

Day 2: Abigail and Daniel

~Prayer~

Heavenly Father,

We come before You today and we are ready to look at the testimonies of people who were found faithful to You. We are ready to understand how their boldness led them to actions that honored You and changed their futures forever. We long to have a testimony that reveals a changed future. We long to be able to boldly share our testimonies without the fear of man holding us back. We want to honor and glorify You. In Jesus' Name, Amen.

During my time of healing and going through the separation and divorce, there have been a few testimonies in the Bible that really challenged me during that season. It revealed the power of God and what He wanted to do in my own life. So today we are going to dig deep into truths and learn about what God is asking of you.

We begin with the testimony of Abigail. We first learn about Abigail in 1 Samuel 25:3 (NIV) says, "[3] His name was Nabal and his wife's name was Abigail. She was an intelligent and beautiful woman, but her husband was surly and mean in his dealings—he was a Calebite."

Already I am getting a glimpse into the life Abigail had to live in. It says that Nabal was surly and mean in his dealings, and I can just see the word abuse shouting out at me. I do not have to imagine what her days looked like, because I have experienced life with someone mean and surly. Another version puts it as evil and mean. Some of you have also experienced this life, and so you know the fears in her mind. You know what she struggled with, the fight to hang onto her identity and who she is.

We read that David sends ten men to Nabal to remind him of how David had protected his men, animals, and goods. David then asked for food (vs. 8). We find that Nabal's response is evil and cruel. Basically, it was a resounding NO. David's response is found in vs 13 (NIV) says, "[13] David said to his men, "Each of you strap on your sword!" So they did, and David strapped his on as well. About four hundred men went up with David, while two hundred stayed with the supplies."

I can just imagine the indignation that arose in David and how fierce he looked. We now have David and his men on their way to bring judgement on Nabal. Yet, back at Nabal's home we have Abigail, a woman who understands righteousness. We find in verses 14-22 that a servant comes to Abigail and begins to explain the situation to her. She hears of the righteous acts of David and how he protected and watched over Nabal's property and servants. She already understands David's character compared to her wicked husband. The servant knows the unrighteous act of Nabal and that it can only be their downfall. So, he humbles himself and asks Abigail to ponder what she can do to bring peace to the situation. Abigail immediately gets up and responds with action. She asks for food, and then tells her servants that they will lead the way and she will follow behind. Although she acts quickly, she keeps her actions quiet from her husband. Abigail finds herself coming into a mountain ravine and behold, right in front of her David is descending towards her. He is loudly declaring his intentions to kill all the males in the house of Nabal. I can only imagine the fear of the unknown that would try to seize Abigail's heart, but we find her boldness and resolve for righteousness pushes her into action.

(Find the answers to these questions and sentences in **1 Samuel 25:14-22**.)

Abigail responded _____.

What did Abigail take with her?

Who did she send on ahead? _____ Who did she not tell?

_____

Who did she meet in the ravine? _____

Read 1 Samuel 25:23-34.

I love what vs. 24-31 says. After she throws herself down before David, who is ready for blood, she begins to bravely speak the truth about her husband and his character, then shifts to talking about David's character, apologizes for her boldness, and then goes on to declare a promise, or what would be considered a prophecy, of what David's future would be.

Because of her boldness, which helped her to respond in righteousness to God, David took what she gave and did not stop there. 1 Samuel 25:35 (NIV) says, "[35] Then David accepted from her hand what she had brought him and said, "Go home in peace. I have heard your words and granted your request.""

What I love is that her testimony does not remain there. No, God does something so amazing. He removes her from her wicked husband. He delivers her out of a horrible life of death and destruction.

When Abigail returns home, she finds the household in full celebration with a banquet. Her husband is drunk and extremely happy. Understanding that it is not the right time, she keeps quiet about what she has done. But when it is morning, Abigail tells him all. When Nabal hears what his righteous wife has done, the Bible says his heart fails and he becomes like a rock. Around ten days later he breathes his last. (1 Samuel 25:36-38) Abigail is now free; she is no longer Held Hostage by a mean and horrible husband. She was set free. Now that she is free, God does something new for her. This next verse absolutely moves my spirit because it is a promise that God has spoken over me.

Read 1 Samuel 25:39-42.

Abigail became the wife of the king. She was not a concubine, but a wife (that is important because a wife carried a different weight and authority then a concubine). Because of her boldness which propelled her into responding in righteousness and truth, God removed her from a horrible marriage and brought her into a place of authority, recognition, and honor. Although I am not promised as a wife to a king, God has promised me that I will marry again and the man will love me and want me, and I will be able to experience a healthy and loving marriage.

Another person whose testimony has inspired me is that of Daniel. We can read in the Book of Daniel that he was wise, obedient to God and His laws, and that he boldly spoke what God gave him to say.

Read Daniel 6:3-5.

What does it say about Daniel?

Write vs 5 out.

How many of us can say that the only way charges and fault can be brought against us is if it has to do with our God? I think for many of us we are finally getting to that place, where it can be said of us. From there, these evil men come up with a plan to destroy Daniel. Their plan is found in Daniel 6:6-9, these evil men went to the king. The talked about their desire for the king to be worshiped as if he was God. The king liked the sound of being worshipped and prayed to, and in his arrogant pride he agreed that if anyone should fail to pray only to him, they would be killed by lions. The king signed and sealed the law, which meant that not even he could reverse it.

I am loving Daniel's response. I pray that the day I encounter situations that put my life on the line, I will have boldness. Daniel 6:10 (NLT) says, "[10] But when Daniel learned that the law had been signed, he went home and knelt down as usual in his upstairs room, with its windows open toward Jerusalem. He prayed three times a day, just as he had always done, giving thanks to his God."

Daniel did not even hide what he was doing. He left the windows wide upon and boldly continued to pray to God. He did not allow his government to dictate what was right and true. He did not cave to the culture's demands but said NO! Obviously since Daniel was not hiding his obedience, the evil men easily found out his "fault." The king could not go back on his decree, and it says he tried to come up with different ways to rescue Daniel. The very king of the country, the ruler of the government, could not save Daniel. We find the king's response when everything failed in Daniel 6:16 (NLT) which says, "[16] So at last the king gave orders for Daniel to be arrested and thrown into the den of lions. The king said to him, "May your God, whom you serve so faithfully, rescue you." The king had been led astray, fallen into a trap, and led his country into sin. He recognized it but could not change the outcome. Only God could supernaturally intervene. (This is exactly where the world is right now, we are needing a divine supernatural reset.)

Read Daniel 6:19-22.

Write verse 22.

I absolutely love how God showed up in a way that only He could. Daniel was safe, with a huge testimony of God's faithfulness that destroyed the plot of the evil men. In fact, those same men were thrown into the lion's den and were eaten before they even touched the ground. Sadly, these wicked men brought destruction upon their own families, because in Daniel 6:24 (NLT) it says, "[24] Then the king gave orders to arrest the men who had maliciously accused Daniel. He had them thrown into the lions' den, along with their wives and children. The lions leaped on them and tore them apart before they even hit the floor of the den."

Daniel's testimony does not end there, though. We find that the king makes a new decree commanding his people that they must fear and reverence Daniel's God. What a powerful understanding this country received that shifted their future during that time. There is more to Daniel and his testimony, and I encourage you to read the whole book of Daniel. What would happen if the Bride became bold for Christ? How would our country change? How many lives would we save from the gate of Hell? Do you feel the stirring in your soul? Is your spirit ready to get out of the box for Christ? I do! "I'm ready, God!"

Read Today: Daniel 6, Acts 4

~My prayer for you today~
Heavenly Father,
I come before You, and I pray for Your child reading this. I pray that they would take hold of boldness and trust and encourage themselves in You. You are asking that they step forward into obedience in You. You have shown that You are faithful and that You will fulfill all Your promises. I pray that Your child would trust in You and boldly move forward and not let fear hold them back.
In Jesus' Name, Amen.

Day 3: Ruth and Shadrach, Meshach, and Abednego

~Prayer~

Heavenly Father,

We come before You and already we can sense a stirring in our spirit, for You are declaring that our time of healing, breakthrough, and shift is at hand. You are declaring that our tomorrow will be better than our past, and for that to happen we need to have boldness in our present. So today, as we learn more from other people's boldness and obedience to You, let that same boldness come upon us as we remember who You are and what You have done. In Jesus' Name, Amen.

Today we will be going into the testimonies of four individuals who showed boldness in very different ways. Yet their testimonies and outcomes are so very powerful and encouraging. They are reminders of what our futures can become. We begin our first testimony with Ruth. Ruth has a whole book in the Bible dedicated to her and her testimony.

Ruth is not a Hebrew; instead, she is from the country of Moab. She had married into the family of Naomi and Elimelek, who were from the tribe of Ephraim (a son of Joseph). We learned about some of that in week 7 when we discussed tribes. We find that Jacob adopted Joseph's sons as his own to give more blessings upon them and because of it they are counted as one of the tribes of Israel. You can read more about it in Genesis 48.

Naomi and Elimelek had left Israel because of a famine and were in Moab. Now Ruth's husband died, along with her father-in-law and brother-in-law. All that was left were the women in the family. During this time there was a great famine and life was very bleak. I can just imagine the situation Ruth was facing. Life was hard, everyday necessities were hard to come by, and on top of that all the men in her family were gone. So, Naomi decides to return home, and both her daughter-in-laws went with.

In Ruth 1:8-9 (NIV) says, "[8] Then Naomi said to her two daughters-in-law, "Go back, each of you, to your mother's home. May the LORD show you kindness, as you have shown kindness to your dead husbands and to me. [9] May the LORD grant that each of you will find rest in the home of another husband." Then she kissed them goodbye and they wept aloud,"

They were now forced to decide. How comfortable and safe would it be to return to their families? They would be in their home country, with a culture and people they understood, and with their families they have always known. A rational person would say it makes sense to go back home. But we find that Ruth's response is completely different. Ruth 1:16-17 (NIV) says, "[16] But Ruth replied, "Don't urge me to leave you or to turn back from you. Where you go I will go, and where you stay I will stay. Your people will be my people and your God my God. [17] Where you die I will die, and there I will be buried. May the LORD deal with me, be it ever so severely, if even death separates you and me.""

Ruth boldly made the decision to go with Naomi. She left all that she had known and chose to attach herself to a new people, a new culture, and a new God. As you read through the book of Ruth, you'll notice that Naomi was not an easy mother-in-law to deal with. In fact, you constantly read about how negative she is towards herself, constantly degrading herself, the pessimistic way she viewed herself. When I first thought of Ruth taking Naomi as family and going with her, I thought, 'wow, it must have been an easy decision because Naomi must have been amazing.' Nope, I got a totally different view of Naomi as I read through it and began to understand Ruth's decision required boldness.

Not only was Ruth's decision to stay with Naomi bold; but understanding more about the culture after reading through Leviticus, Numbers, and Deuteronomy, I understood that Ruth would be faced with judgement and gossip, and she would be treated differently because she was not a Hebrew. Everyone in the city knew about her, all eyes were watching her, and she did not have to introduce herself.

Since all the men had died, Ruth now had to find a way to provide for her mother-in-law and herself. So, she chose to do hard labor and work the fields to get grain. While out working, she ran into a man who was a kinsman redeemer (to keep the bloodline going, a close family relative would take the widow and when the first son was born, he was given to the first husband to receive that inheritance and carry on the bloodline. The children born after that son would then belong to the second husband). Naomi's advice on how to deal with the situation caused Ruth to move in boldness once again.

Read Ruth 3:1-4.
What did Naomi want Ruth to do and why?

My response would have been, "Are you sure about this?" Ruth response is found in Ruth 3:5-6 (NIV) says, "[5] "I will do whatever you say," Ruth answered. [6] So she went down to the threshing floor and did everything her mother-in-law told her to do."

We find out that Boaz then quickly goes and settles the situation. When everything legal had been done, he took Ruth as his wife. He then laid with her, and she conceived a son. But her boldness does not end there.

Read Ruth 4:14-16.
What did Ruth do?

What did Naomi do?

It is revealed that Ruth gives her son to Naomi to raise, and everyone refers to Ruth's son as Naomi's son. I do not know about you, but giving up a child is one of the hardest things I have ever had to do. (I share more about that in week 15.) It is painful and heartbreaking, yet Ruth was obedient.

She gave the bloodline back to her mother-in-law. Her bold obedience led to Ruth 4:17 (NIV), which says, "^{17} The women living there said, "Naomi has a son!" And they named him Obed. He was the father of Jesse, the father of David."

Because of Ruth's bold obedience, King David came from her bloodline, her womb. What a beautiful example of being honored by bold obedience! Because not only does King David come from her bloodline, but so does Jesus. There is something so very powerful about Ruth's life, and the fact that God inspired her story to be in the Bible reveals there are details about Ruth, He doesn't want us to miss. Her testimony is so beautiful.

The next testimony I want to share about it is found in Daniel and it is of the lives of Shadrach, Meshach, and Abednego. In their testimony, we see how government had become wicked and were pushing upon the people vile and wicked laws. Shadrach, Meshach, and Abednego were given the choice to either compromise or obey boldly. We find that King Nebuchadnezzar had decided he wanted to be a god, so he created an image of gold to be worshipped. He brought all the important officials of the country together, and there the image stood.

Read Daniel 3:4-7 and write down the consequences for bold obedience.

Shadrach, Meshach, and Abednego chose bold obedience. They did not cave, they did not surrender, and they held on to truth. So, the king decides to give them one last chance to save themselves. Daniel 3:15 (NKJV) says, "^{15} Now if you are ready at the time you hear the sound of the horn, flute, harp, lyre, and psaltery, in symphony with all kinds of music, and you fall down and worship the image which I have made, good! But if you do not worship, you shall be cast immediately into the midst of a burning fiery furnace. And who is the god who will deliver you from my hands?"

What an intense encounter they were having. The king had every right to do what he was doing, because he was king, but his authority was limited beneath God's. I wonder if they questioned, even just a second; but even if they did, their response takes my breath away.

Read Daniel 3:16-18.
Write down their response.

I think people picture three meek men who are speaking in whispers, shaking in fear, and yet standing firm. I do not see that at all. I see three men boldly claiming truth. Holding firm, standing courageously and boldly, and choosing not to compromise. There are no weak men, no whispers or shaking. There is resolve. There is determination. There is obedience.

The Bible says that the king's attitude swiftly changed towards them, to the point of making the furnace seven times hotter! His strongest men tied up the three and through them into the furnace. Due to the king's anger and urgency, the furnace was so hot that the flames killed the men who threw Shadrach Meshach, and Abednego into the fire. (Daniel 3:19-23) The testimony seems a bit bleak, but truth be told, even if God did not save them, their bold obedience to Him is so amazing that we could stop right here. But that is not the end of their testimony, because God decided to take it even further.

Daniel 3:24-25 (NKJV) says, "^{24} Then King Nebuchadnezzar was astonished; and he rose in haste and spoke, saying to his counselors, "Did we not cast three men bound into the midst of the fire?" They answered and said to the king, "True, O king." ^{25} "Look!" he answered, "I see four men loose, walking in the midst of the fire; and they are not hurt, and the form of the fourth is like the Son of God."

Not only were they saved, but the Son of God appeared in their midst. He did not leave them in that situation alone, but He revealed Himself in the very middle of the furnace. I have seen God do this in my own life over and over. He shows up in the situation and reveals that I am not alone. So, take courage and be bold, step out in faith and obedience.

Their testimony still does not end there; after this, something took place in the country because of their choice. Nebuchadnezzar began to praise God because He saved the lives of Shadrach, Meshach, and Abednego, who trusted in Him. The king sent out a decree saying that no man could come against their God, and if they did, they would be killed and their homes would be destroyed. As for Shadrach, Meshach, and Abednego, the king gave them a promotion. (Daniel 3:28-30

God is wanting to do something amazing with your testimony and give you a future that goes beyond your imagination. All you must do is boldly step out in obedience to Him.

Read Today: Matthew 14, Luke 14

~My prayer for you today~
Heavenly Father,
I come before You, and I pray for Your child reading this. Today, let their boldness increase. I pray that they would take hold of You and run the race set before them, that they would not back down to culture, government, religion, abuse, sin, trauma, or anything that would keep them from You. I pray that You would cover them with Your love.
In Jesus' Name, Amen.

Day 4: Rahab and Peter

~Prayer~

Heavenly Father,

We come before You in expectancy of what You are doing in our lives. We are so very thankful and blessed that You do not leave us in the grave but have brought us into life. Today, we hear Your voice and see You moving. We humble ourselves before You and ask that You would reveal where we need to boldly obey. In Jesus' Name, Amen.

Today we will be looking at Rahab and Peter and reading about their testimonies. The first one we will focus on is Rahab. There is something about Rahab that captures boldness so beautifully.

Her story begins as one in sin. We find Rahab a prostitute. She is living in the promised land, but the true inheritors of the land have not taken possession yet. The land is still currently in the hands of those who do not obey God or love Him. Joshua, who God told to be bold and courageous, is actively doing just that by leading the people to inherit the promised land. They come to the city of Jericho, where Rahab the prostitute lives.

Right here, we are aware of two very important details. The first is that Rahab is in sin, and according to what God has commanded the Hebrews, she should be killed because of her sin. The second thing is that she is not from the tribe of Israel. Two things that she knows full well are against her and her life. The people in Jericho heard stories of the Hebrews who had come out of Egypt, how they were once slaves but were now blessed by God, that signs and wonders followed them, and that they were a chosen nation. It also makes complete sense that the customs, laws, and traditions of the Hebrews had also been made aware to Jericho. Just like Joshua sent two spies into Jericho, I am sure Jericho had spies that kept watch over other nations around them.

Joshua sent two spies to check out the land, and they found themselves in hiding in Rahab's house. The king of the city of Jericho sent solders to find the spies. They came to Rahab with the words of the king, telling her that she needed to bring out the spies. I find it interesting that the king knew the spies had been at her house. Can you imagine how Rahab's heart must have been pounding with adrenaline as she put her life on the line? (Joshua 2:1-3) Yet Rahab understood that God was with Israel and so she boldly hid the men. I love her response to the king's demand.

Read Joshua 2:4-7.

Rahab put her life on the line. She went against the king, stood up to the soldiers, and saved the lives of the spies. Rahab also had wisdom and understood that with her actions she put her family's lives on the line too. So, she makes a request of the spies. Before they all went to bed, she approached them and told them that she understood who the Lord is, and how He has blessed Israel. She knew that Jericho would fall because God was on their side. She spoke about the history of the Red Sea parting, how Israel had already destroyed countries on their way to the promised land and told them that the fear of God was in the hearts of the people of Jericho. She pleaded with them to give an oath to spare her and her family the fate that Jericho would face, and to give her a sign for this oath. The spies agreed. They told her that it would be as she asked. God would spare her and her family, but she had to remain faithful and speak not a word about them to anyone. So with the oath in place, Rahab helped them escape through the window, and after she told them where to hide and for how long (three days), the spies also gave her further instruction. (Joshua 2)

Read Joshua 2:17-21.

Rahab asked that her family and her life be spared, and then she boldly trusted that the spies of Israel would keep their word to her. In Joshua 5, Rahab's testimony is picked back up. The Israelites were given instructions to walk silently around Jericho six days with only the trumpets blaring. Then on the seventh day they were to walk around seven times with trumpets blaring, and on the seventh time around the men were to shout.

First, it does not say how much time passed from when the spies returned to Israel and when they finally came back to Jericho. All that time, Rahab had to be completely aware and discerning, actively waiting every day. Now Israel was here at the very walls. Can you imagine the seven days where Rahab was listening to this? Seven days, without knowing what would happen or if she truly would be safe, and still, she boldly trusted. For seven days Rahab probably stayed in that room, waiting for the coming calamity about to fall on Jericho, never knowing the exact hour, day, or time, but keeping the promise she had made with the spies.

Remember, Rahab did not know what was to come. God had not told her how Israel would take the city. God had told Joshua, and so Joshua gave the people clear instructions when it came to what should take place once the walls fell.

Read Joshua 6:16-19.
Write out vs. 16.

Joshua made it very clear that Rahab and those with her would be protected and saved. When the walls fell and the men had gone in and taken control of the city, Joshua told the spies to do something. Joshua 6:22-23 (RSV) says, "[22] And Joshua said to the two men who had spied out the land, "Go into the harlot's house, and bring out from it the woman, and all who belong to her, as you swore to her." [23] So the young men who had been spies went in, and brought out Rahab, and her father and mother and brothers and all who belonged to her; and they brought all her kindred, and set them outside the camp of Israel."

What took place next was the complete destruction of the city of Jericho. They burned it to the ground. They obeyed God and took all the gold, silver, bronze, and iron, and they took it to the Lord's house. Finally in Joshua 6:25 (RSV) it says, "[25] But Rahab the harlot, and her father's household, and all who belonged to her, Joshua saved alive; and she dwelt in Israel to this day, because she hid the messengers whom Joshua sent to spy out Jericho."

For the rest of Rahab's life, she lived with Israel. She did not remain a prostitute but took Israel's

God as her God. Her past was removed, and she was given a new life and a new future. Later we come to find out that the man she married was named Salmon, and her son was called Boaz. Boaz married Ruth and through their bloodline came King David, and eventually, Jesus.

The next person whose testimony has great impact is that of Peter. Peter is a disciple of Jesus; he denied Jesus three times, he walked on the water with Jesus, he spent most of his time with Jesus, but the part I want to get into happened after Jesus ascended to Heaven. We see the times and season that Peter lived in was very volatile. Herod was arresting and persecuting Christians. We find in Acts 12 that James, the brother of John, had already been killed by the sword. Yet Peter continued to spread the good news about Jesus. Herod realized that Jews approved of his handling of the Christians, and so he went ahead and had Peter arrested. Peter was put in jail, and just to make sure he stayed there, Herod placed four squads of four soldiers each to guard him, a total of sixteen men. Once the Passover had ended, Herod would place Peter on public trial. The church took these days as an opportunity to pray for Peter.

Read Acts 12:6-11.

What was Peter doing? _____

Who was around Peter? _____

Who showed up before Peter?_____

Write out what the angel said in vs 7-8.

What did Peter think?_____

Write out vs. 11

Peter was imprisoned for being a Christian and sharing the Gospel. I love how even though his bold obedience to sharing the Gospel led to hardships like jail, we see how God honored that choice by sending an angel to free him. Peter understood it was not his time yet to die. God had bigger things planned for him and until that day, Peter would choose to continue to spread the Gospel.

What is the end of Peter's testimony? There are two parts to the end of Peter's testimony. The first is that Peter was killed for his belief in Jesus. Although we do not know if it was on a cross, we do know that it was a painful death. Many scholars believe that Peter was crucified, but upside down. Peter's death was prophesied about by Jesus Himself. John 21:18-19 (NLT) says, "[18] "I tell you the truth, when you were young, you were able to do as you liked; you dressed yourself and went wherever you wanted to go. But when you are old, you will stretch out your hands, and others will dress you and take you where you don't want to go." [19] Jesus said this to let him know by what kind of death he would glorify God. Then Jesus told him, "Follow me."

Peter knew that by following Jesus, he would be killed for Him. Yet Peter boldly followed Him anyway. The last part of Peter's testimony are the believers who came to know Jesus because of the Gospel that Peter shared. Because of his boldness, many were saved from hell, and because of him and others who shared the Gospel, we are now part of that testimony.

Read Today: Mark 8

~My prayer for you today~
Heavenly Father,
I come before You, and I pray for Your child reading this. I realize that for some of Your children the boldness You are requiring will put their lives on the line. For some it will radically shift them into new and scary places. I understand that for some it will be a complete letting go of everything. I pray that they would still choose to be bold and courageous, that they would not waver, faint, or grow weary.
In Jesus' Name, Amen.

Day 5: Esther and Stephen

~Prayer~

Heavenly Father,

We come before You, and the realization of Your goodness flows over us. We see that even those who have lost their lives for You counted it worthwhile, not in vain. So many times, we hold ourselves back in fear because obedience means sacrifice; it means facing scary things, and it could cost our very lives. Yet God, our lives are Yours. You are worth losing it for. Let us be mindful today of truth and walk in courage. In Jesus' Name, Amen.

Today we will be talking about Esther and Stephen. Esther's testimony has had such a powerful affect on my life. There are so many truths to it, and God has really used it to impact my life in ways that are still beyond my imagination. Esther is another woman who has a whole book dedicated to herself. She was living in Susa, the capital of the Persian Empire. At that time the Israelites could move back to Israel after being in captivity for a long time. But many Jews chose not to return to Israel. Esther was an orphan and adopted by her cousin Mordecai.

Esther lived in a foreign land, and although she and her people, the Jews, continued to live with their beliefs intact, they were still targeted. People looked down upon them and life was not easy for them. At that time, the king had vanquished his queen and removed her from her position. You can read about that in Esther 1. He was drunk when he made his decision, so once he was sober and wifeless, he brought his leaders together to ask what he should do to fill the empty place in his heart. Their advice was to take all the beautiful young virgins and bring them to the capital for him to choose a queen.

I find it amazing how this meant it would be against the women's choice. Some might think it was okay if they were not chosen; they could just return home. No, they were forced to spend a night with the king, and if they failed to please him, they would become his concubine. Esther 2:14 (NKJV) says, "[14] In the evening she went, and in the morning she returned to the second house of the women, to the custody of Shaashgaz, the king's eunuch who kept the concubines. She would not go in to the king again unless the king delighted in her and called for her by name."

In other words, if they did not please the king, then they would become a concubine who would live her life in loneliness waiting for the king to remember her. This story hits way too close to my own marriage. How many of you were in lonely marriages?

We find that when the king's edict was announced through the land, many young virgins were brought to the capitol. They were taken into the king's harem under the care of Hegai, the eunuch. Esther was one of those virgins, and she was favored among all the women. Hegai gave her special attention in what she ate, her beauty treatments, and he even gave her seven attendants. She was also given the very best room, and yet no one knew she was a Jew. She kept her history private according to her cousin Mordecai's instructions. Her cousin secretly kept track of everything that happened to her. Esther had to go through a whole year (twelve months) of beauty treatments. The year was divided into two six-month increments, the first dedicated to myrrh and the last six perfumes and makeup. (Esther 2:8-12)

Esther, alone in a palace in a foreign land, went through beauty treatments, ate special food, had seven female attendants given to her, and had the best place in the harem. Imagine how she knew that all of it was just because she would be forced to go to the king. Her life and future did not look happy. Yet I believe that Esther used the time wisely to prepare herself, because her future hung in the balance.

Read Esther 2:15-18.
What did Esther request?

What did the king do?

Esther now found herself as queen. I can just imagine the amount of boldness and faith required to lead a harem, the wisdom and understanding she would need to display and hold fast to. Now Esther could have chosen to live a life that was easy, but something happened that caused her to make one decision that would forever impact her future. In Esther 3 we learn that there is a man named Haman, an Agagite who wanted to destroy the Jews. He devised a plan of action that said on a certain day of the year, those who hated the Jews could rise and kill them. He convinced the king to agree and give his royal decree, which, as we learned in Daniel, the king could not change. Mordecai told Esther's servant about the decree giving all of the ugly details. He told Esther that she would need to go to the king and beg for the lives of her people. (Esther 4:6-8)

Esther's response to her adopted father is one of fear. Remember, boldness does not mean there is no fear at all, it just means that it will not hold you back.

Read Esther 4:10-11.
What was the Esther's response?

Esther knew that going before the king uninvited meant that she could very well lose her own life. She had a choice; would she live her life and save herself, or would she choose to lay it down and perhaps save her people? Mordecai understood Esther's fears, but he also called her out on it. He would not let her remain in a place of fear (this shows it is important to have the right spiritual support system around). Esther 4:13-14 (NKJV) says, "[13] And Mordecai told them to answer Esther: "Do not think in your heart that you will escape in the king's palace any more than all the other Jews. [14] For if you remain completely silent at this time, relief and deliverance will arise for the Jews from another place, but you and your father's house will perish. Yet who knows whether you have come to the kingdom for such a time as this?"

Esther was challenged. She could shrink back and die herself, or let God use her to save her people and keep her life. I find it interesting that Mordecai says that her father's house would die, because that meant him to. He was pronouncing what would happen to him as well, that her choices would affect his life too. He wanted her to clearly see what was at stake. Esther 4:15-16 (NKJV) says, "[15] Then Esther told them to reply to Mordecai: [16] "Go, gather all the Jews who are present in Shushan, and fast for me; neither eat nor drink for three days, night or day. My maids and I will fast likewise. And so I will go to the king, which is against the law; and if I perish, I perish!"

Esther boldly made her decision to protect her people and she took her boldness straight to God by fasting and praying. For three days and nights she fasted and prayed to God and asked for His favor. I can sense her resolve when she says, "And if I perish, I perish." Esther understood the importance of her bold obedience to God. She understood her calling and purpose and she chose obedience.

Read Esther 5:1-2.
Write verse 2.

I want to note here that this was a solemn moment. As Esther walked to the king, she had no idea what his response to her presence would be. Each step took her deeper and deeper, closer and closer, to possibly losing her life. When she reached the king, I can just imagine the boldness that radiated from her, her faith in God was secure, yet fear trying to make her turn around and run for her life. Yet, during it all, the king was pleased by his bride and extended the scepter to her. From there, we learn that Esther invites the king and Haman to eat with her twice before she finally tells the king her request is the life of her people. Esther's bold obedience gave her people the chance to survive and protect themselves. Her testimony led to a holiday that is celebrated to this day. We learned about that week 4 day 7.

The next person we will talk about is Stephen. His testimony impacted Saul who would later become Paul. Stephen was known as a man full of the Holy Spirit and a man of wisdom. He was chosen along with six others to care for widows who were not being taken care of. Acts 6 reveals that Stephen is seized. Acts 6:8 (RSV) says, "[8] And Stephen, full of grace and power, did great wonders and signs among the people."

You would think that is an amazing thing, a great thing, but what many probably did not expect was that it would bring opposition. The Jewish leaders rose up against Stephen and tried to argue with him, but God gave Stephen great wisdom through the Spirit, and so they failed. They went and found men who would be willing to lie, and they put forth false testimony against him. But when they looked at him, his face was like an angel's. Stephen's response was to begin to boldly proclaim what the Holy Spirit gave him to say. He did not hold back and declared it forth in power.

Read Acts 7:1-60.
Write vs. 55-56.

What did they do to Stephen?

Who was the witnesses about this event?

What was Stephen's response?

Stephen's life shows his boldness as well as his testimony. His death marked the day a great persecution led by Saul began. Yet, Jesus would get a hold of Saul, He would change his name to Paul, and Paul would become an amazing missionary. Paul himself mentions the effect of Stephen's death. Acts 22:19-21 (RSV) says, "[19] And I said, 'Lord, they themselves know that in every synagogue I imprisoned and beat those who believed in thee. [20] And when the blood of Stephen thy witness was shed, I also was standing by and approving, and keeping the garments of those who killed him.' [21] And he said to me, 'Depart; for I will send you far away to the Gentiles.' "

Because of what Paul had done, God sent him to the Gentiles. Now imagine what would have happened if Stephen had not been bold. He might have lived longer, but he would not have been faithful and obedient. Even though he lost his life here on earth, he glimpsed heaven and led the way for the Gospel to spread to the Gentiles. Our obedience that leads to sacrifice also leads to victories for others and answered prayers in their lives.

Read Today: Acts 7, Acts 22

~My prayer for you today~
Heavenly Father,
I come before You, and I pray for Your child reading this. You are calling Your child deeper into Your ways, into Your understandings, and it is going to cause many to come to a place of decision making. Your child is now at a crossroads of remaining Held Hostage in the old or moving into what is new and unknown. I pray that Your child would become bold and step out in obedience to You no matter the cost.
In Jesus' Name, Amen.

Day 6: My Story and Testimonies

I grew up as a very quiet, shy, and introverted little girl. It was not until I turned nineteen that I began to be pushed out of my shell in communicating in large group settings, or with people I did not know. I made mistakes, I was uncomfortable, but God did not give me the option of staying inside of myself. He was equipping me for the calling and purpose on my life. I say this because 'being bold' was not a part of my vocabulary.

In fact, when I was in a private school, we had a Christmas program and I was so uncomfortable and overwhelmed that when you look at the video or pictures of it, I am practically turned around completely, with my long hair covering my face and my back towards the audience. Bold and courageous were not things I walked in, nor were they a natural strength.

My calling to be bold started when God called me to go to school and bring Him into another country. I left knowing that I might not return, but I was going to be obedient. I ended up going to the Middle East and there were a few situations happening around me that could have easily led to my death. Yet God graciously protected us, and where others were scared, I was not. I knew before I left that I might not return, but I still said yes to God.

After that, my next bold moment was being a lead teacher, or what is now known as the assistant director position at an after-school program. I learned how to have oversight over a hundred kids ages five to eleven, and five or more staff at a time. I had to be bold and courageous and constantly push myself out of my shell. Through those years I was equipped in teaching, worship, discipline, discipleship, united teamwork, and so much more. I am still amazed how God helped me to be bold and courageous all the while and at the same time I suffered at the hands of my ex-husband.

Towards the end of the abuse my boldness and courage had been consumed by PTSD. God knew I needed a shift in atmosphere, so I left my job of 10+ years that had taken me through four ministries: after-school, summer care, preschool, and private school K-6.

My new job was raising my six-week-old niece and watching my eight-year-old nephew after he got off from school. My PTSD was bad, but God used my niece as a healing balm to my heart. She prepared me to become bold, so when the time of separation and divorce came two years later, I was ready. My nephew and niece are truly my son and daughter born from my heart. I will share more about that in week 15.

When God told me a shift with my ex was coming, when I went through the separation and the divorce, He kept saying, over and over, "Stand firm, be courageous, be bold, actively wait, and boldly step!" I had to be bold to face the abuse, to not shove down all the emotions and memories, but to feel it all and process it. I took two months, of intense nights, doing this, then as I gained victory and healing, it became less painful and easier to face and overcome. I had to face it all, I could not run from my past. I had to face my flawed perspective, my sins and mistakes, and become fully aware of the changes I needed to make in order to have a healthy and blessed future.

Since my divorce, that calling has not stopped. Why? Because now God is telling me to share my testimony, be vulnerable and open, and go wherever He sends me. He has given me the blueprints of a ministry to help others get freedom and healing, and then send them out to be bold. God is not just calling *me* to be bold, He is also calling you. It's time we face what we need to face to be healed and set free. It's time to let go of all we have known and step into the unknown. It's time to grasp our

present for a blessed future. My answer is, "YES, God!" What is yours?

Testimonies:

*My challenge in my community is that as a woman you just can't share your ideas, it's a constant nag on how to present the word, etc. Our government has more women now than before; our judge and deputy are women. I am so assertive, so I must tone that down, or when put down or rejected I choose not to be easily silenced when God puts something in my heart. I stand. I know God loves me because every good gift comes from Him. It's not what I do or my weakness. Once I ask God's forgiveness, I am secure and confident. I must silence the accusation in my mind, memorize His Word, pray, and put on the armor of God. It's okay if I don't have it together and I know when it's time to take a break.

Men have hurt me. I had vowed never to get married! In my community a man will have many wives. I remember one time I was teaching that who Christ sets free is free indeed. So, l felt we should take a moment to forgive. Here are a few examples that came from that moment: In my country, I see a man walking and beside him a woman who had a baby on her back and luggage on her head. I felt hurt. God reminded me He is the savior. A western gal had been sexually abused, her mum and grandma shrugged it off. A young African girl was married off, which still happens, arranged marriages, and the man tied her up and raped her. God ministered to us, and the healing process began that day. People you love hurt us the most. Yes, we have scars but that is to show our strength because they are war wounds! I was looking to scripture about God giving us strength and courage. We must do spiritual warfare for our lives, to arise, and do His will, not my feeling. Let's watch out for the negative vibes!

If God is not using someone then I turn my eyes to God, where every good gift comes from. It does not come easy to do spiritual fighting because what if I have no fight left in me? Don't be a loner! One time we went on a safari and a herd of buffalos came to our side. l counted till three and it stopped moving. It's interesting, around two or three of them rested, even when we passed with the car they didn't wake up. The bodyguards gave the go ahead to move on and then out of nowhere came six lions and surrounded one buffalo. Two hours they fought. I must say the buffalo had tenacity. The point is, don't be a loner. Yet be careful, because not everyone has the grace to stand with you. What is my fragrance today? How am l responding to others, to myself...? Yes, we need to forgive others but at times we need to forgive ourselves. ~Habona K.

Day 7: Self-Reflection

~Prayer~

Heavenly Father,

We come before You and we take time today to hear Your voice. Please direct this time of fellowship with You. Reveal to us what You are wanting to say and direct us. Speak to us very clearly and reveal to us what we need to know.

In Jesus' Name, Amen

Today I will be asking hard questions and I want you to write down your answers of what God truthfully and honestly has revealed to you.

Where have you failed to be bold and obedient?

What is God asking you to boldly face from your past?

What is God asking you to boldly face for the future?

How is God Calling You to Be Bold?

~My prayer for you today~

Heavenly Father,

We thank You for revealing to us where we need to be bold and obedient. Thank You for showing us our next steps. Today we boldly say, "YES, God!" We will be obedient, we will be faithful, and we will not let fear hold us back. We hold onto You and we choose to step forward today.

In Jesus' Name, Amen.

Week 9: Get Involved

"[22] let us draw near to God with a sincere heart and with the full assurance that faith brings, having our hearts sprinkled to cleanse us from a guilty conscience and having our bodies washed with pure water. [23] Let us hold unswervingly to the hope we profess, for he who promised is faithful. [24] And let us consider how we may spur one another on toward love and good deeds, [25] not giving up meeting together, as some are in the habit of doing, but encouraging one another—and all the more as you see the Day approaching."
(Hebrews 10:22-25 NIV)

Day 1: Get Involved

Getting involved in church, ministry, your calling, etc. is extremely hard to do when you are Held Hostage. It is also hard to do when you are in the stages of healing, and yet it is so important to do. Satan would like to keep us in darkness and Held Hostage, unable to move forward. If he can keep us alone, walking on a path we were not called to, we will feel defeated and even more stuck than we already are.

This week we will be looking at why we should be involved, how to be involved, and the tools and steps to get involved, which will ultimately lead us to understanding where God is asking us to get involved with personally. Each one of us has a different way of learning this but understanding some of the basics will help us individually understand where God is leading us.

Today I will not be sharing a lot because I believe that today needs to be spent in prayer, getting yourself ready for how God wants you to get involved. Many of you are going to have to be bold, and you are going to have to overcome the desire to remain stuck. You are going to have to make yourself uncomfortable, so prayer is going to be very important for the rest of the week.

Here are some areas you can pray about but you are not limited to them:

1. What am I stuck in?
2. Where does my avoidance of involvement stem from?
3. Who do I need to forgive?
4. How do I need to forgive myself?
5. What are areas I need to repent to God for?
6. What are my motives and my heart?

Read Today: Hebrews 10

~Prayer~

Heavenly Father, we come before You, and we understand that we are not meant to be alone. We are not meant to be distant or separated from other believers. No, God, You are calling us to gather together with other believers, to find our purpose and calling in life, and to walk in it. So today, search our hearts and prepare us to do just that.

In Jesus' Name, Amen.

Day 2: Why Is It Hard to Get Involved?

~Prayer~

Heavenly Father,

We come before You and we humble ourselves before You. We acknowledge that we have lost our way and our purpose and calling. We have allowed the things of this world, our pasts, and other individuals to take us away from You, our first love. Forgive us for where we have disobeyed. Today we choose to get involved again. In Jesus' Name, Amen.

As I mentioned yesterday, there are many reasons that make it hard to get involved in the things of God. Today I want to talk about a couple individuals in the Bible who also struggled to get themselves involved. The first person I want to talk about is Job. Job was a righteous man who had done nothing wrong. Yet everything was stripped from him, till all that was left was his wife. He lost his children, his home, his animals, his possessions, and even experienced a disease that affected his body. The book of Job talks all about it. Honestly, it is probably one of the hardest books to read, because it shows that bad things happen to good people and that God was fully aware of it and allowed it to happen. This can cause a lot of people to want to turn from God, because they do not understand how God can do that, how He can think that is loving. Job spent chapters talking about why God was doing what He was doing, about everything that he had done right, and not comprehending what God was doing. It does not show him being involved, but instead nearly sinking into depression and becoming inactive. God's response is found in Job 38-42. He reminded Job of who He is and His character, and that Job does not have the mind to truly understand God and His ways. Job could have stayed there, but instead he repented and acknowledged that as a human being he cannot fully understand God. I find the next verses so powerful.

Read Job 42:10-13.

What happened after Job prayed for his friends?

What did the Lord do?

How many sons and daughters did God give him?

Those who had once judged him came back together for fellowship. After fellowship, it says the Lord then blessed him greater than he was blessed before. Job had every reason to withdraw and give up, but once he recognized that was not right and repented of it, everything began to change. Job struggled to be involved because of what he had to endure: the loss, the trauma, the sickness, and the struggle to carry the hope of his purpose.

Another person I want to talk about is Jonah. Jonah was a prophet, and God called him to go tell the city of Nineveh to repent and turn from their ways so they could be saved. But Jonah ran away; he fled from his purpose and calling. What happened next was that he was swallowed by a large fish. It took Jonah three days and nights, until he repented. He was then thrown up on shore. Again, God told him to go to Nineveh and tell them to repent or they would be destroyed. This time Jonah obeyed, and the city believed and repented. God forgave their sins and did not bring destruction on them. However, Jonah's story does not have a happy ending for himself, at least not one shown in the Bible. (Jonah 1-3)

Read Jonah 4:1-3.
Write verse 2.

I love God's response to Jonah because He does not just use words, but action as well. First God confronted Jonah and asked what right he had to be angry. Jonah did not respond, but instead he went with his sour attitude to the east of the city, which gave him the perfect view to see what would happen to the city. He fully wanted judgement on them, and he thought his attitude would persuade God to change his mind from showing mercy.

Read Jonah 4:6-9.
What did God prepare?

What was Jonah's reaction?

What did God prepare next?

What was Jonah's response?

Jonah still did not repent or acknowledge his error of misunderstanding God. We are left with the final verses of Jonah 4:10-11 (AMP) says, "[10] Then the LORD said, "You had compassion on the plant for which you did not work and which you did not cause to grow, which came up overnight and perished overnight. [11] Should I not have compassion on Nineveh, the great city in which there are more than 120,000 [innocent] persons, who do not know the difference between their right and left hand [and are not yet accountable for sin], as well as many [blameless] animals?"

Jonah considered the city of Nineveh not worth saving because of their sin and wickedness, but Christ came for the sinful and wicked, so that through Him we can be cleansed, saved, and brought into fellowship with God. Jonah struggled and failed to be involved because of his own perspective and judgement, which he followed instead of God's.

The final person that I want to talk about is Joseph. Joseph was the son of Jacob, the father of the twelve tribes of Israel. God gave Joseph a very specific calling through a set of dreams. You can find it in Genesis 37. Basically, it was that he would rule over his whole family, and they would bow down to him. Instead of using discernment, Joseph went and told everyone about his calling. Obviously, his family was not appreciative of his so-called calling, to the point that his brothers threw him in a well and then sold him as a slave. Joseph ended up in Egypt where he became a slave to the captain of the guard belonging to Pharaoh.

Although this was not what the dream from God told him, Joseph realized that he still needed to live righteously, in obedience to God, even as he waited for the fulfillment of his promised calling. We can see that he did it correctly. (Genesis 38)

Read Genesis 39:2-5.

Who was with Joseph?

Who was blessed?

Although there was blessing, there was also persecution and temptation. This arose from the wife of Potiphar who kept making moves on Joseph, wanting to have an intimate sexual relationship with him. Joseph, however, remained pure and fled from sin. Potiphar's wife used it as an excuse to lie about his character and because of her wickedness, he was thrown in jail. Yet, again, Joseph did not let this time go to waste.

Read Genesis 39:20-23.

Which prison was Joseph put in?

Who was with Joseph?

What was Joseph put in charge of?

Write vs. 23

During this time two men who served Pharaoh were also sent to jail. One was a cupbearer and the other a baker. They each had a dream, and Joseph was inspired by God and able to interpret what the dreams meant. The baker's dream meant he would be killed, while the cupbearer's meant he would freed. It happened just as Joseph interpreted, and he asked the cupbearer to remember him. But as soon as he was released, he forgot all about him. It is later said that two full years passed before the cupbearer remembered Joseph. For two years, Joseph continued to do what he could in the jail, while waiting for his full purpose to come into full alignment. Then one night Pharaoh had a dream and that was when the cupbearer remembered him. Joseph was again inspired by God and able to interpret the dreams. And just like that, he was made second in command under Pharaoh. A great famine came through the land and guess what happened? If you guessed that Joseph's family came for food and bowed down to Joseph, then you would be correct. Sometimes we are not able to get involved in exactly what we are called to right away because we must go through a time of equipping, testing, and refining. But when we have shown we're ready, in seconds we can be shifted into our calling and purpose.

Read Today: Genesis 37, Genesis 39-47

~My prayer for you today~
Heavenly Father,
I come before You, and I pray for Your child reading this. I pray that You would begin to reveal to Your child if the reason they are not in their calling or getting involved because of their pasts, their flawed perspectives, or because they are going through times of testing. Reveal it to them so they have a greater understanding of what You want for their next steps.
In Jesus' Name, Amen.

Day 3: Why Should We Get Involved?

~Prayer~

Heavenly Father,

We come before You, ready to understand the importance of getting involved, how it matters for our futures and the futures of those around us. We ask that You help us to understand, comprehend, and gain insight to help us in our walk with You. In Jesus' Name, Amen.

Today we are going to discuss why we should get involved.

Read Psalm 133.

Write vs. 2

In other words, when we are involved in ministry, in church, in our purpose, and in our callings, there is an anointing that covers us. Matthew 18:19-20 (NIV) says, "[19] "Again, truly I tell you that if two of you on earth agree about anything they ask for, it will be done for them by my Father in heaven. [20] For where two or three gather in my name, there am I with them."

When we are involved and come together and pray, there is a stronger power that is at work. I love what **Ecclesiastes 4:9-12** says; take time to read it.

Just as we described in week 7 about the tribe, the same can be applied to church, to ministry, and to our callings. When we are not functioning in our calling or on the right path God has for us, we become spiritually dead and stagnant. We become weak and easily fall into sin. I will add that when I stepped into the new calling God has on my life, when He placed a mantle upon me, I began to be spiritually attacked like never before. However, I also became fully alive because the more I get involved, the more I draw close to God, for I realize that within my own strength, I am nothing.

Habakkuk 2:2-3 (NKJV) says, "[2] Then the LORD answered me and said: "Write the vision And make it plain on tablets, That he may run who reads it. [3] For the vision is yet for an appointed time; But at the end it will speak, and it will not lie. Though it tarries, wait for it; Because it will surely come, It will not tarry."

Proverbs 29:18 (KJV) says, "[18] Where there is no vision, the people perish: But he that keepeth the law, happy is he."

Jeremiah 29:11 (NIV) says, "[11] For I know the plans I have for you," declares the LORD, "plans to prosper you and not to harm you, plans to give you hope and a future."

God makes it very clear that He has a plan for each one of us, and as we continue to seek Him, He is faithful to reveal each step to take. We must trust Him with the full plan and be content with knowing only when He reveals it. God says that we are to take this vision, our calling, and write it down, stand in it, pray over it, and move in it. Why? Because when there is no vision, we perish. The Bible makes it very clear the reason we need to be involved and move in our gifts and callings.

When you make a decision and say yes to God on something that He has led you to, it is important to follow through. Also, if you say you are going to do something, and you have peace about it, then you need to follow through with it. Before you agree to something you should always pray and be led by God and His peace before giving an answer. I love what Ecclesiastes 5:4-5 (RSV) says, "[4] When you vow a vow to God, do not delay paying it; for he has no pleasure in fools. Pay what you vow. [5] It is better that you should not vow than that you should vow and not pay."

When you say yes to God, you need to be faithful to your word. We should keep our words from leading us into sin and unfaithfulness. Follow through with what you have said you will do. We want to honor God with our words and actions and not make Him angry. Whatever you are being called to do, be obedient and do it. If you have told someone you will do something because you feel led by the Spirit to do so, then make sure you follow through quickly. Our lack of quickness can also be considered disobedience.

In the coming days we will discuss more on how to find what your calling and purpose is, how you can bring the Kingdom of God into that area, and how to get involved with your tribe and church.

Read Today: Ecclesiastes 4, Ecclesiastes 5

~My prayer for you today~
Heavenly Father,
I come before You, and I pray for Your child reading this. I pray that already You would begin to speak to them concerning the church they are to get involved with, the prophetic they are to get involved in, their ministry, calling, and purpose that they are to walk in. I pray for wisdom and understanding for the steps needed to walk into involvement.
In Jesus' Name, Amen.

Day 4: Five-Fold Ministry

~Prayer~

Heavenly Father,

Today we understand that You have a plan for our lives. You are fully aware of all the details that You place before us. You are giving us a vision for our future. Help us to write it down, hold on to it, and run with it, declaring Your faithfulness and truth to all who will listen. Please continue to reveal this vision to us. In Jesus' Name, Amen.

Today we will be talking about the fivefold ministry which is found in Ephesians 4:11-13 (NIV) which says, "[11] So Christ himself gave the apostles, the prophets, the evangelists, the pastors and teachers, [12] to equip his people for works of service, so that the body of Christ may be built up [13] until we all reach unity in the faith and in the knowledge of the Son of God and become mature, attaining to the whole measure of the fullness of Christ."

There is something that I feel God wants to reveal in this. Growing up I had always heard these verses referenced towards the church and what should be taking place within it. Yet, I have week 7's topic concerning the Tribe and the future of the Bride running through my mind. Suddenly God is giving me revelation concerning these verses.

For the western world, most Christians view Sunday as the day to be with God, and then the rest of the week it is about work and family. God is pretty much removed from the day-to-day walk, and at most a few spend a couple minutes or an hour before they start their day, but then as life gets busy, He is once again put on the back burner. Many churches in the western world don't believe in the fivefold ministry, that prophesy, evangelists, and apostles are even necessary anymore. So, they have removed them from their "programs."

I believe that we are now understanding that the fivefold ministry is important to the church, especially in the coming months and years. But the revelation God gave me is that we are to be bringing the fivefold ministry out of the church walls and into our Monday-Saturday life. We are to bring it into our workplaces, into our gifts and talents, and into our callings. The fivefold ministry should be walked out daily, not just on Sunday. I love what https://fivefoldministry.com says about each ministry. There is also a test you can take to see what your strengths are if you aren't sure where you fall into. Another test that you can take as well is https://www.freeshapetest.com. Another test to help you understand your personality and strengths and weakness is found at https://assessment.yourenneagramcoach.com.

We should be taking this Kingdom of God lifestyle into our families, religion, education, media, entertainment, business, and government. Right now, too many Christians are living just like the world, instead of in their calling and purpose. Their lifestyle reflects the culture they are living in, instead of holding true to God's Word and changing the culture. I believe that before Jesus comes back, He will be revealed in every area mentioned above. Matthew 24:14 (KJV) says, "[14] And this gospel of the kingdom shall be preached in all the world for a witness unto all nations; and then shall the end come."

Read Today: Ephesians 4, Matthew 24

~My prayer for you today~
Heavenly Father,
I come before You, and I pray for Your child reading this. I ask that they begin to feel the stirring of Your Spirit burning in their heart, that their eyes and ears would be open to hear and see Your vision. I pray that they would begin to position themselves to engage the present and step into what You are calling for them.
In Jesus' Name, Amen.

Day 5: Ways to Get Involved

~Prayer~

Heavenly Father,

We come before You, ready for there to be growth and movement in our lives. We do not want to be dead any longer, we do not want to lose our way because we lost the vision, and we want to be reset and realigned back into the plan You have for us. In Jesus' Name, Amen.

Today we will be talking about how you can get involved. As was mentioned in previous weeks, it is very important to plant yourself in a church that is alive. Make sure the beliefs and teachings line up with the Word of God. If the pastor is preaching anything contrary to the Word, if the gifts of the Spirit are shut out, and if you can see that the Holy Spirit is not allowed to interrupt them, then that is not the right church.

I have shared scripture after scripture of what a church should be, so you can always return to previous weeks and reread them. It is very important that in the coming months and years, you are in the right position God has for you. If God is leading you to change jobs, then obey. If He is leading you into ministry, even if it is voluntary, then obey.

God is leading each one of us into what He has for us. Here is a list that you can pray over and see if it is an area that you are to be involved in.

1. Nursing Home (Spending time and visiting them)
2. Hospice (spending time and visiting them)
3. Hospital (Spending time and visiting them)
4. Nonprofit organizations that help addicts, victims of abuse, orphans, etc. (What individual groups has God laid on your heart. Could be immigrants, poverty stricken, etc.).
5. Missions organization (global mindset)
6. Entertainment avenues who are wanting to bring God's kingdom into the world.

*The list goes on and on (look up your area and see if there are areas that jump out at you as possible places to get involved.)

The truth is that there are so many options out there. It could be as simple as creating jewelry, and through it you share your testimony of what God has done. You could design a piece of art that does the same thing. You could create music that reveals the Kingdom of God. You could create dances that can be used to further the Kingdom. The point is, while you are healing and going through this, you still need to be involved. Once you are free and healed God does not want you to stop there; no, He wants you to impact the world for Him.

Take time today to ask God to give you a vision for your future and a ministry to connect to, and to show you how to bring the Kingdom of God into your workplace.

Read Today: 1 Corinthians 12

~My prayer for you today~
Heavenly Father,
I come before You, and I pray for Your child reading this. I am so excited for each of them. Father, You have an amazing plan and purpose for their life. It is going to shatter every imagination they ever dared to dream. It is going to go above and beyond, and it will be a blessing to them. So today, strengthen them and encourage them, and I pray that there would be a birthing of passion for this vision.
In Jesus' Name, Amen.

Day 6: My Story

When I began my healing process and to receive breakthrough and freedom, being uninvolved or disengaged would have been easy. One of the hard parts of PTSD is the depression that can creep up and if I don't take care of it right away, it makes me want to pull away from others. Another reason why it is hard is that I am more of an introvert; I can function as an extrovert, but I must be very careful of how much I am exerting of myself. That means there are times where I must pull away and be alone in order to pour myself out to others.

The first couple of months of my healing required facing the abuse and trauma head-on. I had to remember it all, feel all the emotions and fears without pushing them down, and then pray through each one. During that time, I met with my dad almost every night to pray and talk over what God was taking me through. I have been very blessed to have a father who is a pastor, prophet, and full of wise counsel. I would talk with my mom about different things and listened to how to handle situations in life and in God. I met with a spiritual mother who has been a part of my life for fifteen years; we would meet every other week, and I would hear her wise counsel. I would also meet with a sister in Christ every week and we would talk about what God was sharing in both our lives, where He was leading, and we encouraged each other on in the Lord. My siblings would reach out and check how I was doing, and shared ways that God brought them through their own struggles.

I still meet with my dad and mom throughout the week, as well as if things crop up specifically. I meet with my sister in Christ weekly and my spiritual mother at least once a month or every other month.

When I separated from my ex-husband, he decided that he would continue to go to the church that we had been a part of. I decided that I would no longer continue going and I had no desire to visit churches to find the right one, especially because I was finding that many churches did not meet the scriptures and were not alive in the Holy Spirit. But until I found the right church, I still wanted to be involved and knew that my freedom and breakthrough meant staying in the presence of God. I found a couple of churches that I could watch online, and it was exactly what I needed. I would watch all three sermons on Sunday and allow the truth to resonate within my soul.

I found prophets who are declaring what God is speaking to His people, and I followed the Word of God and tested them before agreeing with the word given. I still continue to listen to what they are speaking, and I love how they confirm things God has also spoken to me. It shows me that I can hear from God and that He has an amazing plan for me.

A year after everything began, God revealed that I was to write Held Hostage and then later, Beyond Held Hostage. On top of that, He revealed the blueprints for a ministry that will have global impact. I am also involved in my dad and mom's ministry and church that began recently. I am excited about the future, because I know I have a purpose and the past will not stop my favored future.

Day 7: Self-Reflection

~Prayer~

Heavenly Father,

We come before You and we take time today to hear Your voice. Please direct this time of fellowship with You. Reveal to us what You are wanting to say and direct us. Speak to us very clearly and reveal to us what we need to know. In Jesus' Name, Amen.

Today I will be asking hard questions and I want you to write down your answers of what God truthfully and honestly has revealed to you.

Are you struggling to get involved with church, ministry, bringing the kingdom of God to earth?

What has kept you from getting involved?

Where have you failed to be obedient to step when God told you?

(Take time to pray, repent for this, and then obey.)

What has God been speaking to you concerning His vision for you?

What is your gifting He wants you to use?

How is God calling you to get involved?

~Prayer~

Heavenly Father,

We thank You for sharing with us the vision and plan You have for us. Thank You for making us aware of where we have missed it and how we can correct it. Thank You that You have not given up on us, but You have taken us out of the grave and into life. So today, we choose to say yes. We will obey and we will begin to live a lifestyle that reveals Your glory Sunday-Saturday.

In Jesus' Name, Amen.

Week 10: Walking in The Opposite Spirit

"[16] So I say, walk by the Spirit, and you will not gratify the desires of the flesh. [17] For the flesh desires what is contrary to the Spirit, and the Spirit what is contrary to the flesh. They are in conflict with each other, so that you are not to do whatever you want."
(Galatians 5:16-17 NIV)

Day 1: Walking in The Opposite Spirit

This week's topic is going to be one of the hardest ones to follow through on. It will go against everything you are feeling, and at times take you out of your comfortable box. The topic is walking in the opposite spirit. Galatians 5:16-17 (RSV) says, "¹⁶ But I say, walk by the Spirit, and do not gratify the desires of the flesh. ¹⁷ For the desires of the flesh are against the Spirit, and the desires of the Spirit are against the flesh; for these are opposed to each other, to prevent you from doing what you would."

One of the biggest areas that satan hits us during our healing process is around emotions and feelings. If you have been betrayed, abused, and abandoned, that leads to desires for revenge, anger and resentment, and the list goes on and on. As we process memories, we will be tempted to move from the Spirit into our flesh. Galatians truly sums up what we should do in times of healing, but it will go against everything we are feeling. At times it means going against what we believe, and we will get into that next week.

I am going to share a small portion from my book, 'Held Hostage,' that explains this a bit better.

I once had a friend ask me, "Doesn't that mean you are not being true to yourself and how you feel?" We live in a culture and world that tells us to do what we want according to how we feel, and that is how to live. But that is a lie! Our war is spiritual. We belong to God and so we do not live like the world. Anger, depression, bitterness, etc., if acted upon will hurt us in the long run. It will become my baggage, my open wounds for all to see, and I will live with them for a long time. As we walk with God in His Spirit, we must choose what is right and align our spirit with His. What is right does not change with our feelings and emotions. When we choose to walk in the opposite of the negative, we begin to change and heal, and we no longer have wounds and baggage, but hope, joy, and love. Take every negative feeling and emotion to God.[8]

How many of you, after reading that, had your flesh rise and say, "NO! I don't want to!"? However, this step is necessary for your growth, healing, and freedom. Our healing is not based on the other person. It does not matter if they are sorry, it does not matter if they repent, and it does not matter if they change. Our healing is based upon ourselves and if we will let the Holy Spirit do the work in us. My ex-husband said he was sorry, but it was because he got caught. He never truly repented and changed. If my healing and breakthrough is because of him, I would still be waiting. No, my healing and breakthrough came because I walked in the Spirit instead of the flesh.

We will begin by looking at what God says about walking in the Spirit and what He says about walking in our flesh. From there we will talk about different ways found in the Bible where people walked in the opposite of how they felt. Finally, we will get into examples of how we can apply this to our own lives.

Read Today: Galatians 5

---

[8] Aubrey Dawn Weinzetl, "Held Hostage," 2022.

~Prayer~

Heavenly Father, we come before You, and we understand that this week is going to break us. It is going to be hard, and we will have to cling to You through it. We understand that this idea of walking in the opposite Spirit is going to make us face things about ourselves that we would rather run from. Even so, we understand that where You lead us, You will not abandon us, and we will cross through.

In Jesus' Name, Amen.

Day 2: What Does the Bible Say About Our Spirit Man and Our Flesh Man

~Prayer~

Heavenly Father,

We come before You and we are ready to push through our pasts and pain. We are ready to take up our cross and follow You. We recognize that we need You through this process, because in our own strength we will fail. So today, come and fill us anew. Give us boldness to face what we need to face and walk in the opposite of what we feel when it is contrary to You. In Jesus' Name, Amen.

Today we will be looking at what God says about our Spirit man and our flesh. It is important to understand the difference. Walking in the opposite spirit is really a form of spiritual warfare. We will talk about spiritual warfare in week 14. But I really wanted to give walking in the opposite Spirit its own week, because of how powerful this step is. So, let's first begin by understanding what the flesh is.

I absolutely love how Romans 8:4-9 (NIV) explains the flesh and Spirit.

(Read and then write down what the verses say about the flesh and about the spirit.)

When Christ is in us, we are given life because of the Spirit of God. The very Spirit who brought Jesus out of the grave and gave back His breath, is living inside of us. So how can we live by the flesh, which leads to our spiritual death and hell? If we live by the Spirit, then sin is put to death and our spirits live. I love what Romans 8:15-16 (RSV) says, "[15] For you did not receive the spirit of slavery to fall back into fear, but you have received the spirit of sonship. When we cry, "Abba! Father!" [16] it is the Spirit himself bearing witness with our spirit that we are children of God, [17] and if children, then heirs, heirs of God and fellow heirs with Christ, provided we suffer with him in order that we may also be glorified with him."

I think it is important to discuss what the soul, spirit, and Spirit is all about. I think for many they have not heard about this and so I want to bring understanding and clarification. Every human being has a soul, spirit, and body, making us different from animals. Our soul consists of the mind, will, and emotions. The flesh is you making decisions about your life without your spirit being alive. When we have not received Christ as Lord and Savior, then our spirit is dead, and we are separated from God. Our spirit then comes alive when we receive Christ as Lord and Savior, and the Holy Spirit comes into our heart. Then the Holy Spirit begins to renew our spirits according to the will of God. Remember how we talked about that in week 3? So, our flesh is about our soul and who we were before our spirit came alive through Christ. Now the Holy Spirit resides in us and communicates with this new spirit man within us, and that helps us put down the flesh in our soul. Now we are called to be free, and with this freedom we should not abuse God's grace and continue to serve the flesh, but instead we should work in the Spirit and in our spirit man. We should be careful in how we treat one another because we do not want to be a tool of satan's and destroy one another.

Galatians 5:24-25 (RSV) says, "[24] And those who belong to Christ Jesus have crucified the flesh with its passions and desires. ^{25} If we live by the Spirit, let us also walk by the Spirit."

(Answer these questions.)

What are the acts of the flesh? (Galatians 5:19-21)

What is the fruit of the Spirit? (Galatians 5:22-23)

Now in our minds as we think about the flesh, it is almost a no-brainer. Like, of course we do not want to live in sin, darkness, and do those things. Yet is it truly easy to walk in the fruit of the Spirit towards someone who betrayed you, lied to you, hurt you, abused you, abandoned you, etc.? If you answer this truthfully, you answered, "NO! It is not easy, and it breaks my heart to do it." God does not give us a pass to walk in our flesh feelings and emotions when someone wrongs us. No, the Spirit is to always be in operation and shown to all, even those who persecute us.

I started applying this step throughout my whole marriage because I wanted to honor God. I realized that I wanted my actions and heart to always reflect God and honor Him, regardless of my husband's (ex-husband's) choices. Can you imagine doing this during the abuse and betrayal? It was so hard and painful but doing anything in my flesh only caused me greater pain and separation from God. Did I always do it right? No, I made mistakes, but I learned from them because I truly want to get to Heaven and have God say, "Well done, good and faithful daughter."

Having that mindset already in place when it came to the separation and divorce, I continued to live in the Spirit. My ex-husband did not deserve it, but it wasn't about him. No, I did it out of my love for God and obedience to His Word. My feelings and emotions did not always line up with my actions, but after a while they did. Those negative feelings and emotions that wanted to push my flesh to the front no longer Held me Hostage.

I know that right now many of you are struggling with this step and the desire to follow through in it. So today I want you to **read Psalm 23** and let it encourage you. Our God is a good God, and He will be our strength and our comfort.

~My prayer for you today~

Heavenly Father,

I come before You, and I pray for Your child reading this. I pray that You would bring comfort and peace to them. Let Your light shine through where their minds are in torment from memories and negative feelings and emotions. I pray that they would begin to see the Light at the end of the tunnel. Let it stir in them the passion to continue through this healing process, so they can have a future that is thriving and bright.

In Jesus' Name, Amen.

Day 3: Jesus, Paul, and Joseph

~Prayer~

Heavenly Father,

We come before You and we are ready to see how walking in the opposite Spirit has been applied throughout the Word. We understand that their testimonies will encourage us and spur us on to do the same. Help us to keep the right heart, attitude, and mindset. In Jesus' Name, Amen.

Today we will be looking at a couple of different testimonies of individuals who walked in the opposite spirit when everything screamed at them to do it differently. The first one is Jesus, and honestly there are so many ways that Jesus showed us this. Yes, He was God yet also man, but He still had a choice to act in the flesh. I want to set the stage for this part of His testimony. For a couple of years, Jesus had been spending quality time with His twelve disciples. During this time, He was equipping them and revealing more of Himself to them, and they had become a family. We find that right before this part of His testimony takes place, Jesus was with His disciples celebrating the Passover, the promise of what He was about to fulfill. While with them, He shared how one of them would be the one to betray Him.

Already I understand what Jesus was feeling. I have been betrayed by the one closest to me, and I understand the feelings, emotions, and pain that brings. While in the Garden praying, a group approached Jesus, and leading them was Judas. One of His own went up to Him and betrayed Him with a kiss. Immediately Jesus confronted him and asked him if he was truly doing this. (Luke 22:47-48) I can just see the heartbreak taking place at this moment. The pain and wounds went deep. We can see the disciple's response to the situation was not one of the Spirit. Luke 22:49-50 (AMP) says, "[49] When those who were around Him saw what was about to happen, they said, "Lord, should we strike with the sword?" [50] And one of them struck the slave of the high priest and cut off his right ear."

But Jesus response is one of great love. It goes beyond the situation, the pain, the betrayal, and beyond whether the slave deserved it or not. Luke 22:51 (AMP) says, "[51] But Jesus replied, "Stop! No more of this." And He touched the ear and healed him."

Jesus went above and beyond and healed the servant of the high priest. This high priest would play a part in the very brutal persecution that would require Jesus to lay His life down. Yet He did not let His flesh rule. He walked in the Spirit and loved.

Paul is another one who showed the spirit in multiple situations, but the one we will talk about today is found in Acts 16. Paul was on his way to pray; they were met with a slave who had a demonic spirit that told her the future. Her owners used the demon to make money for them. Acts 16:17-18 (AMP) says, "[17] She followed after Paul and us and kept screaming and shouting, "These men are servants of the Most High God! They are proclaiming to you the way of salvation!" [18] She continued doing this for several days. Then Paul, being greatly annoyed and worn out, turned and said to the spirit [inside her], "I command you in the name of Jesus Christ [as His representative] to come out of her!" And it came out at that very moment."

She was completely set free, but that meant her masters would no longer be able to make financial gain from her. Furiously, they took Paul and Silas before those in authority and laid their accusations against them. The crowds also joined in the anger, and the stage was now set. Paul, through Jesus Christ, had delivered a woman from an evil spirit. Talk about being set free!!!! Yet, because of this they were seized and taken before those in authority, and with false testimony, the one in authority commanded that they be stripped naked then flogged and beaten. I can only imagine the embarrassment, shame, and physical pain they were enduring. Our minds would say they had every right now to respond in their emotions and feelings. Yet, their response shouts out love.

Read Acts 16:25-28.
Write verse 25.

Because of their actions done in the spirit, the jailer and his whole household got saved and baptized. What would have happened if Paul responded in the flesh? How many lives would have been sent to Hell? Also, look at the wisdom Paul applied in dealing with the magistrate; in a wise way he revealed their identity and fear seized them. The outcome of walking in the opposite spirit led to a powerful time of worship, lives saved, the wicked realizing their mistake, and in the end, to Paul's freedom.

Finally, we are going to look at Joseph. We talked about Joseph last week and how he had to be tested before he walked into his calling. But this week we are going to look at his response to the brothers who had betrayed him. Joseph's brothers had thrown him in a well, sold him as a slave, and then had gone back to their father and told him he had died. This meant the father would never go and look for his son. Many people would say that Joseph would have every right to treat his brothers wrongly. But we find that Joseph does not. Joseph is now second in command; Pharaoh is the only one higher than he is. He is using the wisdom and knowledge God gives him to allocate food during a severe famine. His brothers, in need of food themselves journey to Egypt, and Joseph takes them through a time of testing, wanting to see if they had truly learned from their mistakes, or if they would harm their father again. After the testing, we learn Joseph's response. (Genesis 42-44)

Read Genesis 45:1-7.
(Write down verse 2.)

(Fill in the blanks.)
Do not be _____ nor _____, it was not you, but _____ God who _____ me _____.
But God sent me ahead of you to _____ for you a _____ on earth.

I was meant to _____ your lives by a _____

_____.

Genesis 45:14-15 (NIV) breaks my heart, "[14] Then he threw his arms around his brother Benjamin and wept, and Benjamin embraced him, weeping. [15] And he kissed all his brothers and wept over them. Afterward his brothers talked with him."

How many of us could respond this way willingly? How many of us has God been asking to live in the Spirit, but we have been controlled by our flesh? Why are we here on this earth? Are we not meant to save lives and keep people from hell? Are we not to be an ambassador for Christ no matter the situation we are in?

I want to be one of those who treats others the way the Holy Spirit calls me to. I want my love and compassion to reveal to the world the love of the Father at work in me, to cause them to long for a relationship with God, because who I am is so very different from the world around them.

Read Today: Luke 22, Acts 16, Genesis 45

~My prayer for you today~
Heavenly Father,
I come before You, and I pray for Your child reading this. I can sense the struggle that many are facing with this step of working in the opposite Spirit. I understand the struggle, but I also know the freedom they will receive if they obey You. So today, I pray that You would encourage their hearts, that they would see the truth and the truth would set them free.
In Jesus' Name, Amen.

Day 4: Jesus and David

~Prayer~

Heavenly Father,

We come before You and we repent for the times we have been in the flesh but were meant to be in the Spirit. Forgive us for how we failed to see what You were doing and how You were bringing our freedom and deliverance. We repent and we choose today to walk in the Spirit instead of our flesh.   In Jesus' Name, Amen.

Today we will be looking at two more testimonies. As I mentioned yesterday, Jesus lived so many examples of this. Yesterday we left off when the soldiers seized Jesus. His disciples abandoned him, and one even went so far to deny Him three times. He was taken before the religious leaders, slandered, and falsely accused. Guards mocked Him and made fun of Him, all while physically wounding Him. From there, He faced Pilot and Herod. He was whipped and beaten beyond recognition. His fellow people asked for a murderer to be released instead of Him; He who had done nothing but heal them, set them free, and give them life. (Luke 22) Luke 23 then goes on to say that two men, both of whom had reason for the death penalty, was crucified along with Jesus. The crowd mocked him, and even one of the criminals beside him joined in. Jesus' response was, "Forgive them, Father." Yet, one of the criminals clearly saw Jesus for who He is.

Read Luke 23:40-43.

What did the criminal say?

Write verse 43.

Jesus allowed Himself to be hung on a cross; He allowed others to throw insult while suffering severe pain we cannot even imagine. Despite this, His response was to tell one of the sinners that he would be joining Him in paradise. What amazing love the Father has for us. Luke 23:44-47 (NLT) says, "[44] By this time it was about noon, and darkness fell across the whole land until three o'clock. [45] The light from the sun was gone. And suddenly, the curtain in the sanctuary of the Temple was torn down the middle. [46] Then Jesus shouted, "Father, I entrust my spirit into your hands!" And with those words he breathed his last. [47] When the Roman officer overseeing the execution saw what had happened, he worshiped God and said, "Surely this man was innocent."

Jesus understood that if He responded in the flesh, everything that He had done up to this point would be for nothing, that to completely save us and give us the opportunity to be with the Father, it required Him to purposefully give up His life. He laid it down for us; they did not take it from Him, He gave it. If Jesus would have chosen flesh, we would still be separated from God. We would not have communication with Him nor the Holy Spirit within us. On top of that, even the soldiers would not have seen the faithfulness and love of God.

David is another one we have talked about. Remember he was anointed king, and yet Saul was hunting him down, ready to take his very life. Saul had taken his daughter, who was married to David, away from him and had given her to another man. Talk about experiencing some betrayal and pain. Even so, David's response was not out of flesh but in spirit. Saul was returning home when news came that David was close by. David was hiding in a cave, and Saul just so happened to pass by this very exact cave to use the bathroom. David's men encouraged him to take Saul's life and end their suffering. But David only cut off a piece of Saul's clothing, and his small action brought deep conviction. He rebuked his men and ordered that no harm come to Saul. Later on, he confronted Saul. (1 Samuel 24)

Read 1 Samuel 24:11-12.

1 Samuel 24:15 (NLT) says, "[15] May the LORD therefore judge which of us is right and punish the guilty one. He is my advocate, and he will rescue me from your power!"

David could have easily taken Saul's life. No one would have blamed him, especially because Saul again turned around to kill David only a couple of chapters later, but David's obedience was not based on whether or not Saul would change. His obedience and choice to walk in the Spirit were based upon his relationship with God. David's action pleased God, and God blessed him. He would become king and through his bloodline the Messiah would come. I love that even after all Saul had done and he was finally gone from this world, David still remembered his own promise. In 2 Samuel 9, we find that David takes in Jonathan's son, restores his father's land back to him, and then has the son eat every meal with him. How many of us are willing to keep our word even towards those have hurt us? (Obviously if you are being abused there needs to be wisdom on how to act on this, because letting them go and releasing them to God is more loving than staying with them.)

Tomorrow we will be talking about ways to apply walking in the opposite spirit in our own lives.

Read Today: Luke 23, Luke 24, 2 Samuel 9

~My prayer for you today~
Heavenly Father,
I come before You, and I pray for Your child reading this. I pray that Your child is ready to begin taking steps to walk in the Spirit instead of the flesh. No matter how hard, no matter what emotion or fear wants to control them, I pray that they would overcome by the Blood of the Lamb and the Word of their testimony.
In Jesus' Name, Amen.

Day 5: Ways to Walk in The Opposite Spirit

~Prayer~

Heavenly Father,

We come before You and right now we submit ourselves to You. We command every lying spirit, demonic agenda, and strongman to be gone in the name of Jesus. You have no authority over us, and you cannot keep us from the love of God. Father, we ask that You now come and bring truth, understanding, and boldness, as well as the desire for obedience into our lives. In Jesus' name, Amen.

Today we are going to be talking about ways to walk in the opposite Spirit. James 1:12-15 (RSV) says, "[12] Blessed is the man who endures trial, for when he has stood the test he will receive the crown of life which God has promised to those who love him. [13] Let no one say when he is tempted, "I am tempted by God"; for God cannot be tempted with evil and he himself tempts no one; [14] but each person is tempted when he is lured and enticed by his own desire. [15] Then desire when it has conceived gives birth to sin; and sin when it is full-grown brings forth death."

Here are some situations and ways to handle them.

1. You find out your friends have been gossiping or lying about you behind your back. In this situation, you can confront them in a loving way and let them know how their actions have hurt you, that you have chosen to forgive them, but you also no longer trust them to keep things confidential, so you will be guarding what you say to them.

2. Your church abused their power and because of it you were hurt. Confront the ones who hurt you in an honoring way. If the situation cannot be resolved or if it was done by a pastor and there is no one above him/her and it does not change, pray about leaving that church and then explain your reason to them. Let them know their actions were not Biblical, that you forgive them, but that you will be finding a church that lives according to the Word.

3. Your spouse has an affair. If the spouse is just sorry because they were caught, prayerfully consider what your next step should be. If there is true repentance, begin to have counseling sessions together. It will take time to build back the trust and heal, but if both parties are truly following God again, He will give you what you need for this. If there is no repentance and the affairs continue, then it is time to let this marriage go. Throughout the whole thing you should keep your heart right before God. Make sure that your words and tone are honoring. Be wise when you talk about things. Make sure you're careful in a moment of anger or resentment. The goal is to show your spouse an image of Jesus.

4. You are being triggered by specific things (you possibly also have PTSD). When you are triggered, the goal is to remain calm and not respond. If you need to get away until you are calm, then do so. I usually wait a day before I confront the person who triggered me or explain to them what was going on. I must make sure that I am in my right mind, so when I am triggered, the goal is not to give any response until it is one I won't regret.

5. One example that I often use is depression, because it is something I have lived with for a long time. Although it has been almost two years since I had a big bout of depression, there are plenty of others that I can use for this example. Many times, I have no desire to dress up, wear makeup, go places, spend time with God or family and friends, and I mainly just want to stay in bed. So, I get

dressed up, I put on makeup, and I go places, even if it's just for a walk, but anything other than staying in bed. I spend time with God, family, and friends. The goal is to do the opposite of what my flesh wants. It's having the resolve to continue even when your flesh says to give up.

6. Your spouse had an affair; the mistress or the other party involved is making life hard for you. But you continue to forgive them, no matter how long it takes. For four years, I had to continually speak forgiveness over the mistress because the pain or memories would overwhelm me, along with the anger and resentment. I continued to choose forgiveness until I realized I had truly forgiven her and no longer thought about her. You can also write or call them and, with honor, tell them they need to stop and if they won't, you will be getting another person involved, whether it's a police officer, lawyer, pastor, or their parent. The point is this: with honor, you tell them the effects of their actions, that you forgive them, and that their behavior needs to stop. Make sure you receive wise counsel in how you say this because you never know the mind of the other person involved and you want to make sure you are safe.

These are just a few examples, but I am sure that in your own life God has already been revealing areas your flesh took over when you needed to walk according to the Spirit. It is important to continue to live in the spirit and not by flesh.

Finally, I want you to **read Romans 12:3-21**, because it clearly states what our spirit response should be. Make every effort to follow the Holy Spirit and put down the flesh that would try to keep you in death. Romans 12:21 (NIV) says, "[21] Do not be overcome by evil, but overcome evil with good."

Read Today: James 1

~My prayer for you today~
Heavenly Father,
I come before You, and I pray for Your child reading this. Sometimes our situations want to override what we know is true. Sometimes we would rather take the easy way out and follow our flesh rather than oppose it and move in the Spirit. Today, I pray that You would encourage Your child not to take the easy way, but to fight the good fight of faith, and to remain faithful and true to You, regardless of what has happened to them.
In Jesus' Name, Amen.

Day 6: My Story

This has been one of the hardest tools to use, but it has been one that has brought so much freedom. Through my marriage I really struggled to act in the opposite spirit when the abuse, trauma, betrayal, and pain was happening. When the anger surged in my heart, I had to choose not to follow through, but to walk in honor.

As I mentioned in Held Hostage, I did not want to become an abuser myself, so when the anger came, I would get away and cry and scream, and it would usually end as I cried out to God. When hurtful words were said, I chose not to respond in turn. (Although there were times I failed in that, and had to repent.) When my past was brought up as a weapon against me, I would be careful of what I said about his. There were times when walking in the opposite of how I felt failed. But I didn't give up. I wanted to honor God regardless of how I was being treated; I didn't want my responses to be based on another person but based off my relationship with God.

As my relationship with God in November of 2020 was strengthened, this became easier and easier to do. (When his last betrayal came to light in February, four days before my birthday.) I walked in peace, gentleness, and honor. When he chose not to wish me happy birthday and make the day fun, only to turn around the next day and wish me a happy birthday because he claimed he couldn't remember the actual day (after fourteen years of knowing me), I walked in gentleness and honor. To say I wasn't hurt or that the situation wasn't painful would be a lie. But I chose to walk in love and honor out of my relationship with God.

For one month we stayed in the same house and in the same bedroom, although I was usually only in the room four hours at most. The rest was spent at work and on the downstairs living room sectional, where I would spend hours with God. That spot is now known among my family and friends as an anointed spot. When we come together to pray or talk, you will usually find me in that spot. I also wrote Held Hostage in that place because it is where I meet with God.

During that month of living in the same house, instead of taking out my pain, anger, or feeling like I needed to avenge myself, I would go to my spot and cry, read my Bible, pray, and worship. That month was one of the hardest of my life as I battled through fourteen years of abuse, trauma, betrayal, and brokenness, not to mention fighting the triggers of my PTSD these memories brought. It is also the place I began to find healing and freedom from PTSD. It would have been so easy to respond in hurt and anger, but I chose to love and honor.

I stood firm on my decision to separate, but I was not harsh or ugly about it. When I told him that I was going to get a lawyer to start the divorce process, I spoke in love and honor, without anger and hate. When I wanted to justify myself or make him feel my pain, I refrained and spoke the facts covered in grace.

I had overseen all the bills and finances through our dating and marriage years. So, I taught him how to do it, instead of letting him suffer to learn. I wrote down the information, I took pictures, and helped fill out paperwork. Why? Because I wanted to honor God, not because my ex deserved it. I wanted him, my nephew and niece, my family, and my friends to see Jesus as I walked through the separation, divorce, and the aftermath. I wanted God to be glorified by my actions and heart.

I get asked often, "Doesn't that mean you are not being true to yourself and how you feel?" In many countries we are taught to do what we want, what "feels" right, and not worry about the outcome. We are taught to be selfish. However, our feelings lie all the time. Our perspectives, especially the ones that are based on our own experiences and thoughts, cause our feelings and ideas to flow in a selfish direction. Which is why I addressed 'perspective' in week 11, because our perspectives urge our flesh to respond, instead of letting our spirit respond. Paul is so right when he says there is a battle taking place inside of us. (Gal. 5:13-26)

So, walking in the opposite spirit means dying to my flesh and its responses, and moving in the Spirit with righteous responses. As I began to apply this to my ex, I was given great freedom, because I understood the abuse, betrayal, and abandonment were not my fault. It was a heart issue within my ex-husband. If I responded out of my flesh, I would've remained Held Hostage. But when I respond in my spirit, I give room to God to work in the situation and bring freedom. Soon my feelings fell into alignment with the Holy Spirit. (Anger was gone, pain was removed, and I was no longer broken, but walking in royalty.)

Before I move on, I want to mention that when I met with my ex during the separation and divorce, my dad was close by, and made sure we met in a busy location. I also asked God if I was to meet him or not.

Walking in the opposite spirit is not something that stopped after my ex and I went separate ways. Due to life experiences from childhood up until now, I have default responses that try to take over when my PTSD is triggered. When a family member, friend, or stranger responds in a certain way that reminds me of my past experiences, my negative response takes over. So, I work in the opposite of that. Sometimes I can catch it right away, other times I must repent and seek their forgiveness. Other times I must challenge and correct them in honor. It's something I continually work on because I do not want to use PTSD as an excuse to let my flesh reign and keep me hostage. I fully desire to overcome PTSD so that even when I might be triggered, I will still respond in the Spirit.

Day 7: Self-Reflection

~Prayer~

Heavenly Father,

We come before You and we take time today to hear Your voice. Please direct this time of fellowship with You. Reveal to us what You want to say, and direct us. Speak to us very clearly and reveal to us what we need to know.

In Jesus' Name, Amen.

Today I will be asking hard questions and I want you to write down your answers of what God truthfully and honestly has revealed to you.

What are the situations you failed to walk in the opposite spirit?

When are times that you were able to walk in the opposite spirit?

Going forward, how does God want you to implement walking in the opposite spirit?

What steps are you going to take to put the flesh down? (Colossians 3)

~Prayer~

Heavenly Father,

We thank You for revealing to us how to work in the opposite spirit in our situation. We are blessed to have You leading us in this path. We know that when we make a mistake, You will lovingly correct us and show us how to do it differently. Continue to teach us and help us to mature.

In Jesus' Name, Amen.

Week 11: Perspective

"⁸ Be alert and of sober mind. Your enemy the devil prowls around like a roaring lion looking for someone to devour. ⁹ Resist him, standing firm in the faith, because you know that the family of believers throughout the world is undergoing the same kind of sufferings. ¹⁰ And the God of all grace, who called you to his eternal glory in Christ, after you have suffered a little while, will himself restore you and make you strong, firm and steadfast."
(1 Peter 5:8-10 NIV)

Day 1: Perspective

Romans 12:1-2 (RSV) says, "[1] I appeal to you therefore, brethren, by the mercies of God, to present your bodies as a living sacrifice, holy and acceptable to God, which is your spiritual worship. [2] Do not be conformed to this world but be transformed by the renewal of your mind, that you may prove what is the will of God, what is good and acceptable and perfect."

This week we will be talking about perspective. Now, there are many different opinions on this topic, but I think it is important to explain what I mean when I talk about perspective. Perspective to me is how my brain takes in information and then directs me to respond. It is the thought processes, the habits, and the belief systems that my brain functions in.

In other words, (as we talked about last week in walking in the opposite spirit), my perspective can either be in alignment with the Spirit, or it can be in alignment with the flesh. Perspective is where our views of others, situations, and experiences come to life. In Romans 12, we understand that God wants us to live our lives in a way that is holy, pure, righteous, and by doing this we worship Him with our lives. We also learn that our mind needs to shift from the world mindset, and it is our responsibility to renew our minds for what is righteous in the will of God. God will not force us to change our mindset and perspective but leaves it a choice for us. Even so, He commands us to do it because the consequences if we don't will be a life Held Hostage and can lead to separation from Him for eternity.

The Bible makes it very clear that our mind is a powerful weapon. It has the power to destroy ourselves and others. Micah 4:12 (RSV) says, "[12] But they do not know the thoughts of the LORD, they do not understand his plan, that he has gathered them as sheaves to the threshing floor."

In 1 Corinthians 2, there are some powerful verses that spread light on perspective. They explain how God's wisdom has been hidden, like treasure, and that many will not receive this gift.

Read 1 Corinthians 2:10-13, 16.

_____ searches _____.

Who searches the depths of God? _____

Who knows the thoughts of man? _____

Who knows God's thoughts? _____

What spirit have we received? _____

Remember when we talked about how we all have a spirit, but the spirit only comes alive when we receive Jesus Christ and the Holy Spirit comes to live in us? Since our spirit is now alive, and we have the Holy Spirit inside of us, we can make judgements concerning everything: situations, problems, etc. But the person who is dead in spirit cannot accept or understand spiritual truths and principles, because the Holy Spirit is not inside them to give discernment.

This week we will be talking about our thought patterns, if our minds are in carnal mode or in the Spirit, how to renew our minds, and finally, how to look through God's eyes and see different perspectives before making a decision.

Read Today: Romans 12

~Prayer~
Heavenly Father, we come before You, and we ask that You begin to reveal to us where our perspectives are in alignment with You and where they are not. We want to have renewed minds that are not Held Hostage, but free to discern Your voice, thoughts, and ways.
In Jesus' Name, Amen.

Day 2: What Is God's Perspective?

~Prayer~

Heavenly Father,

We come before You and we ask that You help us to renew our minds and give us Your thoughts. We want to live for You, we want to be godly examples of You to the world, and we want to change the world for Your kingdom. So come and remove everything that is not of You. Tear it down, take out the roots that would cause our minds to be moved by the flesh, and give us a new mind and perspective. In Jesus' Name, Amen.

Today we will be talking about what God's perspective is. The fact is that many believers feel it is okay to respond to individuals who have hurt us in a harsh way, because they deserve that response. But God very clearly shows us that He disagrees. His perspective of the person and the situation is different than our own.

Read Isaiah 55:6-11.

Who are we to seek and call out to? _____

Who should forsake their ways and thoughts? _____

What do we need to do to receive His mercy?

Write out verse 8.

What does not return void but will accomplish God's desire and purpose?

The Old Testament and New Testament are filled with God's thoughts concerning the future and His plan for us, and if we want to walk in it, we need Him to strengthen us so we can renew our minds. Renewing our minds is a battle; it is the spirit fighting against the flesh. We need God's help as we fight the battle to reclaim our minds.

Read Ephesians 2:6-9.

Write verses 8 and 9.

We used to live our lives in the world, with selfish and wicked desires and thoughts. Our actions gratified the flesh and did not bring honor to God. But when we come to the understanding of who Jesus is, and we accept Him as Lord and Savior, we are taken out of the world and brought into the Kingdom of God. Although we still remain in the world, we are no longer a part of it. He has a plan to show the world, through His Bride, that He is good, loving, kind, and is faithful. The world is seeing the greatest love story lived out through the Bride and Jesus.

I love David's understanding of God's thoughts. I especially love the way he explains it. In Psalm 139, he begins by telling God he knows that God knows him better than anyone else. That God has looked deeply into his very being, and God knows every single detail about him. David acknowledges that this deep knowing God has of him makes it impossible to run and hide, for he is always found.

Read Psalm 139:13-18.
Write down what God knows about you.

What a beautiful imagery that David gives. We forget that God knows every detail about us, from our physical bodies to our soul, mind, will, emotions, and spirit. He knows it all. He knows our battles, our struggles, our temptations, our sins, and our desire for Him. He knows us better than we know ourselves, and I absolutely love what David says next.

Psalm 139:23-24 (NIV) says, "[23] Search me, God, and know my heart; test me and know my anxious thoughts. [24] See if there is any offensive way in me, and lead me in the way everlasting."

My heart is crying out these words even now. "Father, I long for you to search me and to know me. I long to be known so deeply and still be accepted and loved by You. So search me, Father, and reveal to me the areas that are not of You, that separate me from You. Then give me the strength to turn from the world and to fear You, living my life in Your ways. In Jesus' name, Amen." It doesn't stop there; the Bible directs us even further regarding our perspective.

Read Ephesians 5:10-11, 15-20.

God's perspective for us is found in verses 10-11, 15-20. We hear what to stay away from, but also what to replace the flesh with. God desires that we find out what truth is and He walks alongside us to teach us how to apply this to our actions. He does not leave us alone on this journey, but is constantly leading, directing, and giving comfort through it. I love how it mentions twice to find out, to understand God's will, or what pleases Him. Proverbs 25:2 (NIV) says, "[2] It is the glory of God to conceal a matter; to search out a matter is the glory of kings."

When we search for God's thoughts and perspective, it is our glory. Although God has hidden things, He chooses us to reveal the truth. Matthew 11:25 (NIV) says, "[25] At that time Jesus said, "I praise you, Father, Lord of heaven and earth, because you have hidden these things from the wise and learned, and revealed them to little children.""

No matter our past, our present, or our future, God desires that our responses reveal Him to the world. Jesus explains that everything He knows and does has come from the Father Himself. He shares how it is His choice to reveal the Father through His life. So then, what does that have to do with us? The Father reveals to us who He is through the Son, and the Son is constantly choosing people to reveal Himself to. Jesus goes on to say this in Matthew 11:28-30 (NIV), "[28] "Come to me, all you who are weary and burdened, and I will give you rest. [29] Take my yoke upon you and learn from me, for I am gentle and humble in heart, and you will find rest for your souls. [30] For my yoke is easy and my burden is light."

I can hear God saying this to me today. That although the battle to renew my mind will have its challenges, He is still with me. The fight might make me tired, but He will give me rest in the midst of it. What He calls me to will not be a burden as long as I remain in Him and continue to fear Him.

Read Today: Isaiah 55, Matthew 11

~My prayer for you today~
Heavenly Father,
I come before You, and I pray for Your child reading this. I pray that You would bring them comfort and peace. Where their minds are in torment from memories and negative feelings and emotions, I pray that Your light would shine through and that You would give them Your perspective on these situations. The truth is the enemy has tainted these memories and feelings in order to control them and keep them bound. So today, reveal Your truth and renew their minds.
In Jesus' Name, Amen.

Day 3: Why Should My Perspective Align with God's?

~Prayer~

Heavenly Father,

We are ready to be renewed, changed, and established in our callings. We are ready to move forward and break out of the mindset that has held us in captivity. We are excited for the future You proclaim over us. We surrender to You, we acknowledge Your ways, and we say yes to You today. In Jesus' Name, Amen.

Today we will be talking about why our perspectives should align with God's. As I mentioned yesterday, our past life experiences have influenced our thought patterns. We will discuss more of that in week 13. God really wants us to be aware and present during each moment so we can know how we should think and respond in every situation. Our pasts, sins, mistakes, abuse, traumas, etc. do not give us a license to go against what is right. When we get to heaven God will not say, "oh it's okay, child. I know you treated them that way because of what they did to you, and so I am just going to cover it and say it's not sin." As much as we would love that, true love says, "My child, I understand the pain and hurt you were experiencing, but your responses were still a sin against Me."

God makes it very clear that our own minds are tainted and unable to grasp His ways by ourselves. Therefore, it is so important for us to ask Him to help us renew our minds and direct our paths. I love Paul's understanding of this.

2 Corinthians 12:7-10 (NIV) says, "[7] or because of these surpassingly great revelations. Therefore, in order to keep me from becoming conceited, I was given a thorn in my flesh, a messenger of Satan, to torment me. [8] Three times I pleaded with the Lord to take it away from me. [9] But he said to me, "My grace is sufficient for you, for my power is made perfect in weakness." Therefore I will boast all the more gladly about my weaknesses, so that Christ's power may rest on me. [10] That is why, for Christ's sake, I delight in weaknesses, in insults, in hardships, in persecutions, in difficulties. For when I am weak, then I am strong."

Paul chose to be humble because he knew everything was in God's hands. I love his perspective; we truly see that he lives it, especially in the times he experienced hardships, jail, persecution, etc. We see a godly perspective that gave godly responses. I hear so many people who say they are unable to do that and follow Jesus' example because He was also God, and we are not. I think they are weak and choosing the easy way in life, which will keep them in bondage. If Paul could live like Jesus did, why can't we? Why can't we live like Ruth, Esther, Joseph, Daniel, Matthew, John, Peter? And the list goes on and on.

We are here on this earth, made in the image of God, with a burning desire for intimate relationship with Him. Our calling is to bring His kingdom to the world and set the captives free, to keep many from entering hell, to keep many from entering hell so that they can grasp eternal life in heaven instead. How can we do that if we hold to our fleshly perspective instead of the Spirit's perspective? Our perspectives need to be aligned with God's.

Read Today: 2 Corinthians 12

~My prayer for you today~
Heavenly Father,
I come before You, and I pray for Your child reading this. I pray that Your child would begin to take their thoughts captive, surrender their ways and ideas to You, and begin to see Your thoughts and ways flow through them. I pray that they would have an amazing testimony that will save many from the gates of hell.
In Jesus' Name, Amen.

Day 4: How Should We View the Earthly Realm and the Spiritual Realm Around Us?

~Prayer~

Heavenly Father,

Today we want to understand a better glimpse of what You want us to see. Our perspective keeps us so focused on ourselves that we fail to see what You are doing. So today, change our perspective regarding the Earthly Realm and the Spiritual Realm. In Jesus' Name, Amen.

Today I want to talk about the physical (or earthly) realm and the spiritual realm. Although this could be in week 14 for spiritual warfare, I want to talk about it here because it affects our perspective so much. If we are not aware there is a spiritual realm around us, our perspective will always fall short.

The best example of failing to see the spiritual realm is found in 2 Kings 6. Israel is being targeted, but God gives spiritual insight of this plan to Elisha who then warns the king of Israel. God continually gave Elisha insight and frustrated the evil king's plan. The evil king was angered by this, so he figured out where Elisha was and then sent his men to surround him to capture him.

Read 2 Kings 6:15-18.

(Write out verse 17.)

Elisha then led the army into the city, but told the leaders to give them food and drink and then send them on their way. When those who'd been taken had returned to the evil king, they no longer raided the land.

Some people do not believe in the spiritual realm or that there are still demons and angels today; however, if you travel outside the western world, you will find that many other countries not only believe, but have seen them.

Read Revelations 12:7-9.

What happened in Heaven? _____

Who fought against who? _____

How did the war end? _____

Where is he at now? _____

So not only are there angels all around, but also satan and his followers. Our natural eyes do not see them, but our spiritual eyes can. Genesis 1:27 (NIV) says, "[27] So God created mankind in his own image, in the image of God he created them; male and female he created them."

We are created in God's image, which means our soul and spirit is within us. Our soul and spirit is what will go to heaven and is able to connect to the spiritual realm. What takes place in the spiritual realm affects the natural realm around us. We will go further into that in week 14.

Our thoughts and our responses are to keep the spiritual realm in view, not base things off of the physical realm. We have talked a bit about prophesy and the gifts of the Spirit. If we keep our perspective in the physical realm, we will always be missing information, understanding, and wisdom. I do not want to be foolish; I want to see things clearly for what they are, so the spiritual realm is very important.

Read Today: 2 Kings 6

~My prayer for you today~
Heavenly Father,
I come before You, and I pray for Your child reading this. I pray that You would give Your child understanding about the spiritual realm, that they would begin to really see what You are doing, and understand that the natural realm does not have the answers. The truth is that before we see You move in our physical realm, You have already been moving in the spiritual realm.
In Jesus' Name, Amen.

Day 5: What Does That Look Like?

~Prayer~

Heavenly Father,

Today is a new day for us. It's stepping out of the old and into the new. Today we take hold of a new mind, and we take captive the flesh mind. Help us today to view You and what You are doing differently than what we have in the past. We want to see You accurately. In Jesus' Name, Amen.

Today we will be talking about what God's perspective looks like and how it applies to our lives.

Read 2 Corinthians 10:1-6.

(Write verse 5.)

Read Philippians 4:4-9 (NIV), because our perspective should have these actions as our response. Fill in the blanks.

_____ in the Lord always. Let your _____ be evident to all (even those who wound, betray, and hurt you.). Do not be _____ about anything, because in every _____ you should _____ and _____. In _____ present your requests to God.

When we respond with the right perspective it says that the _____ of God, which goes beyond our own understanding, will _____ our hearts and our _____. We are to think about whatever is _____, whatever is _____, whatever is _____, whatever is _____, whatever is _____, whatever is _____, and if anything is _____ or _____.

For us to have God's peace with us, we should put into practice all that we have learned, received, heard, and seen God do.

How does this truth apply to the situation you are in right now? Have you been looking at it in your own perspective instead of through God's? Have your responses been glorifying to God, or have you sinned? Is your flesh trying to keep you Held Hostage (when is our flesh not?), and have you learned to take it captive and move in the Spirit instead?

One of my recent struggles that has affected my perspective is when I am around a narcissist, and I am triggered; however, I was also being triggered by believers who were not narcissistic. God revealed that I needed to research the difference between a narcissist and a strong-willed person. I was to see what the similarities are because I am sometimes triggered by them and need to learn how to respond in a way that is glorifying to God, instead of allowing anxiety to overcome me. Here is a link to read about the narcissistic personality. https://www.mayoclinic.org/diseases-conditions/narcissistic-personality-disorder/symptoms-causes/syc-20366662

I loved this explanation of narcissism and a strong-willed nature. Here is the link for it. https://narcissistabusesupport.com/strong-willed-or-willful/

It allows me to see the differences and similarities between both. This is when having the right perspective of individuals, as well as understanding what spirit the person is walking in (flesh, demonic, or Spirit-filled) comes into play as well. There is a reason God wants us to be able to discern the spirits, and we will talk more about that in the week on spiritual warfare.

Read Today: Philippians 4

~My prayer for you today~
Heavenly Father,
I come before You, and I pray for Your child reading this. Sometimes our situations want to override what we know to be true. Sometimes we would rather take the easy way out and follow our flesh, than oppose it and move in the Spirit. Today, I pray that Your child would receive Your perspective, and that they would take their thoughts captive and cling to what is true.
In Jesus' Name, Amen.

Day 6: My Story and Testimonies

Not many people know how one innocent (or not-so-innocent) decision can quickly influence future choices. We can set ourselves up for great victories or terrible defeats.

My parents are amazing. My dad is a pastor and has a prophetic gifting. My mom has the gift of a seer. I was homeschooled most of my life and my siblings were always my best friends. My oldest sister was eight years older, my second oldest sister two years older, and my younger brother is almost two years younger than me. We also have three siblings who are in heaven; we never got to hold them, but they are with our Father. When I was around eleven, I began taking over the roles of the older sister. My siblings would come to me for advice, and I would try to keep them out of trouble. In fifth grade I was teased because the boys liked seeing my face turn red, and because of that I was homeschooled the following year. Seventh grade I returned to school, but it was hard. I only had a couple of boyfriends during that time, but honestly, they were more like good friends I hung out with. There was one boy who kept giving me inappropriate letters, and it only took one time for me to learn that it was not okay to write one back. A teacher found it, my dad was called, and I got detention. The good news, though, was that we broke up. But a demonic agenda from satan was planted: the lie that says that guys only care about sexual stuff and not my heart. At the age of thirteen, this thought was destructive.

Feeling such a big responsibility, being bullied in middle school, and then lies from satan began to change my perspective of God, myself, and others. I turned inward. In three years, I read over eight hundred novels. I barely socialized. When we moved to Georgia, my brother and I became super close. I consider him my very best friend. I still carried the responsibilities of the eldest and took care of many family dynamics for my parents. I continued to stand strong for my sisters and did my best to hold them up. The innocent choice of a boyfriend at thirteen led to a mindset that men only cared about one thing, which led to the decision of a relationship at eighteen with someone who only confirmed that lying agenda. I never took care of those spiritual lies, and it wasn't until after I was ready to get divorced at the age of thirty-four that I understood all the steps I thought were insignificant actually played a huge role in my choices.

We were living in Georgia because God called my dad to start a church. Having only lived there a year, I didn't have many friends. Besides my brother, my cousin (who I remain close to), and then a guy friend. I knew the red flags right up front. He was manipulative, blamed everything on me, and was very forceful. I did not want to date him, but he wouldn't leave me alone. I tried to get others to make the decision for me, but it was always put back into my hands. After months of being pressured, I agreed to date him. It was the worst decision I could have made. His intent was based on sexual desire and not love. Yet, I resolved to maintain my morals on sex before marriage, although we would kiss often. I was not attracted to him, I did not like his character, and I did not like how I was treated. I made the decision to go to a school that would take me into the ministry I felt called to. I decided the first thing I wanted to do when I got to school, was to break up. It was UGLY! He sent me a very abusive email; I sent it on to my dad who met with both the ex-boyfriend and his dad. My dad took care of it and I left it all behind.

God took over my time at school and made it all about my identity in Him and how I was His precious daughter. So much healing took place, and my character began to grow into who I was supposed to be. But there were lies and faulty perspectives that I did not address. So, when I met my ex-husband, whereas before I saw the red flags with the ex-boyfriend, I did not with my ex-husband. They were more hidden. At first, that was due to cultural differences. It was not until after I was married that I saw the flags for what they were.

During our time at school, I saw that he was very friendly with other girls, but I thought it was just a cultural difference. He also said many times that nothing was going on with them. (RED FLAG) During our dating time, he began grooming me. He would tell me something bad happened to him because he wanted to see my reaction, and then would later say it never happened, things like his health, cheating, getting hurt in rugby, etc. He would make everything sound true, so when I would say 'it's okay' or 'I forgive you, I'm sorry, I still want to be with you,' he would say, "I'm just teasing. I just wanted to know what you would say." He kept saying that was how guys get to know girls in his country. But for me, it stole my trust because I never knew when he was being serious or joking because it all sounded the same. (RED FLAG)

After two years of dating, I sent him a promise ring and a book I wrote about our story, filled with both the good and the bad. He lied and said he never got it, and then he told me that a team had come to their location for ministry and one of the girls had ended up kissing him in the kitchen. He kept saying it was just a joke, but he brought it up so many times and I didn't trust him. (RED FLAG) It was then that I made another choice that led me deeper into darkness. A family friend that I had known since I was around ten let me confide in him. So I shared my woes, hurts, and concerns. He was there for me, and slowly, he led our friendship to overstep into a relationship. He would send me sexual images, and I would send risqué ones. I did not see how he was manipulating me in the relationship till the end of it. I still remained a virgin, but it did lead me further into the sexual drive of the world.

I ended up breaking up with my boyfriend (ex-husband) as well as with the male friend who overstepped. I mentioned in my book 'Held Hostage' that it led to my attempted suicide two weeks after my twenty-first birthday, and six months of deep depression and return to God. I bring this up because the choice to cheat led me to go further sexually than I wanted; even though we didn't have sex, I was still guilty for going beyond what Christ was pleased with. Second, it led me to almost take my own life, and then to a depression that tried to disable me. But another huge one was sexual images. Just those few images tainted my view of myself. It made me believe that if I wanted a guy to love me, I needed to respond to him.

When my ex-boyfriend (ex-husband) got back together almost seven months later, I confessed my sin and mistakes, and asked for forgiveness. I felt cleansed and free, but I had no idea that he would use everything as a weapon against me for the next thirteen years. (RED FLAG).

The grooming and emotional and spiritual abuse began in 2006 but intensified in 2009. (RED FLAG). I took it because I was the one who had cheated. What I wasn't aware of at the time was that he was conditioning me to take all his mistakes on myself. When I finally saw him in person in 2009, my flawed perspective that said guys only liked me for sexual reasons and not my heart came into its most damaging influence. My thinking created a force to my actions, and during my time there with him he said to me, "You did stuff with the other guy, so does this mean you do not love me?" Sadly, during that trip I lost my virginity. The guilt, shame, and my relationship with God shattered. I felt powerless to say no. Midway through the trip he brought up my mistakes and said we should just break up.

I pause my story to share one of the mistakes the church has made. The church has taught that we are to stay pure and holy until we get married, and that being a virgin is very important. While this is good and true, they have made it impossible to share your mistakes because you will be judged, talked about, and at times even excluded. I understand if someone continues to sin there should be different consequences, but they usually put everyone into the same boat, and they fail to talk about God's forgiveness and second chances. In fact, I know many who made one mistake and after that one night got pregnant. Not only was the girl judged, but so were her children. They wouldn't let her children be dedicated to God even though the parents' true repentance had taken place. Although it makes sense because they do not want single girls falling into temptation, they also missed an opportunity of a testimony.

Back to my story. Being a pastor's daughter, I was always under pressure, because whatever choice I made the congregation would put on my parents. So how could I break up? How would another man ever want me when I wasn't a virgin? How could I ever tell people that I was not a virgin? I felt like I had no power to say no because he would always threaten to break up (RED FLAG). So, I gave myself and died spiritually every time. What I did not know was that sexual manipulation is also a form of sexual abuse. This continued until we got married. In 2011 when his visa was running out, the only option to not have to wait years for him to return was to get married right away so he could get a green card to stay. So, we got married. His sister knew, but I was not allowed to tell my family, so we technically eloped. Six months later I finally told my family against his wishes. He directed a lot of emotional abuse at me for that. (RED FLAG)

I mentioned in my book, Held Hostage, that he had an affair and I found out the day before our second anniversary; during that time, I found out he had had another girl in 2008. She broke up with him when she found out about him and I, and it is unknown if she is the girl from the kitchen.

During our dating and through marriage, my ex-husband enjoyed watching R-rated movies filled with sexual imagery. (RED FLAG). I would look at him during each of these parts and break inside. If he could watch this in front of me, what would he do behind my back? It usually led to us having sex, where through it I mentally questioned if he was thinking about me or the girl he just watched. And the demonic agenda of, 'I must be like them to be loved' began to change my perspective even more. Eventually the sexual manipulation changed and he started withholding sex for long periods of time, lasting up until our eighth year of marriage. I was not given the answer to the question of whether or not he had more affairs, since I wasn't the one meeting his needs.

So, to finish this section I will summarize the facts.

1. Sexual relationships outside marriage destroy you and your relationship with God.

2. Sexual images, videos, etc. have horrible affects in relationships and distort views of ourselves and our partner.

3. Listen to the red flags.

So, what does this have to do with perspective?

My perspective of past situations altered how I perceived and viewed myself and others. It made me lower my guard and choose sin instead of Christ. I gave satan one step, but he took miles. In week 14 I will talk about the steps to overcome demonic agendas, but now I want to go into another area of perspective.

As I mentioned in my book, Held Hostage, I was in an abusive (verbal, emotional, spiritual, and sexual) relationship with my ex-husband for three years dating, and ten years married. In week 5 I talked about how my perspective changed about hearing God's voice, but let me focus today how my perspective of others, myself, and the world changed.

During this time, I perceived that I had to be strong all the time and that showing any weakness was wrong. I questioned peoples' characters constantly, especially if they claimed to be a believer, because saying it and living it are two very different things. My perspective on life became negative and hopeless. I no longer believed I had a purpose or that I was wanted and protected. I was dead on the inside and my head was numb. Depression was something I carried with me all the time. It was a very dark and painful time.

Three months before everything started happening to get me to freedom, God started to work on my perspective. First, He changed how I viewed Him and how I viewed myself. He showed me how to view our relationship and that His plan for me had not changed. He changed my perspective of my ex-husband and marriage, and then my view of family and friends.

There are so many times when my perspective dictates how I should respond. When I feel alone, forgotten, or misunderstood, I respond from the perspective that I am not loved. So, I become defensive and protective of my heart, which comes across as harshness. Yet, my perspective is usually not correct. The individuals did not even mean to come across that way. They were struggling with something and so they appeared harsh or uncaring. We are all going through things, so it's so important that we seek God's perspective and move in the Spirit instead of the flesh. Our feelings and perspectives can be our biggest failures.

Testimonies:

*My wife and I committed to serve two years in missions in Kenya, Africa. We were so committed to serving God and wanted to help people to find Jesus and know Him. When one year was just about up, we noticed life was getting harder. Felt like everything was getting to be a drain on us personally and with ministry. We sat down and said, "If something doesn't change, we are not going to make it." We didn't want to quit, but we were close to it.

Come to find out that we began to do the work in our own strength. We lost sight of the purpose. The purpose was not the work of the Lord, but rather our love for the Lord and the love for the people who we were serving. We turned our eyes back to God, and it changed our perspective for being there in Kenya. It turned out that the second year was easier, and we had greater success in helping the people. ~Douglas W.

Day 7: Self-Reflection

~Prayer~

Heavenly Father,

We come before You and we take time today to hear Your voice. Please direct this time of fellowship with You. Reveal to us what You are wanting to say and direct us. Speak to us very clearly and reveal to us what we need to know. In Jesus' Name, Amen.

Today God is asking you some hard questions and you need to be truthful and honest. Write down your answers of what God has revealed to you.

When it comes to God:

1. What does the Bible say about My character?

2. Are you listening to satan's lies?

3. What have I said to you?

4. Will you trust Me?

When it comes to yourself:

1. Who do I say you are?

2. Are you seeing yourself through My eyes or satan's?

3. How are past experiences trying to keep your mind from breaking free?

4. Look at the past through My eyes, do you see how I was with you?

5. Will you claim your identity in Me?

Questions about your relationship with God:
1. Do you know I love you?

2. Do you know that in My eyes you are special?

3. Are you walking out of covenant relationship or the past?

4. Will you let Me take you out of the box and reveal truth to you?

Questions concerning a spouse or boyfriend/girlfriend and future marriage with someone else:
1. Are you carrying his/her mistakes or giving them back to him/her?

2. Do you recognize that his/her actions stem from heart issues, sin, and the flesh?

3. Can you give Me the need for revenge and let Me handle the judgement?

4. Do you know you can and will be loved?

5. Do you know you will have a healthy marriage?

Questions about family, friends, and other people:
1. Are you understanding them out of your past abuse and pain, or through My perspective?

2. Are you projecting your own thoughts of why they say or do something onto them and misunderstanding them?

3. Is your PTSD causing you to react instead of respond?

4. Can you see them through My eyes?

Final question:
What areas do you need to change your perspective?

~Prayer~
Heavenly Father,
We thank You for revealing to us the importance of Your perspective and how we need to apply it to our lives. Thank You for revealing Your thoughts and ways to us.
In Jesus' Name, Amen.

Week 12: Thankfulness

"[15] Let the peace of Christ rule in your hearts, since as members of one body you were called to peace. And be thankful. [16] Let the message of Christ dwell among you richly as you teach and admonish one another with all wisdom through psalms, hymns, and songs from the Spirit, singing to God with gratitude in your hearts. [17] And whatever you do, whether in word or deed, do it all in the name of the Lord Jesus, giving thanks to God the Father through him."
(Colossians 3:15-17 NIV)

Day 1: Thankfulness

This week we will be talking about thanksgiving, or thankfulness, and the importance it will play through your healing and breakthrough process. The reason I have thankfulness after the topics of walking in the opposite spirit and perspective is that each of those play a part into our mind and spirit's choice to be thankful regardless of the situation. To actively pursue thanksgiving, we need to be in the Holy Spirit and have God's perspective about every situation.

In Hebrews 13:15-16 (NKJV) says, "[15] Therefore by Him let us continually offer the sacrifice of praise to God, that is, the fruit of our lips, giving thanks to His name. [16] But do not forget to do good and to share, for with such sacrifices God is well pleased."

Did anyone catch the first part of vs 15? Through whom? Through Jesus, therefore, offer to God sacrifices of praise. So many people try to do this in their own strength, but we are going to find that thankfulness requires God's strength running through us. We will not be able to do it on our own in our fleshly minds, and it will require us to dig deep into God and who He is.

Starting today, I want you to pick three things a day that you can thank God for. Make sure it is not the same thing every day, but be very aware and focused on how God is moving and what you should be thanking Him for.

Write down three things for today and spend time in prayer thanking Him.

Read Today: Colossians 3, Hebrews 13

~Prayer~
Heavenly Father, we come before You, and we ask that You begin to reveal to us how You are moving in our lives. We want to be able to have thankful hearts, we want to be aware and awake. So today, open our eyes to see You.
In Jesus' Name, Amen.

Day 2: What Does the Bible Say About Being Thankful?

~Prayer~

Heavenly Father,

We thank You for Your goodness, Your faithfulness, and Your great compassion for us. We are so blessed that You see our pain and suffering, yet You do not let us remain there, but call us to greater living in You. We are so thankful that Your love conquers all. In Jesus' Name, Amen.

Today we will be looking at what God says in the Bible about thanksgiving, or being thankful.

Psalm 107:1 (NIV) says, "[1] Give thanks to the LORD, for he is good; his love endures forever."

I love that we are to give thanks because He is good, and that His love will go on into eternity. It does not stop when we are no longer on this earth, but will last through our time with Him in heaven. However, a sad realization in that is if God loves us so much and that love does not stop even when we die, then He doesn't stop loving even those who are in hell. His heart will always feel that separation they chose. As I mentioned in a previous week, the world is seeing the greatest love story being lived out through Jesus and the Bride, but it is also seeing the greatest heartbreaking story played out when people choose to separate from Him forever.

Knowing this makes me want to be thankful even more, to shower my gratitude upon Him. Take some time to **read Psalm 95 and Psalm 100.**

For many of you, you will find that being thankful right now is very challenging. As I mentioned yesterday, thankfulness has to do with our perspective. I love what 1 Thessalonians 5:18 (NIV) says, "[18] give thanks in all circumstances; for this is God's will for you in Christ Jesus."

(Fill in the blanks.)

Give thanks _____ all circumstances; for this is God's will for you _____ Christ Jesus.

Did you catch it? God is not saying to thank Him for all circumstances, He is saying thank Him IN all circumstances. It means being aware of the things He is doing amidst the situation and thanking Him for that. I did not say, "Thank You, God, that my husband is having an affair and abusing me." To thank God for that would be a slap in His face because He has no desire to hurt me, and why should my ex-husbands sin be thanked for? No; in that situation, find how God is moving (which takes His perspective to do), and then thank Him for that.

Tomorrow we will see why being thankful in these hard situations is so important for our present and future.

Read Today: Psalm 107

~My prayer for you today~
Heavenly Father,
I come before You, and I pray for Your child reading this. I pray that they would begin to seek the things that they can thank You for. Sometimes they will not be able to see it right away, and it is going to require them to search deeply. I pray that they would take the time to look and search, so they can in turn thank and praise You. In Jesus' Name, Amen.

Day 3: Why Is Being Thankful a Powerful Weapon?

~Prayer~

Heavenly Father,

We come before You, recognizing that there is power in thanksgiving. When we have a grateful heart, everything changes: our attitudes, actions, and circumstance. Thank You for not giving up on us. Thank You for passionately and relentlessly running after us in love. In Jesus' Name, Amen.

Today we will be talking about how thanksgiving and a grateful heart are powerful weapons that shift our heart and focus, but also shift the seasons and situations we find ourselves in. I love what Paul says to Timothy about this.

Read 1 Timothy 2:1-4.

Write verse 1.

If we want to live in peace and enjoy quiet lives in all godliness and holiness, then thanksgiving is a huge part of that. I want to give an example of how being unthankful can lead to further hardship and trials. This example is shown through the lives of the Israelites when they had escaped Egypt, the place that Held them Hostage.

Remember how God brought them out? There were signs and miracles that took place, not to mention the parting of the Red Sea for them to pass through. We find in Exodus 15 that Moses had just let the people away from the sea and into a desert. They had been traveling for three days and during that time they had nothing to drink. Once they reached a place that had water, they found the waters unsafe for drinking. Exodus 15:24 (NIV) says, "[24] So the people grumbled against Moses, saying, "What are we to drink?"

In verse 24 it says the people grumbled; there was no gratitude. In fact, it's as if they forgot who was taking care of them. Moses stepped in and interceded, asking God to provide, and God revealed what to do in order to have clean water. God gives them a promise in verse 26 that if they listen to Him, do what is right, and keep His commands, there will be no disease. I would hope that if I was there, I would immediately start getting a thankful heart, but we find that many do not. In fact, in Exodus 16 we find that their heart condition remained the same. Around two months since their release from Egypt we see the ugliness of an ungrateful heart. Exodus 16:2-3 (NIV) says, "[2] In the desert the whole community grumbled against Moses and Aaron. [3] The Israelites said to them, "If only we had died by the LORD's hand in Egypt! There we sat around pots of meat and ate all the food we wanted, but you have brought us out into this desert to starve this entire assembly to death."

Again, the Israelites grumbled and yet God still faithfully provided food. He caused the food to literally fall like rain from heaven. If you are like me, maybe this question jumped to your mind like it did mine: after everything God had done for them why didn't they ask Him, in love, for food and water? Why, instead, do they grumble? Why can't they just ask God? It doesn't make any sense. Yet how many of us, when we are going through our own healings, begin to grumble about the situation and take our eyes off God and what He has done?

Again, in Exodus 17 we find the community traveling wherever God tells them to go, but along the way there was no water again. Exodus 17:2 (NIV) says, "[2] So they quarreled with Moses and said, "Give us water to drink." Moses replied, "Why do you quarrel with me? Why do you put the LORD to the test?"

If I was Moses, I would be extremely angry with the people who are totally missing what God is doing too. His frustration can be read in verses 3-4. Isn't interesting how again, the people took out their frustration on Moses, instead of asking their loving God? Again and again, there are examples of their lack of trust, faith, and gratitude. So then, what is their outcome?

It comes time for them to explore their promised land. They send twelve men to check out the land. Two had good reports and the rest spread lies and negative opinions. Israel's response is that they got together and wept with loud voices. They grumbled and even wanted to find a different leader than Moses.

Numbers 14:2 (NIV) says, "[2] All the Israelites grumbled against Moses and Aaron, and the whole assembly said to them, "If only we had died in Egypt! Or in this wilderness!"

God's response is found in **Numbers 14:26-35.**

What are the consequences for their grumbling?

What is God's heart on the matter?

What would have happened if Israel had been grateful? How would their testimony have turned out differently? Everyone over a certain age died in the wilderness, and their children had to wait and watch them die before they could enter the promised land. Talk about suffering and pain, all because of the ungrateful hearts and attitudes that gave them an earthly perspective of their situation.

How many of you are stuck in your situation because you have become depressed, worn out, drained, and only able to see the negative? How many of you view people around you with earthly perspectives, instead of seeing them the way God does? How many of you need a shift in your perspective and attitude? Thanksgiving causes everything to change.

Read Today: Numbers 14

~My prayer for you today~

Heavenly Father,

I come before You, and I pray for Your child reading this. I pray that they would have hearts filled with gratitude, and that they would not miss their promised land. I pray that they would enter in. Where there are things keeping them from being grateful, break it off them, in Jesus' name. I proclaim freedom from the enemy's lies and from earthly perspective.

In Jesus' Name, Amen.

Day 4: Ten Lepers

~Prayer~

Heavenly Father,

So many times, we fail to have grateful hearts. In fact, I rarely hear those around me thanking others who have done something for them. It has become such a rarity to show gratitude. It makes sense why satan has attacked it. Forgive us, Father, and help us to make gratitude a constant part of our hearts. In Jesus' Name, Amen.

Yesterday we talked about what happens when we are not grateful, but today I want to talk about the power of being thankful.

Read Luke 17:11-19.

(Fill in the blanks.)

How many lepers were healed? _____

How many came back when they were healed? _____

What nationality was he? _____

I love Jesus' response here. Then he said to him, "_____ and

_____; your _____ had made you well."

What a powerful declaration. I once heard Hank Kunneman preaching on this, and he gave an insight from his studies that blew my mind away. He talked about how all ten were cleansed from the disease so that they could return to live inside the city with their family and friends, but the one who returned received an even greater blessing because of his thankful heart. Not only was he cleansed of the disease, but he was then made well; in other words, his body now looked normal, as if he had never been sick, completely restored, whole, and realigned to what it was before the sickness.

So, our true thankfulness causes Jesus to want to pour out even more blessing on us. Because when we are thankful, it reveals our love to Him, and He feels it deep down. His response then is to reveal His love to us even more. In February of 2023, it will have been two years since everything happened, and the separation and divorce took place. It hasn't even been two years yet, but already people see me, and they cannot believe what I have been through. Why? Because I don't look wounded and I don't act wounded; instead, I am thriving and walking in favor, anointing, and blessing. God not only healed me, but He restored me like it had never even happened.

I am telling you, there is power in a thankful heart. Thankfulness changes our situations and how we view our lives.

(Today, memorize a verse about thanksgiving.)

Read Today: Luke 17

~My prayer for you today~
Heavenly Father,
I come before You, and I pray for Your child reading this. I pray that as they begin to apply thanksgiving into their lives, they would begin to see themselves completely restored in the name of Jesus. I pray that everything satan has stolen from them would be returned with triple blessing.
In Jesus' Name, Amen.

Day 5: Jehoshaphat and Hannah

~Prayer~

Heavenly Father,

We are now beginning to understand the power of thanksgiving. I pray that as we go even deeper today, every single one of us would be stirred into active faith, that our hearts would begin to search for You, and in thanksgiving we would be overcomers. In Jesus' Name, Amen.

Today we will be studying two more testimonies of thanksgiving found in the Bible. I personally don't have much to say because these testimonies truly speak for themselves. The first one is the testimony of Jehoshaphat and how he applied thanksgiving, which allowed God to turn the tide. In 2 Chronicles 20 we see that two countries are waging war against Judah. When the king of Judah, Jehoshaphat, heard that an army was descending towards them, he immediately went to the Lord. He told God everything he knew about God's character, what He had done in the past, and that He had given them promises. He asked God to intervene for them, and to bring justice swiftly. God responded and told him that the battle was the Lord's, and to stay strong and watch Him move. The king and the people fell on their faces before God in worship. The next morning, Jehoshaphat encouraged the people to have faith in God.

Read 2 Chronicles 20:21-24.

Jehoshaphat appointed men to do what?

What did God do as they obeyed?

What happened to the army?

Look at the power of praise and thanksgiving and what God did on their behalf. I am telling you, there is something so powerful and beautiful that takes place as we praise and thank our Father. They did not even have to wage ware. They received vast amounts of plunder, joy was felt throughout Judah, and the fear of God seized the hearts of the surrounding countries.

The last testimony we will get into is found in 1 Samuel 1. Hannah was loved by her husband, and he doubly blessed her. However, the Lord had kept her from having kids. Her husband's second wife mocked her and treated her unjustly because she could not give birth. For many years she had to endure this torment. Hannah would go to God and weep and be unable to eat. The bitterness was so extreme that Hannah made a vow to God.

1 Samuel 1:11 (NIV) says, "[11] And she made a vow, saying, "LORD Almighty, if you will only look on your servant's misery and remember me, and not forget your servant but give her a son, then I will give him to the LORD for all the days of his life, and no razor will ever be used on his head."

The priest at that time misunderstood Hannah and, thinking she was drunk, he put her in her place. But Hannah would not allow the misunderstanding of her heart to remain and clarified that she was praying. She explained her situation and her desire for a child. The priest sent her on her way and told her that God would answer her prayer. Relief filled her and she was able to eat. I love what 1 Samuel 1:19-20 (NIV) says, "[19] Early the next morning they arose and worshiped before the LORD and then went back to their home at Ramah. Elkanah made love to his wife Hannah, and the LORD remembered her. [20] So in the course of time Hannah became pregnant and gave birth to a son. She named him Samuel, saying, "Because I asked the LORD for him."

Hannah's thanksgiving led to active faith, and in her thanksgiving, she gave her son back to God. When the boy had been taken off of breastmilk, Hannah fulfilled her vow and gave her son back to God. Samuel became a famous prophet in the Old Testament, and he was also the one the Lord used to anoint David as king. Hannah's thanksgiving led to blessings upon the nation of Israel through her son's life, and it is important to remember that our thanksgiving does not stop when things get better. Our thanksgiving should be a natural and daily response to God that lasts for the rest of our lives.

Read Today: 1 Samucl 1

~My prayer for you today~
Heavenly Father,
I come before You, and I pray for Your child reading this. I believe that Your child is ready to see amazing miracles take place in their lives because of their thankful heart. I pray that they would have discerning eyes to see how You answer their situations. It will most likely be different than what they are expecting or imagining, but it will be exactly what they need. I pray that they would trust You.
In Jesus' Name, Amen.

Day 6: My Story

When hard times come, when there is trauma, abuse, sin, heartache, depression, mental strain, and the list goes on and on, thankfulness to God is not natural or easy at first.

As we begin to heal from what Holds us Hostage, our focus is mainly consumed by all of the bad and hard stuff. When I began my process of healing, I didn't realize a key tool would be thankfulness. In March of 2021, when my ex and I officially separated, I heard a sermon on thankfulness by Paula White-Cain. It was so powerful hearing the Biblical importance of thankfulness, that I immediately started to apply it.

Every day I would tell God three things I was thankful for. It wasn't easy at first, but after a couple of weeks I noticed that when I thanked God it changed my attitude for the day. It realigned my thoughts back onto God's goodness and faithfulness. I would look for the positives instead of the negatives.

The more I thanked Him, the more I was aware of what He was doing in my life, my family's life, my friends' lives, and in the Remnant (Bride). It changed the way I viewed my situation. It changed my outlook for my future. It led me to greater victories because I was willing to face everything, for my hope for tomorrow urged me on.

Thankfulness should be a natural and loving exchange between us and God. Every day we should be applying it in our relationship with Him.

Day 7: Self-Reflection

~Prayer~

Heavenly Father,

We come before You and we take time today to hear Your voice. Please direct this time of fellowship with You. Reveal to us what You are wanting to say and direct us. Speak to us very clearly and reveal to us what we need to know. In Jesus' Name, Amen.

Today I will be asking hard questions and I want you to write down your answers of what God truthfully and honestly has revealed to you.

Make a list of things God is doing, people in your life, and things in your life that you can thank God for.

Find ten verses that talk about thanksgiving or thankfulness. Write down the references and summarize.

~Prayer~

Heavenly Father,

We thank You for revealing to us the need for a thankful heart. Now we understand the great importance of it and the weapon it is to deal with demonic agendas and bondage. We look forward to applying this tool and to the day when thankfulness is natural and easy.

In Jesus' Name, Amen.

Week 13: Health

"^{22} A cheerful heart is good medicine, but a crushed spirit dries up the bones."
(Proverbs 17:22 NIV)

Day 1: Health

The term health has so many different meanings to it, and I find that more and more people have become unbalanced in health. Through the years, trends have changed. One year mental health is important, another year physical health, and then finally, for some, spiritual health. But one thing God revealed to me through my healing journey was that I was called to have health in all three areas.

In Held Hostage I wrote, "When someone looks at me, I do not want them to see someone who was abused (broken), I do not want them to see a survivor (still carrying baggage), but someone who thrives (favored and blessed)."[9]

To have true healing and freedom means that we are healthy in our minds, souls, and physical bodies. We talked a bit about mental health when we learned about having God's perspective. We will talk more about the importance of keeping our minds healthy. We will look at how spiritual health allows our bodies to be healthy. And finally, we will talk about what God says about our physical bodies.

The truth is, especially in the western world, we have been taught that love is turning the other cheek. They use **Matthew 5:38-40 (NIV)** as a reference.

Write down verse 39 and 40.

This is true, but I am realizing most people swing to extreme opposites. There are those who love themselves too much and have become selfish and unloving. Then you have those who hate themselves so all they do is turn the other cheek. The truth is, God calls us to a life of balance. I have a feeling this week is going to stretch some of us in uncomfortable ways. But if we want the complete freedom and healing from what Holds us Hostage, then this is necessary.

Jeremiah 30:17 (NIV) says, "[17] But I will restore you to health and heal your wounds,' declares the LORD, 'because you are called an outcast, Zion for whom no one cares.'"

You see, not only are we longing for healing and freedom, but God is also longing to restore our health and heal our wounds to where it has never even happened. This isn't just a longing that we alone desire; no, it's there because it's the heart of the Father for us. He has been crying out to us, relentlessly pursuing us, and loving on us, because He longs for us to be released from captivity.

Read Today: 2 Chronicles 7:13-15

~Prayer~

Heavenly Father, we come before You, and we ask that You begin to reveal to us how health is important. Open our eyes to see how mental, spiritual, and physical health all are connected and affect each other. Reveal truth to us and we will obey.

In Jesus' Name, Amen.

---

[9] Aubrey Dawn Weinzetl, "Held Hostage," 2022.

Day 2: What Does God Say About Mental Health?

~Prayer~

Heavenly Father,

We recognize that our mental health is probably not always healthy and balanced. What we think about has negative or positive responses to our health. Help us to be wise and discerning, so that we would see the importance of our health. In Jesus' Name, Amen.

Today we will be talking about mental health. As we talked about in week 11, our minds are a great battlefield. Romans 12:2 (RSV) says, "[2] Do not be conformed to this world but be transformed by the renewal of your mind, that you may prove what is the will of God, what is good and acceptable and perfect."

Take time to read **Philippians 4:8-9**, because it gives the steps on how to renew your mind. Write it down on a piece of paper and put it somewhere that you see every day as a reminder to check your mind throughout the day.

What we think about has the power to pull our steps in many different directions.

Read Proverbs 4:23-27.

What should we guard and why?

What should we do with our mouths?

What should we do with our eyes?

What should we give careful thought to?

Our minds need to be used to give careful thought about the directions we take in life. It can lead us to freedom and healing or take us into further bondage and captivity. Our minds give the words to voice what is going on in our hearts, and that is where the spiritual health comes into play. Proverbs 16:24 (RSV) says, "[24] Pleasant words are like a honeycomb, sweetness to the soul and health to the body." Also, Jesus reminded the people that it's not about the food, but it is what we say that defiles us. (Matthew 15:10-11) So, what comes out of our mouths has the power to affect our very bones, both physically and spiritually. This is a great example of why all three areas need to be healthy in our lives. If we keep our minds on God and what is right, when Jesus returns, we can go into heaven with Him. Colossians 3:5-6 (NIV) says, "[5] Put to death, therefore, whatever belongs to your earthly nature: sexual immorality, impurity, lust, evil desires and greed, which is idolatry. [6] Because of these, the wrath of God is coming."

To make sure our physical bodies do not walk in sin, our minds need to be healthy, and we need to be fully aware of what we are thinking about. Examples: if you continue to think about another person and lust after them, soon your body will follow your mind. If you are thinking negatively about an individual, soon your actions will be negative towards that person. Our minds have the power to lead us. Therefore, we need to be on guard with what we watch, what we listen to, and what we entertain in our minds. We need to actively guard our minds in Christ and keep out that which is not of Him.

So, what happens if we fail to guard our mind and we keep sinking further and further into sin, bondage, and captivity? Romans 1 states that God will bring wrath against all those who are in sin and try to hide truth. God and His truth have been relevant from the beginning of creation. The world sees Him, but many ignore Him and become ignorant fools. Sadly, they worship others and serve their agendas.

Read Romans 1:24-28.
What did God give them over to?

What was exchanged and what did they worship?

What word is now used to describe those in sin in vs. 26 and 27?

What kind of mind were they given over to?

Wow! They are taken over by their sin, their actions go from gossip to murder. (To read the full list of things they do, go to **Romans 1:29-32**) I do not want to be given over to a depraved mind. Depraved means wicked and morally corrupted. That is not the mind that I want. I do not want to suffer in my thoughts. I have experienced a mind filled with pain and suffering. Memories that would try to keep me captive. Nightmares that would plague my sleep. My mind would steal my joy and cause me to question God and myself. It kept me in an active battle for 10+ years.

Now, by renewing my mind and walking out the steps I have mentioned concerning your mind and thoughts means that I have found freedom in my mind. I am healthy, I am on guard and aware of what I am putting in, and I get to experience a healthy mind.

The mind is very powerful. Science has shown that our brain can cause our body not to work the way it was made to and can bring about many diseases and sickness. I would encourage you to listen to Dr. Avery Jackson's message he gave at Lord of Hosts Church. Here is the link: https://lohchurch.org/service-archives/. Go to February 27, 2022, and become in awe of God and how He made us.

Read Today: Philippians 4, Romans 12

~My prayer for you today~
Heavenly Father,
I come before You, and I pray for Your child reading this. I ask that today their minds would be renewed, that they would begin to guard their minds and protect their hearts. I ask that they begin to dwell on positive and righteous things that will lead to freedom and victory. I pray that every memory that would come up and try to Hold them Hostage would be dealt with in the name of Jesus. Bring truth to those memories, so when they think about it, they would see You.
In Jesus' Name, Amen.

Day 3: What Does God Say About Spiritual Health?

~Prayer~

Heavenly Father,

Today we are going to learn about our spiritual health and why it is so important. We understand that there have been times when we have failed to keep our spirits healthy, and we almost completely died on the inside. We were living yet walking dead. So today, open our eyes to You. In Jesus' Name, Amen.

Today we are discussing spiritual health.

Read Ephesians 4:20-25.

How are we taught?

_____

What do we put off? _____

What is made new? _____

Summarize vs 24-25.

When we put off our old self, we will no longer sin when we are angry, we will not compromise and give room for satan to work in our lives, and everything we put our hands towards will be used to glorify God. We will guard our tongues, our thoughts, and we will speak forth that which brings blessing to those around us. We will work in kindness and compassion and forgive those who hurt and persecute us. Our spiritual health has to do with our spirit overcoming the flesh. If our soul is downcast, our mind and body will also be downcast, and depression can come into play.

Romans 5:20-21 (NIV) says, "[20] The law was brought in so that the trespass might increase. But where sin increased, grace increased all the more, [21] so that, just as sin reigned in death, so also grace might reign through righteousness to bring eternal life through Jesus Christ our Lord."

I love this passage in Romans (take time to read **12-21**), because it really reveals that because of sin, our souls are of the flesh. It is not until we believe in Jesus and make Him our Lord that our spirit comes alive, and our soul is healed. Yet, we still have the power to make our souls sick.

I love what 1 Timothy 4:8-10 (NIV) says, "[8] For physical training is of some value, but godliness has value for all things, holding promise for both the present life and the life to come. [9] This is a trustworthy saying that deserves full acceptance. [10] That is why we labor and strive, because we have put our hope in the living God, who is the Savior of all people, and especially of those who believe."

Our spiritual health is very important to how we live. In the last days, we see people deceived by lying spirits and they no longer hold to Jesus and the truth. They come up with rules that are meaningless and contrary to who God is. We are to speak boldly of their error and their need of Jesus. We should stay away from myths and fables. If we want to live in freedom, wholeness, favor, blessing, abundance, and experience the good things in life, then our souls need to be healthy. For many of you reading this, your soul is not healthy. And because your soul is not healthy, it is having great impact on your mind and thoughts, and then your physical body is responding to it with sickness, tiredness, exhaustion, and deep sadness. It is time to get your spirit healthy. If you are spiritually healthy then you should be teaching and preaching to others how to have spiritual health. You should be using your gifts and making a difference. You should be guarding towards deceiving spirits and let others know when you see them at work.

Read Today: Ephesians 4, Romans 15

~My prayer for you today~
Heavenly Father,
I come before You, and I pray for Your child reading this. I ask that today their souls would become healthy. I pray that they would begin to apply all the truth we have been learning about in the last twelve weeks, and that their souls would come alive in You. I pray that they would not stop until they are fully healthy in You.
In Jesus' Name, Amen.

Day 4: What Does God Say About Physical Health?

~Prayer~

Heavenly Father,

We come before You and we admit our physical bodies are not healthy. Many of us are overweight, have no muscle or strength, and our organs are handling so much stress that it causes them to struggle and not to work together for our good. So today we seek You and long to understand the truth that comes from You. In Jesus' Name, Amen.

Today we are discussing physical health. In all honesty this is the one that I am struggling with right now. My body is still not healthy, and I am actively doing what I need to do to be obedient to God. For so long I had this mindset that if I truly loved my ex-husband then I needed to stay with him and try and love him through the abuse, affairs, and trauma. This is where I continually heard that to show love means turning the other cheek. I have heard it said the Bible doesn't talk about loving oneself so much, because it is a given that we already love ourselves.

But for a person who has been betrayed and abused, loving themselves is pretty much nonexistent. I can honestly say that in those fourteen years I was with my ex, I did not love myself and I did not love him. True love would have dealt with the issues, and if he didn't listen to me and others in the church, then I should have removed myself from him. Because staying with him and letting him continue with the abuse became a stumbling block to him in his relationship with God. He needed to be corrected and to deal with the consequences.

There needs to be a balance when it comes to loving others, and we also need to understand what God's love is. I disobeyed God because I allowed my temple (body) to be hurt instead of keeping it sacred. By staying with my ex, I became unbalanced. 1 Corinthians 3:16-17 (NIV) says, "[16] Don't you know that you yourselves are God's temple and that God's Spirit dwells in your midst? [17] If anyone destroys God's temple, God will destroy that person; for God's temple is sacred, and you together are that temple."

Our bodies, our physical bodies, are God's temple and He dwells within us. Yet, how many of us treat our physical bodies as holy? **1 Corinthians 6:7-10** speaks into how many live, and it's full of wickedness and compromise. 1 Corinthians 6:11 (NIV) says, "[11] And that is what some of you were. But you were washed, you were sanctified, you were justified in the name of the Lord Jesus Christ and by the Spirit of our God."

Read 1 Corinthians 6:17-20.

What does it mean to united to the Lord?

What are we to flee from?

Write vs.19 and 20.

I love how it is very clearly saying our 'bodies'. We should honor God with our physical bodies and not just our mind, will, and emotions. What a powerful message. How many of us use our bodies for His honor and glory?

I have a hard time with working out because of my trauma. But I realize that if I am going to go wherever God sends me, then I need a healthy body. I need to be strong, I need strong lungs, and I need my body to work the way it is meant to work. Proverbs 31:17 (NIV) says, "[17] She sets about her work vigorously; her arms are strong for her tasks."

Acts 27:33-34 (NLT) says, "[33] Just as day was dawning, Paul urged everyone to eat. "You have been so worried that you haven't touched food for two weeks," he said. [34] "Please eat something now for you own good. For not a hair of your heads will perish."

Truthfully, I am still overweight and doing my best to lose it. The weight has caused my joints to hurt, and my muscles need to be strengthened. The fat around my stomach puts heavy pressure on my lungs and organs, causing the inside of my body to struggle to function the way it is supposed to. If my body is the temple of God, then this is an area I need to change.

We are to use our bodies to glorify God because when we use it for sin it will affect our spiritual health. We are to be strong so that we can run the race set before us. We need to be eating the right food so that we can survive and thrive.

As I mentioned above, I did not have a good balance of health when I was with my ex. I sacrificed myself to the point I was almost dead inside, and my PTSD was consuming me. Years passed in blurs as I just tried to survive. It wasn't until a friend asked me if my ex-husband got right with God and pursued me again if I would go back to him that I fully understood this point. My answer was and is, "NO! I will never get back together with him." God Himself also spoke about this when He gave me Galatians 5:1 (NKJV) says, "[1] Stand fast therefore in the liberty by which Christ has made us free, and do not be entangled again with a yoke of bondage."

Our bodies should not be used to entangle us in bondage. Our physical bodies should help us complete our goal, our mission, and our purpose. We should be doing everything in our power to be physically healthy. We should be eating healthy, working out, and then trusting God with the rest.

Read Today: 1 Corinthians 6, Proverbs 31

~My prayer for you today~

Heavenly Father,

I come before You, and I pray for Your child reading this. I ask that Your child would begin to take the steps needed to have physically healthy bodies, that they would be aware of what they need to eat, what their weight should be, and that they would use their bodies to glorify You.

In Jesus' Name, Amen.

Day 5: Ways to Apply Health

~Prayer~

Heavenly Father,

We understand that to honor You means that we keep our mind, spirit, and bodies healthy; we know all three work together to give us a long and favored life. Help us to start making right choices that will lead to greater health. In Jesus' Name, Amen.

Today we are going to look at ways that you can apply healthy steps into your life. We will break it up into the three different categories. The first category is health for the mind. The second is health for the soul. The third is health for the body.

Ways to have health in your mind.

1. Guard what you think about
2. Keep watch over what you listen to and what you watch
3. Think on things that are holy and righteous and good
4. Read
5. Play games that build mind strength
6. Stay social
7. Tobacco, alcohol, and drugs will affect your brain in negative ways- stay away from it
8. If under a lot of stress, find ways to relax yourself

Ways to have health in your soul.

1. Read the Bible
2. Pray everyday
3. Spend quality time with God
4. Obey all that the Bible says to do
5. Obey what God gives you to do for your life
6. Walk in your spiritual gifts
7. Walk in the fruit of the Spirit
8. Keep your soul strong in God
9. Get involved with your tribe
10. Get involved with a church
11. Walk in your calling

Ways to have health in your body.

1. Get enough sleep
2. Eat healthy
3. Drink lots of water
4. Watch the amount of processed foods and drinks you consume
5. Exercise
6. Take vitamins

7. Get enough sunlight

8. Rest

It's time to start looking at your health and see which areas you have been unhealthy in. When I was going through my separation and divorce, I was getting healthy in all three ways. I was beginning to feel good, but then life got busy. I started writing Held Hostage and now I am writing the Beyond Held Hostage, so I have limited time. That means I have not been working out and keeping my physical body healthy. I can really tell the difference and how it is affecting my soul and mind. In a couple days I will be done writing the revelation in this book and then I will earnestly begin to workout and exercise again. While writing this week on health, God really brought conviction to me that I had started out strong, but along the way I stopped doing what was healthy for my body.

Read Today: 1 Corinthians 3

~My prayer for you today~

Heavenly Father,

I come before You, and I pray for Your child reading this. I ask that You begin to impress upon Your child the areas that their health is lacking, that they would understand what things they need to add, and that they would choose every day to be healthy in all categories.

In Jesus' Name, Amen.

Day 6: My Story and Testimonies

Truthfully our health is probably the last thing we are thinking about when going through difficult times of being Held Hostage, and yet it is an important role in recovery and healing. As we learned this week, God wants us to be healthy spiritually, mentally, and physically. He created all three to function together.

For many years I suffered from depression. I have been overweight for what my age and height require for the last 11+ years. During my first year of marriage, working out was not something I had time for. I was the only one working. I had two jobs and worked 50+ hours a week. There was no time because I had limited hours to sleep, and my ex was doing a lot of drinking during that year, so sleep was important, because it was an area I was lacking.

Then leading up to our second anniversary my ex went away to get help and the school was supposed to get him freedom. Although I didn't have a peace about it, especially knowing he lied about being married, yet I had no power to do anything about it. The only thing I could do was get healthy. I began to workout diligently and lost over thirty pounds. Then the day before our second anniversary, at 3am, I found out he was having a sexual affair. Later I learned that they had gotten close through working out together in the mornings.

Two things that affected my health happened: first, working out became a trigger and I have struggled ever since with it. Exercising with my ex was just as bad. The second is that I have bad insomnia ever since then. It did not help that when my ex was home, he would go to the gym at 3am. Every time he left, I struggled. Other times I would be so tired because I had barely slept that I wouldn't hear or remember him leaving and would wake up startled, panting, and consumed with fear. I would call him to see where he was, and why he didn't tell me he left, because on top of all that he kept telling me that one day, while I was sleeping, he would up and leave me and never tell me where he was going. That he would never return. I would end up having nightmares about his affair and the abuse. I had them around 3am or after 3am. The nightmares were vivid and accurate. Later the nightmares turned into the fears of him doing it again or leaving me for good.

For me, a good night's sleep is getting at least five hours, and by the grace of God He has allowed me to function at full capacity without having enough sleep. I praise God that through my healing the nightmares have pretty much gone away. I still have insomnia, but I am working on finding healthy solutions to overcome it.

I have been forcing myself to work out and lose weight, because I don't want it to be something that Holds me Hostage and remains a trigger. Also, the weight puts pressure on my joints, muscles, and organs. It also affects my breathing and digestive system. So, I am forcing myself to overcome this trigger.

As I mentioned in week 11, my ex and I were sexually active before marriage. (Praise God for redemption! It is something I have always regretted, and now I know that when God brings my future spouse, it is not a choice I will repeat.) However, I do want to share a bit more about this. I have always had a very normal woman's cycle (period) throughout all my life, even during the times of abuse and trauma. But after one of our times together, I began to experience changes in my body and when looking up some information, I saw that the signs could be an indication of pregnancy. A huge part of me was so scared that I would be pregnant out of wedlock, but another part of me really wanted to be a mother. My time was very late, and I took a test, but it showed negative and then later the following day I ended up getting my time. However, it was a very abnormal period with excruciating pain. The amount of blood was also scary. A month later I was still experiencing aching in my body, depression, and feeling very down. My appetite was gone, and it was such a rough time that I decided to go to the doctor. They found that I was anemic, or low in iron. I was also very low in vitamin D. I was immediately put on vitamins, high dosage at first, and then as the months progressed, I went to a lower dose.

To this day I do not know if I had a miscarriage or if it was side effects of the low iron and vitamin D, but what I do know is that not knowing has always been hard and traumatic. Not knowing if I was grieving over an actual child or one in my mind. I never told my ex or family about it. Only one friend, who was a nurse, knew about it. After that, the trauma, abuse, and always living in adrenaline rush made it impossible to have kids. I see now that it was by God's grace, but not being able to have a child has broken my heart. In my last two years of marriage, I went and got tested, because I wanted to make sure it was possible for me to have children. The only thing that came back was that I was low in iron. So as hard as it was not having a child, I know it was God's protection over me and my future children. I look forward to a healthy marriage and the opportunity for kids in the future.

As I mentioned before, I have had depression. The side effects of having low iron and vitamin D is that your body becomes unbalanced and aches, and it throws off how your organs function. By not taking care of my body, I was adding to the depression. Also, I was spiritually dying, which also affects our bodies' health and how we handle healing.

So now a big way I have found to overcome depression and anxiety, etc. is by making sure my spiritual man, is strong and healthy in God. Second thing is I make sure I am eating healthy, drinking water, working out, and taking the vitamins I need. The third step is, I put my mind on the things of God (getting God's perspective and being thankful).

By doing all of these steps together I am becoming the healthiest I have ever been, and I will be able to go wherever God leads me and face life full on, in favor and blessing.

Testimonies:

* When it comes to God's healing, I have a few different experiences to share. It wasn't until I was in college that I realized I was not physically healthy at all. I never worked out, I ate more than I needed, and I didn't like myself—both who I was as a person, and how I looked outwardly. I wanted to get started on losing weight and growing healthier right away, but every time I tried, I reached a dead end. I kept trying and failing, over and over, and now I look back and realize that it was because the Lord was working on the inward healing, I needed first. He began to teach me who He was, and who I am. He first healed my mind and thought patterns (this took a long time; about four years, to encourage anyone who's going through this, it takes time), He healed me spiritually in teaching me about who He is because I didn't truly know Him, how to know His voice, how to trust Him; and He healed me emotionally, for my emotions have always been an overwhelming tidal wave I could never break free of. As I finally released my need to focus on how I looked and let Him heal me mentally, spiritually, and emotionally, my physical health began to follow suit naturally, without my even trying. My skin began to clear up. I was starting to take better care of myself. I was eating what I needed

without feeling the uncontrollable urge to eat more. I was moving more, going for walks with friends. Now I look back and I can see how I needed to be healed inwardly first. I needed to be taught of my brokenness and unholiness, but also that because of Jesus, I am chosen and beloved. Even now, I am still learning to take care of my physical health, but the Lord has brought me so far, and I know that He will help me to come even farther.

I have two other powerful experiences with healing. One Sunday several years ago, my family was getting ready to head to church. But my brother was not feeling well, so he decided last minute to stay home and rest. My mom said, "Alright, we'll be praying for you!" And I felt the Holy Spirit prompt me forward. I decided I would pray for him right then before we left for church. I put my hand on his arm and prayed for him. When I got done, he suddenly surged forward and said to our mom, "Mom, when Krystle touched me, I felt completely normal." He was able to come to church and felt totally fine. It was an incredible experience to see God heal so immediately and so quickly, before I had even prayed at all. I had only touched my brother, and God moved.

Another time was while I was in college. I and a few other fellow students were working together to prepare a lesson for kids' church that upcoming Sunday. One student looked pale and was sitting by the wall. He said he was feeling sick. I sat beside him and put my hand on his shoulder and prayed for him. When I was done, he told our group leader that he felt much better after I prayed for him.

The Lord is our healer. Sometimes, as with me, the way He heals takes time. It takes years. Other times, He heals immediately. Either one is nothing short of miraculous. God is our healer and He heals us in every aspect of our health. ~Krystle V.

*Growing up, I had always assumed and had been taught that God may allow, permit, or grant us to get or to remain sick in order that He may be glorified. For instance, I always heard that God allowed Satan to make Job sick even though Job was a righteous man who didn't necessarily do anything wrong. But because God is still sovereign, trustworthy, all-knowing, and good, we can trust that He will make it better in the end, even if one must die and get to heaven first.

I applied this view of God to my own situation when it came to a diagnosis of congenital hypothyroidism. Since we live in a fallen world due to Adam's sin, I presumed that this generational disease was just happenstance. Since I could easily manage this condition with cheap medication for the duration of my life, I considered this medically "incurable" disease to be no big deal.

About seven years ago, however, I had a conversation with a pastor where he challenged some of my assumptions about healing. This started a journey through the Scriptures and science where I started to dig deeper into the realm of health, healing, disease, and sickness. Throughout this journey of research and seeking God through His Word, I have learned more insightful information about where sickness comes from and how healing manifests. By learning from the experience of ministries with proven results in the areas of healing and discipleship, I have gained a deeper appreciation how the mind set on the flesh (fear, bitterness, envy, pride, anxiety, shame, guilt, and mindsets like these) is death, but the mind set on the Spirit is life and peace (see Romans 8:6).

Throughout this healing journey, I have discovered how worry, fear, anxiety, guilt, and shame release excess stress hormones (like cortisol), which compromise the immune system so that corresponding sicknesses will manifest accordingly. I have also discovered how God's perfect love casts out fear and how the good news of God's grace can renew our minds, change our DNA, restore bone marrow, repair the immune system, remove disease, and bring health to the body (see Proverbs 17:22; 15:30; 16:24; 14:30; 1 John 4:18; Ephesians 4:22-24).

Growing up, I inadvertently fell into accusing, blaming, or placing the responsibility on God for not healing a person's body, when it is actually human ignorance, immaturity, and unbelief that often plays a greater role in permitting the thief to steal, kill, and destroy this broken world via disease and sickness (see John 10:10; Acts 10:38). Only God's grace can equip and train us to keep moving forward and to endure until we see God's promises and provisions manifest as we become doers of the Word and not hearers only (see Hebrews 10:35-36; James 1:21-22). ~Steve D.

Day 7: Self-Reflection

~Prayer~

Heavenly Father,

We come before You and we take time today to hear Your voice. Please direct this time of fellowship with You. Reveal to us what You are wanting to say and direct us to do. Speak to us very clearly and reveal to us what we need to know.

In Jesus' Name, Amen.

Today I will be asking hard questions and I want you to write down your answers of what God truthfully and honestly has revealed to you.

How have you not been keeping your mind healthy?

What are ways that God is telling you to keep your mind healthy?

How have you not been keeping your spirit healthy?

What are ways that God is saying to keep your spirit healthy?

How have you not been keeping your physical body healthy?

What are the ways that God is saying to keep your physical body healthy?

~Prayer~

Heavenly Father,

We thank You for revealing to us the need for a healthy mind, soul, and body. Thank You for reminding us that we need balance in our lives and that it is important we take care of our temple.

Help us now to implement this truth into our everyday life.

In Jesus' Name, Amen.

Week 14: Spiritual Warfare

"^{13} Therefore put on the full armor of God, so that when the day of evil comes, you may be able to stand your ground, and after you have done everything, to stand."
(Ephesians 6:13 NIV)

Day 1: Spiritual Warfare

Spiritual warfare is one of those terms you do not hear much about in the world we live in. In fact, there are many Christians who do not even believe there is a spiritual realm. This has left them at a big disadvantage when it comes to the attacks of the enemy.

So many Christians place more importance on the physical realm and what they can see with their eyes. This means that when negative situations occur, they direct their fight and focus on the individuals who are involved, instead of understanding what is truly going on.

2 Corinthians 10:3-5 (RSV) says, "³ For though we live in the world we are not carrying on a worldly war, ⁴ for the weapons of our warfare are not worldly but have divine power to destroy strongholds. ⁵ We destroy arguments and every proud obstacle to the knowledge of God, and take every thought captive to obey Christ."

There is a reason that I waited to discuss spiritual warfare until now. The truth is that many of you have been experiencing spiritual warfare this entire time, but because you lacked a strong foundation in God, digging deep into the matters of spiritual warfare would have set you up for battles you weren't ready to fight.

In week 11, we talked about when Elisha asked God to open his servant's eyes to the truth of what was really happening. The servant looked and beheld a great multitude of angels, ready for battle. In fact, angels are all around us, which means that demons—the fallen angels—are also around us.

Ephesians 6:11-12 (RSV) says, "¹¹ Put on the whole armor of God, that you may be able to stand against the wiles of the devil. ¹² For we are not contending against flesh and blood, but against the principalities, against the powers, against the world rulers of this present darkness, against the spiritual hosts of wickedness in the heavenly places."

Our battle is not against man; it is against the one that man serves. Our battle is against the powers of the dark world, but not against man himself. Why is that? Our heart's desire is that every man will be saved and go to heaven. Our heart's desire is that every child is redeemed and renewed. If we fight against man, it won't change their future because they are under the control and influence of satan.

This week we will be talking about what spiritual warfare is, what tools to use, and learn about the demonic agenda.

Read Today: 1 Corinthians 10

~Prayer~

Heavenly Father, we come before You, and we ask that You begin to reveal to us about the spiritual realm. Show us who we are truly fighting against, and how we are Your warriors. Give us understanding, wisdom, and discernment over spirits so that we can set captives free.

In Jesus' Name, Amen.

Day 2: What Is Spiritual Warfare?

~Prayer~

Heavenly Father,

We come before You and we are aware that there have been many times that we wrongfully attacked those who have hurt us. But we did not battle in the spiritual realm and we lost the battle! Thank you that true victory can still be ours. Help us to understand true spiritual warfare and how we and others can gain freedom. In Jesus' Name, Amen.

Today we are going to be talking a little bit more about what spiritual warfare is. It is interesting that our temptations, arguments, strife, gossip, sins, and even warfare often stem from our own desires. James 4 puts it this way: we do not ask God for our desires, and sometimes when we do ask, it's with the wrong motive, for our own pleasure. Too many believers are trying to be accepted by the world, but those who do that are now enemies of God.

Read James 4:5-10 (NIV).

What do these Scriptures reveal to you?

We are given clear understanding that many of our battles come from our own desires and the war within us. I love how this expresses God's desire and heart for us. He longs to be close to us, closer than even our own families. He desires that we long for Him above all others.

(Write out vs. 7-8)

So many Christians today do not believe in demonic spirits or that people can be possessed. However, the Bible gives many examples of demon—possessed people set free when Jesus, and the church that followed, cast them out in His name. Many cultures around the world have a great understanding of the spiritual realm and seeing demon-possessed people is quite normal. But for many in the western world this idea has been ignored and has become nearly nonexistent. Today, demons think they are in complete rule of the culture, family, and country. But God is fully aware of their limitations and so He calls us forward to fight against them, take back the ground, and conquer new ground for His Kingdom.

Matthew 12:43-45 (RSV) says, "[43] "When the unclean spirit has gone out of a man, he passes through waterless places seeking rest, but he finds none. [44] Then he says, 'I will return to my house from which I came.' And when he comes he finds it empty, swept, and put in order. [45] Then he goes and brings with him seven other spirits more evil than himself, and they enter and dwell there; and the last state of that man becomes worse than the first. So shall it be also with this evil generation."

It is so very important that when someone is freed, they are filled with the Holy Spirit, who comes through acceptance of Jesus as Lord and Savior. When the Holy Spirit fills you, you are no longer unoccupied and cannot be taken back down. But if one who is free turns away from God, it will be far worse for them, because the demons will return with many, and that individual will live in worse captivity than before.

As I mentioned in week 11 on perspective, some of our greatest spiritual battles take place in our minds.

Read 1 Peter 5:6-10.
(Write out vs. 8-9)

It is very important to remember that our final victory has already been decided. Jesus will return, and He will reign and bring the New Kingdom of God into the world. Therefore, we do not need to fear these small battles, though large in our eyes, because satan has already been defeated and he is just throwing a tantrum to keep it from happening. I love how this version of this Scripture says to take a decisive stand. In other words, don't be swayed by temptation and sin. Remain firm in the fear of the Lord, holding firm to your salvation, and clinging to purity and righteousness. Stand! When you are being attacked in your thought life, think on God. When you are being aroused, stand in purity. When you are struggling with others and want to gossip about them, pray blessings over them. Stand in what you know to be right, regardless of how you feel. Keep your thoughts in alignment with truth.

Romans 8 addresses our responses to spiritual warfare. God is all powerful, and with Him, what can take us down? Nothing. Nothing can. God is our justice, He has chosen us, and Jesus is actively interceding for us. No matter the hardships, temptations, or persecution (whether to us physically or spiritually) God is with us.

Read Romans 8:36-38 (NIV).
(Write out vs. 38.)

Spiritual warfare is very important for our healing and freedom. My greatest victories took place on my knees before God. It is when we are praying that God shows up to give us answers, victories, and understanding. He sends out His angels to do what we ask of Him. When we stand our ground, we continue to hold that ground because the spiritual battle has already been won.

Read Today: James 4, 1 Peter 5

~My prayer for you today~
Heavenly Father,
I come before You, and I pray for Your child reading this. I ask that today they would know that their fight is not against another human being, but against the darkness they serve. Their battle is against the lies and bondage found in satan. I pray that You would begin to reveal truth and discernment to them.
In Jesus' Name, Amen.

Day 3: Ways to War Against the Demonic

~Prayer~

Heavenly Father,

We come before You and we are longing to make ourselves ready for battle. We want to be victorious overcomers and we desire to see Your kingdom in this world. Show us today the ways that we can begin to fight boldly. In Jesus' Name, Amen.

Today we are going to be looking at different ways that we can fight against the demonic agenda that surrounds us and tries to Hold us Hostage.

Read James 1:12-15 (RSV).

(Summarize these verses.)

Working in the opposite spirit is a way to fight the demonic agenda that is out to destroy your future. If your responses to struggles (sin, mistakes, and traumas), lead you further into darkness, then it is time to walk in the opposite spirit. We do not want to be deceived into believing that everything God has given us is bad or evil. We need to remember God's heart and character; His gifts are good and for a purpose, and He does not change.

Read Colossians 1:9-11 (RSV).

Write verse 10.

Prayer is the best way to fight against satan and his demons. When we boldly pray, things shift in the spiritual realm. The heart of the person we are praying for begins to soften. Each of us have a spirit, and our spirits completely understand the spiritual realm. Therefore, when we pray for people or even ourselves, we are praying concerning their spirit, and since our spirits are not of this world they are affected by prayer. We should make sure that we are thankful and celebrate God's goodness with joy. He calls us sons and daughters, and we will be with Him for eternity. He rescued us from the demonic forces here on earth, and we can walk in righteousness in Jesus' forgiveness (if we have asked Him and made Him Lord and Savior).

We need to be fully aware of what God has done in our pasts, understanding the ways of escape that He has given us. 1 Corinthians 10 talks about the Israelites knowing all that God had done for them, but because of their lack of faith and trust, they clung to the old flesh, so God was not pleased with them. We need to stay away from sin, temptations that would want to drag us back into bad habits and sins and should cling to what is true. We need to be thankful and keep a heart of gratitude, to stay far from pride, and to realize that every victory comes from God alone.

1 Corinthians 10:12-13 (RSV) says, "[12] Therefore let any one who thinks that he stands take heed lest he fall. [13] No temptation has overtaken you that is not common to man. God is faithful, and he will not let you be tempted beyond your strength, but with the temptation will also provide the way of

escape, that you may be able to endure it."

It is very important to fight with discernment. Remember how we addressed the importance of discerning spirits in individuals and who they serve? We need to understand the spirit we are dealing with, even in our own lives, so that we understand how to escape temptation. We need to discern the way that God has provided for our great escape.

Ephesians 6:10-20 teaches us how to wage spiritual warfare. The first thing we need is the full armor of God; not just parts of it, but the whole of it. It all must be active in our lives. Each week that we studied together has needed the full amor. If we choose to ignore the topics of the other weeks, we will not win our battle for freedom and healing. After having the full armor, we are called to stand, to STAND FIRM!

(Look up the verses and fill in the blanks.)

Belt of _____

Breastplate of _____

Feet fitted with _____

Shield of _____

Helmet of _____

Sword of the _____

Pray in the _____; TONGUES!!!

Pray on all occasions with all kinds of _____ and _____.

Be _____ and always keep on praying for _____.

We need truth to fight lies and deceit. We need the righteousness found in Jesus and walking in Him (opposite spirit). We need to share the Gospel of peace, how Jesus came, died, rose again, how He will return for us, and how we are to bring the Kingdom of God to the world around us now. We need to have faith that God is who He says He is and walk in that. We need salvation, and we need to walk according to the Word of God. In every situation, we need to walk in this way. No matter the person, no matter the situation, no matter what our feelings and emotions and memories cry out for us to do. Tomorrow, we are going to take a closer look at how to apply these steps to our current situations and the people around us.

Read Today: Ephesians 6

~My prayer for you today~

Heavenly Father,

I come before You, and I pray for Your child reading this. I ask that You begin to show them how to apply these tools when dealing with spiritual warfare. I pray they would not run from the battle, but would be ready to take on the enemy with You. Please reveal to them Your truth and give them discerning hearts.

In Jesus' Name, Amen.

Day 4: How to Use Tongues and The Word as a Weapon

~Prayer~

Heavenly Father,

We come before You and we are ready for battle. We are ready to overcome and be victorious in all that You have called us to. No longer will we give satan room to work in our lives. We will stand against his schemes, and we will hold fast to You. In Jesus' Name, Amen.

Today we will be talking about how the gift of tongues and the Word can be used to battle the spiritual attacks we face. One of the best examples of using the Word was given to us by Jesus Himself. If Jesus did it, how much more should we incorporate it into our fights as well? Matthew 4 gives us this example in which satan tempts Jesus three times: 1. with food and drink, 2. with God's protection, and 3. with power and authority.

Matthew 4:4, 7, and 10-11 (RSV) says, "[4] But he answered, "It is written, 'Man shall not live by bread alone, but by every word that proceeds from the mouth of God.'"

"[7] Jesus said to him, "Again it is written, 'You shall not tempt the Lord your God.'"

"[10] Then Jesus said to him, "Begone, Satan! for it is written, 'You shall worship the Lord your God and him only shall you serve.'" [11] Then the devil left him, and behold, angels came and ministered to him."

Three different times Jesus used the Word to tear down the lies of the enemy and break out of temptation. How often are you using the Word to fight? Do you have verses memorized to know what to use in warfare? Do you know how to find verses you can use? The truth is that many do not know the Word by heart. Many do not know how to find verses to help in the fight. The church has done a horrible job equipping the body of believers for war. Instead of mature seasoned fighters, we have infant Christians told to go into battle who end up casualties because they refused to grow in maturity. So, when you face a battle, begin to declare the Word to the situation and the demonic spirit you are dealing with. Let the Word do the fighting as you stand in Truth. Get a Bible concordance that gives different words and the verses to find them in. (For example, find the word anger; you will find verses that deal with that topic, and so forth.)

Tongues is an important weapon in fighting against the demonic. Remember, tongues is the private language between our spirit and the Holy Spirit, who is in us. When we pray in tongues our spirit is strengthened and made firm. Not only that, but the battle plan is being arranged without the enemy (satan) aware of what is going to happen. Because remember, satan cannot understand tongues. Finally, the Holy Spirit, God the Father, and Jesus the Son in perfect trinity command the angels to move on our behalf. The angels are given words to speak to us, weapons to battle against the demons, and they hold the ground once we have taken it. 1 Corinthians 14:2 (RSV) says, "[2] For one who speaks in a tongue speaks not to men but to God; for no one understands him, but he utters mysteries in the Spirit."

It is through tongues that our spirit learns to hear the Holy Spirit. Jesus said that His sheep will know His voice, and we are able to do that by the gift of tongues. So, the next time you are in a spiritual battle, begin to pray in tongues, and then speak forth what the Holy Spirit gives you to win the victory.

Prayer is an important part of spiritual warfare. In fact, without prayer, you suffer through it silently, or maybe you let your emotions run wild when you face it. But when you pray through the attacks, mountains in the spiritual realm fall, demons are bound, chained, and restrained. Every place satan has delayed will be released through your prayers, and your answer and miracle is on the way. I love what Matthew 18:18-20 (RSV) says, "[18] Truly, I say to you, whatever you bind on earth shall be bound in heaven, and whatever you loose on earth shall be loosed in heaven. [19] Again I say to you, if two of you agree on earth about anything they ask, it will be done for them by my Father in heaven. [20] For where two or three are gathered in my name, there am I in the midst of them."

Prayer is a very important weapon in battle; without prayer, we try to fight on our own, without God, so we lose. Not only is prayer important, but when you incorporate fasting and giving, the victories keep on coming. When we give financially (tithe ten percent and financial gifts), our time, or what God tells us to give, we are positioning our hearts into a place of thanksgiving and gratitude, and that opens the heavens to us. The Father is truly pleased when we give. When we fast, we are humbling our hearts before God, and battles are won on our knees before Him. Bring all three together and the heavens are opened wide to us. The Father's heart and our heart connects on a deeper level in those moments, and nothing satan throws at us can stand. I find it interesting that every time I go to pray and fast, (which I do every other month for two days), I experience extreme spiritual warfare leading up to it. Now that I am fully aware that satan is afraid of what God is going to do on my behalf during that time of fasting and praying, I have become aware and am discerning of the time leading up to it, so I am not surprised by the enemy's attack.

So how can we apply these weapons to the battles we face? When dealing with individuals, first I recognize that what is taking place has to do with the spirit man, or the flesh man. Instead of responding in anger or out of my own perspective, I ask God to reveal to me how He sees the situation. Then I pray against satan and whatever demonic spirit is trying to work in this person. I pray that the Holy Spirit would fill this person and that they would walk in truth. I pray that the individual would begin to fight against the demonic spirit trying to pull them down. When I feel released, I move on. I incorporate prayer and tongues, I speak the Word, and then I declare forth what God gives me to say. Afterwards, I work to treat that individual in a way that is honoring to God, regardless of how they are acting. There will be times when you yourself will need to apologize to others because you were used as a weapon of the enemy against them.

Other spiritual battles do not involve people at all. Instead, they involve the temptations or demonic spirits themselves directly coming against you. Once again, pray, stand firm, speak the Word, speak in tongues, and then declare what God gives you to say. Everything that we have learned in the last thirteen weeks is meant to be applied to this week. Understanding the Father, Son, and Holy Spirit gives us the understanding of who we belong to. Understanding covenant relationship, hearing the voice of God, and using the gifts of the Spirit allows us to boldly stand firm in our faith, unwavering and unafraid of the enemy, for we understand that we have been given the power in God to overcome. Using thanksgiving and our health to work together for the glorifying of God, understanding tribes, being bold, getting involved, walking in the opposite spirit, and changing our perspective (or renewing our minds) leads us into stronger unity to fight together against the enemy. We are not meant to fight alone, so when we apply all the weeks together, nothing can stand against us because we are fully in the Father, and He leads us.

Tomorrow we will be looking at some of the demonic spirits that are out there, as well as temptations that are sweeping around the world.

Read Today: Matthew 18

~My prayer for you today~
Heavenly Father,
I come before You, and I pray for Your child reading this. I ask that Your child begin to take steps to battle courageously for You, that they would plant their feet, stand in Your truth, and boldly fight and take back the ground. I pray, that they would not stop there, but keep conquering new ground for You.
In Jesus' Name, Amen.

Day 5: What Are Some Demonic Spirits Around Us?

~Prayer~

Heavenly Father,

Today we understand that everything we face has to do with the spiritual realm, not the physical realm. For even the evil we face in humans is because they serve satan. But our battle is not against them, for they are captives. We choose to begin fighting in the spiritual realm so that others can find freedom. In Jesus' Name, Amen.

Today we will be talking about some of the temptations and demonic spirits that are at work in the world today. I would like to first discuss what demonic attacks can look like, and the spirits that are attached to them.

*Seeing demons in natural eyes or in dreams and visions.

*Sexual and seductive movies, books, tv shows, songs, and games. There are demonic spirits connected to them that cause sexual lust. They destroy marriages, relationships, and lead to death. As a Christian, this also means wearing revealing clothes, sex, and other sexual behaviors (outside of marriage), and lewd comments. There is a spirit connected to these as well. We need to be able to fight against it spiritually because we cannot live our lives hiding with our heads in the sand. We still must live in this fallen world and be surrounded by people who don't care about morals. But we also need to hold ourselves accountable and avoid watching, reading, speaking, or listening to such things as a form of entertainment and pleasure.

*Self-gratification- this has to do with sexual desire and finding the means to fulfill it without waiting for the one God has for us in the sanctity of marriage.

*Fear - The Bible says that there is a spirit of fear

*Anxiety

*Confusion

*Mental battles

*Words spoken that come against us and our character and purpose

*Anger

*Resentment

*Sex before marriage

*Affairs

*Abuse

The list goes on and on

(On a global scale), these are some of the demonic agendas that are contrary to God, that have been researched and found to be tied to demonic spirits.

*Homosexuality

*Transgenderism

*Woke Culture

*Abortion

To learn more about this topic and the demons that go with them, go to http://www.hopeoftheworld.org or you can look for Rabbi Jonathan Cahn's sermons on his book, "The Return of The Gods." The knowledge God has given him is truly eye-opening for how we are to fight the spiritual battles concerning the world we live in.

*Divorce - not all divorce has a spirit to it. For some of us divorce was right because the spouse was unfaithful, abusive, and harmful. But for many others, divorce has been an easy way to get with someone and then move on to someone else. It takes away the covenant commitment and instead makes marriages weak. There is a demonic spirit attached to this movement as well.

*Mental disorders - there are some mental disorders that the world believes are just medical related, but in fact are of a demonic spirit. Therefore, we should always respond with spiritual warfare for that person's mind.

*Witchcraft

*Palm readings

*Horoscopes

*Crystals

*Religions

*Sickness - In many countries we just assume it is a natural problem but fail to recognize that there is a spiritual realm where sickness is demonic. We gladly admit there are angels and demons, but we live like they are not around us. Instead, we should first view the world through the spiritual realm, waging spiritual warfare against the demonic spirits, and then take physical action.

Many times, spiritual steps are taken last or never taken at all. It's time we rise as warriors and boldly take the Kingdom of God forward.

~My prayer for you today~
Heavenly Father,
I come before You, and I pray for Your child reading this. I pray that their heart would not be hardened against You and the truth You want to reveal. I pray that they would be willing to let go of the flesh and walk in the Spirit. Give them wisdom and discernment.
In Jesus' Name, Amen.

Day 6: My Story

Spiritual warfare is something that people in the western world don't think about. When you go to the Middle East, Asia, Africa, South America, and to Polynesian islands you do not have to explain darkness, demons, or the spiritual realm. They understand the darkness and so then you share about God, angels, light, truth, and they understand it. They have a better grasp of the spiritual realm than most western countries.

Demons, curses, angels, and God are all things that the western world is clueless about. In the last few days, we have been studying what God's Word says about spiritual warfare, and now I will share my own experiences.

Self-gratification has been something I had the most shame and guilt with and had to overcome. It led to sex before marriage, but it also influenced my view of my ex-husband and myself. During the times my ex withheld sex for months to years during our marriage, he found ways to meet his needs (but I suffered). So, self-gratification led me to meet my own needs, but it also became a form of rebellion towards my ex. At the same time, it couldn't hide the pain of the truth that my husband did not love me enough to fill my needs. This broke my view of intimacy. We are not meant to take care of our own needs. It's why in Song of Songs 8:4 (RSV) says, "⁴ I adjure you, O daughters of Jerusalem, that you stir not up nor awaken love until it please."

In 1 Corinthians 7:5 (RSV) says, "⁵ Do not refuse one another except perhaps by agreement for a season, that you may devote yourselves to prayer; but then come together again, lest Satan tempt you through lack of self-control."

From our eighth anniversary to our tenth, my ex wanted children, so we were active for that purpose, (as I mentioned in Held Hostage, I felt completely degraded during those times and cried throughout many of them) so the physical body's needs were being met, meaning there was no self-gratification. However, now that I am single, the sexual desire does not miraculously go away. Therefore, I must fight the good fight and remain free from self-gratification.

I have mentioned some of the spiritual attacks in the weeks before, but there are a couple more that I will discuss here. As I mentioned, my dad is a pastor. When I was seventeen, we moved from South Dakota to Georgia to start a church. Most people are unaware of the spiritual attacks we faced in obedience to God. The church I had grown up in told us we were not hearing from God, that we were in the wrong. They implied that we had a Jezebel spirit and by going we were sinning. They talked behind our backs, they ignored us, and they refused to send us out with their blessing. In fact, God used an entirely different church we were involved in when I was a little girl to send us out. That time left deep hurts and wounds, but God took us through a time of healing. I know that if we had remained in South Dakota, we would have died spiritually. I'm so glad my parents chose obedience over of fear of man.

After we had lived a year in Georgia, it became very hard. Our support system was small, yet powerful, but those lies we heard, before the move, began to attack us in different ways. Each one of my family members dealt with it in different ways, and there were times the light at the end of the tunnel seemed very far away. During this time, I left to go to school, but I honestly have regretted that I didn't stay and help them through that rough season, especially for my younger brother, who had few friends. It seems that satan likes to isolate us and get us alone. I praise God that He has taken each of us through a time of strengthening, and healing from that season, which clearly showed me the demonic agenda satan has toward families and covenant relationships. I realized the importance of knowing how to battle in the Lord and not against each other. Because I didn't battle correctly, I dealt with long lasting effects. To this day I must watch how my responses to my family members are, because they can reflect the trigger I feel from that year.

When that happens, I go back and pray, forgive, repent, and remind myself we are not who we were then. That situation showed me we need to know the right way to fight and overcome. We need to see with our spiritual eyes and hear with our spiritual ears. We need a tribe, a support system, because when we fight alone, we will grow weary and tired. There is a reason we need other believers. I praise God for the things He has revealed to each of my family members about that time, what we were learning, how we were growing, and that He truly did have a reason for us to be there. I am truly thankful that we obeyed, but also sad that the church became a weapon for satan to use.

When I went to my school, I ended up traveling to the Middle East to teach for a couple of months. I had to constantly stand in my identity in Christ, because as a woman I was not treated with respect most of the time. I was generally treated like an object. When I walked alone to class, men would call out to me, whistling, and follow me. The first month I was fearful, but I began to hold onto who God said I was, and then I walked in complete boldness as a woman of God. The last month I was there, I was walking alone and had to cross a busy road without lights. The cars have the right of way and so pedestrians must bravely make their way through. I remember boldly stepping forward and holding out my hand in a gesture to slow down or stop, and then I walked. I remember a man from the bus that did not slow down, (but I passed in time) and he said, "You are a true (member of the country I was in)." When I left, one of my students gave me a letter saying, "You showed your beliefs and your relationship with God through your actions. My first judgments of you were wrong. I see that you are a white (member of the country I was in) in a sea of brown."

I remember very clearly one night when the Muslim call to prayer went off around 3am. Right before it went off, I had a dream that I was being chased. I climbed a ladder to get inside a treehouse, but once I reached the top, my pursuers showed up, and in front of me, their heads turned into wolves. They gnashed their teeth and lunged for me. I woke up, startled, awakened by the call of prayer going off. I sensed demons all around me, and I immediately went into a time of prayer to God, and I repeated the name of Jesus over and over. Within minutes the demons were gone, and peace and light flooded my room.

Another time we went to Israel for a couple of days before returning to the US. We went to one of the locations where they thought Jesus had died, was buried, and rose again. As we walked inside these churches there was a strong demonic presence. Many of us felt suffocated and couldn't breathe. We went outside and waited for the rest of the group. Later we went to a different location where it was also thought Jesus had died, was buried, and rose again. We all experienced the power of God, His peace, and a holy reverence. God showed me that just because a location was considered holy, individuals bring the spirit they are involved with. There are many Christians who have been deceived and carry demonic spirits with them, because they hold fast to false teachings. We either bring the presence of God with us, or we bring satan. Plain and simple!

In week 6 we talked about the gifts of the Spirit. I want to talk a little more about tongues. It wasn't until 2022 that I fully began to understand that tongues is my spirit communing with the Holy Spirit.

We are talking and having deep revelations that satan cannot understand. In fact, psychiatrist Andrew Newberg did a study, where they had individuals speak in tongues while their brains were scanned. The images showed that when speaking in tongues the area of the brain that keeps us in control is shut down, while the area that reflects on ourselves and the world around us increases.[10] Here is the link for the study. https://robertwimer.com/wp-content/uploads/2020/04/The-scientific-evidence-of-speaking-in-tongues.pdf.

Our brains function differently when we speak in tongues. Tongues allows us to speak without satan understanding the plans. Our spirits become lighter, and heaviness is removed. We receive the blueprints and steps to take. That means when all of a sudden, we're given a step and we have peace, it's because our spirit already knows what to do. Then when you add the interpretations of tongues you have just wiped out satan's plans and brought them into the light. His agenda cannot stand. One of the biggest attacks in the Christian Churches is the removal of the Holy Spirit and the condemning of Tongues. Why? Why does satan push against it so heavily? Because he knows that when we remove the power of the Holy Spirit from our lives and displace our way of communing with the Holy Spirit, our battles are harder, and complete victories are limited.

Satan is trying to destroy the power of the Bride of Christ by removing the gift of tongues and the Holy Spirit. It's time the churches take back the truth and bring the Holy Spirit back into the midst. Far too long people have believed the lies of the enemy and it's time for them to be broken off. It's time to receive the power of the Holy Spirit and take back our fellowship with the Him through tongues.

---

[10] CONSTANCE HOLDEN, "Tongues on the Mind," American Association for the Advancement of Science, 2006. https://www.science.org/content/article/tongues-mind

Day 7: Self-Reflection

~Prayer~

Heavenly Father,

We come before You and we take time today to hear Your voice. Please direct this time of fellowship with You. Reveal to us what You want to say, and direct us. Speak to us very clearly and reveal what we need to know. In Jesus' Name, Amen.

Today I will be asking hard questions and I want you to write down your truthful and honest answers of what God has revealed to you.

(Apply these to every area that you need freedom in.)
What is the spirit, demonic agenda, or spiritual battle connected to this area?

Take time to pray in tongues concerning it, cast satan and his demons out, and ask the Holy Spirit to come and help you fight this battle. Pray and speak the Word over that spiritual attack. When you feel released, write down what God is saying about this situation and declare forth what He gives you.

How did you handle this attack in the past?

How does God want you to begin fighting the battles?

(Apply these steps to every area that you need breakthrough, healing, and freedom in.)

~Prayer~

Heavenly Father,

We thank You for revealing our need to be ready for battle. Thank you that we are Your royal warriors ready to take the ground for You. We thank You that we do not fight alone, but that You are with us and go before us.

In Jesus' Name, Amen.

Week 15: Reclaim Yourself

"[9] For this reason, since the day we heard about you, we have not stopped praying for you. We continually ask God to fill you with the knowledge of his will through all the wisdom and understanding that the Spirit gives, [10] so that you may live a life worthy of the Lord and please him in every way: bearing fruit in every good work, growing in the knowledge of God, [11] being strengthened with all power according to his glorious might so that you may have great endurance and patience, [12] and giving joyful thanks to the Father, who has qualified you to share in the inheritance of his holy people in the kingdom of light."
(Colossians 1:9-12 NIV)

Day 1: Reclaim Yourself

This week we will be looking at how to reclaim yourself. If you have been like me along this journey you've traveled, you have lost yourself. The things you once enjoyed you either laid down or had stolen from you; the relationships you once were a part of are no longer the same, and your hobbies are a struggle to pursue. Not only that, but your very purpose and calling has all but become extinct, and you are just barely getting through each day.

Through my healing process, I realized this: Because I met my ex when I was very young and was still trying to learn what my identity and purpose was, and because of everything that happened throughout the marriage, I never truly found my identity. So, part of my healing process was finding myself, what I enjoyed, and what I was being called into purpose. For many of you this will be new, or it will be going back to something you once knew.

After reading **Colossians 1:9-14**, write down in your own words how God wants us to live our lives.

I find these verses so relevant, and I recognize that many believers are not praying for those around them. Sometimes it seems that all our prayers are focused on ourselves. As I was going through my time of healing and started fasting and praying, I began to reach out to those around me and find out how I could be praying for them. I diligently prayed for them and their needs. God would reveal things to pray about, and later the individuals would confirm I was praying accurately.

James 1:23-26 (NIV) says, "[23] Anyone who listens to the word but does not do what it says is like someone who looks at his face in a mirror [24] and, after looking at himself, goes away and immediately forgets what he looks like. [25] But whoever looks intently into the perfect law that gives freedom, and continues in it—not forgetting what they have heard, but doing it—they will be blessed in what they do. [26] Those who consider themselves religious and yet do not keep a tight rein on their tongues deceive themselves, and their religion is worthless."

Look up vs. 27 and write it down.

When we reclaim ourselves, it should also benefit those around us, because it's not just about us. The way we reclaim ourselves, so we can go out into the world and bring His Kingdom, is an important key. If I reclaim myself for only myself, then I have missed the mark and lose my calling entirely. When I understand that reclaiming myself will allow me to walk into my purpose and calling, this allows Jesus to give back all that satan stole for God's Kingdom to grow.

Read Today: Colossians 1

~Prayer~
Heavenly Father, we come before You, and we ask that You begin to reveal to us how we are to reclaim ourselves. Show us the gifts we laid down or were stolen, what relationships need to be built back up, and what our calling and purpose is for our futures. This week, come and open our eyes and ears to understand all that You want us to know.
In Jesus' Name, Amen.

Day 2: How to Reclaim Yourself

~Prayer~

Heavenly Father,

We come before You, and we long to understand how to reclaim ourselves. Please give us understanding and leading. Direct our ways, lead us on the path that You have for us. We trust in You, and we acknowledge that we long for Your ways and Your thoughts. In Jesus' Name, Amen.

Today we will be talking about how you can reclaim yourself. As I said, this can be a very hard thing to do. In fact, not only is it hard, but also very confusing. I had no idea what my identity was because I was still learning who I was when I met my ex, and then we had a relationship and a marriage. My identity became 'wife' and 'financial provider.' You can imagine the identity crisis I faced during the separation and the time leading up to the divorce. My whole identity was so wrapped up in my ex that I had no idea who I truly was and where I was supposed to go. I had to mourn what could have been in my marriage, how I could have been a mother, and I had to release all the dreams that never came to pass. I had to realize that my identity does not come from my job or my relationships, but my identity is found in Christ.

As I mentioned in Held Hostage, it was during that time that I started to proclaim who I was in Christ. I am His warrior bride, ready for battle, and ready for the future He has for me. I recognized myself as a daughter of the Father. I began to claim the spiritual gifts God had given me and began to walk in them.

Because of the abuse, I had a hard time remembering what hobbies and things I felt called to as a teenager and in my young adult years. So, I had to take a lot of time praying and asking God to reveal things to me. And He did, in big ways; He revealed dreams that I had forgotten about, a calling to write a book, a calling to minister to the world, and once He started revealing everything that I had given up or that had been stolen from me, I began to see the steps to reclaim them.

I began to workout and also lose weight, to paint, design furniture and create them with my dad. I began to learn new skills that I always wanted to do, such as shooting and I have many more that I will be pursuing throughout this coming year, such as learning Korean, dance, etc.

When it comes to reclaiming yourself, here is a list of questions you might find beneficial.

1. Is your identity found in God?

2. Begin the process of reclaiming your identity by learning who you are in God.

3. What relationships do you need to invest in again?

4. What hobbies did you stop doing?

5. What clothes, makeup, hairdo, etc. did you give up?

6. What are ways you can create a safe and peaceful environment for your healing?

7. What spiritual gifts are you no longer using?

8. Pray and ask God to reveal dreams that have long been dead.

9. Begin to walk out the steps God tells you to take to reclaim yourself.

Read Today: James 1

~My prayer for you today~
Heavenly Father,
I come before You, and I pray for Your child reading this. I pray that they would begin to hear Your voice leading them in the ways to reclaim themselves. I pray that You would reveal to them any areas their identity is based in satan's lies instead of truth. Help them to begin discerning and walking in the path You have for them.
In Jesus' Name, Amen.

Day 3: Habits to Incorporate

~Prayer~

Heavenly Father,

We come before You today and we understand that everything we are doing today is because You have taken us through a process. You are leading us through a time of great healing and deliverance. We choose to rest in Your embrace and sit at Your feet. In Jesus' Name, Amen.

Today we will be talking about habits that we can incorporate to help us reclaim our gifts and callings. Some of you right now might feel as if you have completely missed it and that there is no way that God would allow you to fulfill the calling that He gave you in your youth. I love what Romans 11:29 (NIV) says, "[29] for God's gifts and his call are irrevocable." The term irrevocable according to the Merriam-Webster dictionary means "not possible to revoke: UNALTERABLE."[11] In other words, the gifts and calling God gives us cannot be changed or altered. It means that they remain, and now we have a choice if we will of whether be obedient and walk in them or not.

The day I realized that not only was I healed, redeemed, and restored, but also realigned to my original calling and purpose from God was truly a day that I will never forget. As I was reading through my journals, I saw that everything God was speaking to me now, He had also spoken to me before and during my marriage. I still had the chance to walk in it now. This has brought a joy and a passion to be obedient no matter the cost. So, when God told me that I would have a ministry where I would be using my past to help others, I said "Yes!" When He told me that it would take me to the world, my answer was, "Yes, no matter the country, if You say go, I will go." And I am now fully ready to see God move in this area.

Read 2 Timothy 1:6-14.

Summarize what these verses mean.

So, what are some of the habits we should be incorporating to reclaim our identity, gifts, and calling?

1. Understand who the Father, Son, and Holy Spirit is, and understand Their character

2. Understand how your relationship works with the Trinity.

3. Begin to live each day by hearing Their voice

4. Begin to apply the gifts of the Spirit in your life daily, not just on Sundays.

5. Begin to be active in your tribe and get involved with the ministries around you that God calls you to.

6. Be bold and passionate about what God calls you to.

7. Walk in the Spirit and not in the flesh.

---

[11] "Irrevocable," Merriam Webster Dictionary. 2023. https://www.merriam-webster.com/dictionary/irrevocable

8. Renew your mind and change your perspective through God.

9. Keep a thankful and grateful heart.

10. Continue to keep your mind, body, and spirit healthy.

11. Fight every spiritual battle and don't let satan take ground from you.

As you follow these habits and steps, you will begin to see that all along you have been finding your identity, purpose, and calling. Right now, you should have a great passion for the things of God and for your relationship with Him. Everything that we have learned through the last 14 weeks has led us to this week.

Read Today: Romans 11, 2 Timothy 1

~My prayer for you today~

Heavenly Father,

I come before You, and I pray for Your child reading this. Right now, Your child is beginning to see that all along You have been revealing their identity, value, and worth to them. You're calling on their lives has not changed. I pray that they would walk boldly into all that You have for them.

In Jesus' Name, Amen.

Day 4: Reclaiming Creativity

~Prayer~

Heavenly Father,

We recognize that we are created to create. But how many times have we followed the world's ways of creating, instead of letting You direct our gifts and callings? Today we desire to create with You, to break out of the box that would try to control You, and we boldly begin to create new things. In Jesus' Name, Amen.

One of the hardest things for those who need healing and have been deeply wounded to do is be creative. Our minds tend to go through the past over and over, but creativity requires us to think ahead, to push ourselves to see things from a different view. That is a truly hard thing to do when everything in us is just trying to deal with the past. However, it makes complete sense that this is an area satan wants to destroy. Nehemiah 9:6 (NIV) says, "[6] You alone are the LORD. You made the heavens, even the highest heavens, and all their starry host, the earth and all that is on it, the seas and all that is in them. You give life to everything, and the multitudes of heaven worship you."

God, the Creator of everything, the one who took nothing and made it into something beautiful. He created the vast heavens and the stars that shine for all the world to see. He created landscapes that take your breath away, the sunsets and sunrises that even the best painter cannot come close to capturing, animals and plants that can bring joy and amusement to those who walk in this world. He created you and I. In His image, we are created. God is the Creator, and since we're made in His image, it's why we desire to be creative too. It is how God made us.

Creativity can be used in any field, but I specifically want to get into the field of art. That means dance, music, painting, pottery, acting (movies and shows), etc. I feel demons have taken over this field in a stronger way than most other 'mountains.' Remember how we discussed the seven different mountains in week 9: families, religion, education, media, entertainment, business, and government. You can read more about this topic from the book 'Invading Babylon: The 7 Mountain Mandate' by Lance Wallnau and Bill Johnson. Although we understand how each mountain has truly been in darkness and it is time for believers to take back all seven of them, I specifically feel called toward the arts or entertainment. Why? Because we find our rest and happiness through entertainment. It is an area that draws many to be a part of and easily sways culture. I believe that God is calling believers to take this mountain back. His desire is for us to become creative and lead the way in coming up with new things that will draw the world to God and glorify Him.

For far too long, believers have been following the mainstream and trying to keep up with them. Yet now God is asking for us to be the ones to take the lead. He is saying that it is time to be creative and take the lead for His Kingdom.

If you are an artist and satan stole it from you, and you can barely pick up your tool to create because of the trauma, it's time to breakthrough and reclaim your calling. Enough is enough! Do not allow satan anymore power and control in your life. Be bold, PICK UP your tool and create!!!!! Do not stop! Do not give up! Do not give in to satan and his lies! It is time to push back, to take back, to reclaim, and to create with God once again. Dance like no one is watching, sing and play your instrument unto the Lord, paint, draw, mold, act, and do everything unto the Lord. Break out of the box and boldly lead this mountain into the ways of God.

Read Today: Nehemiah 9

~My prayer for you today~
Heavenly Father,
I come before You, and I pray for Your child reading this. I ask that they would begin to be creative with You. Where the enemy has used the past to keep them from being creative, I break it off in the name of Jesus. Satan, you have no power or authority over them; you will no longer control them through fear, anxiety, and creative—blocking, in the name of Jesus. Today I proclaim over you, child of God, that it is time to create. It is time to take back and reclaim the gift God has given you, and it is time to lead the way instead of following the world.
In Jesus' Name, Amen.

Day 5: Why Big Changes Should Not Be Made Quickly

~Prayer~

Heavenly Father,

We come before You and we are ready for the future You have called us into. We are ready to pursue all that You call us to. We recognize that You make us ready in the right time to take on bold new things. Help us to be aware of the season and the time for everything. In Jesus' Name, Amen.

Today we will be talking about why big changes should not be made quickly when one is healing but should be given time until you are ready to handle that decision. During my healing process, each step was clearly directed by God. My first big step was separation and then from there, divorce. After that God had me wait a year and two months before my next big step, which was leaving both of my jobs and stepping into ministry.

During that time, as I mentioned previously, I took many small steps to reclaim myself. I decorated my room, got piercings, dyed my hair, and spent time with family and friends. As I continued to take small steps, He led me to write Held Hostage and then to bigger steps. I left both my jobs, let go of my kids (nephew and niece), and stepped into ministry.

So many of us would want to make big decisions right away, especially financial ones, and if you are in an abusive situation and need to move for your safety then you do to make that big change. But I am talking more about changes that no longer involve the abusive person, traumatic event, or temptations to sin. I am talking about things that have to do with your future, not your past.

So why should we wait before making big life changes? I love what Dr. David Jeremiah says about this topic of life decisions. He gives five principles for decision making.

1. Your decisions reflect your values.
2. They are birthed in prayer.
3. Heed wisdom from others.
4. Take time.
5. Commit to God[12]

When you are going through a time of healing, our minds are not ready yet to make big decisions. It is as we heal that our minds begin to process, grow, and finally connect to the future. In our eagerness to reclaim ourselves, we still need to be wise in our decisions. We need to make sure they reflect our true values found in God. We need to make sure each is birthed through prayer. We need to be willing to heed the counsel of the wise. We need to take time to let the right time for the decision to come to pass and not step ahead of God. And ultimately, our decisions need to be committed to God as we follow Him. 2 John 1:8 (NIV) says, "[8] Watch out that you do not lose what we have worked for, but that you may be rewarded fully."

---

[12] Dr. David Jeremiah, "5 Principles for Biblical Decision Making," David Jeremiah Blog, 2023. https://davidjeremiah.blog/5-principles-for-biblical-decision-making/

Read Today: Joshua 24, especially vs. 15.

~My prayer for you today~
Heavenly Father,
I come before You, and I pray for Your child reading this. I ask that You begin to reveal to them how they need to start making future decisions. I pray that they would wait upon You for the right time, but that they would also be ready for when it's time to take those big steps. Keep them from becoming lazy, and help them to actively live out their faith, taking small steps that lead to big steps.
In Jesus' Name, Amen.

Day 6: My Story

Having walked through fourteen years of abuse and trauma, I had completely lost myself, my hobbies, my joys, my friends, my relationships with family, my calling, my ministry, and my relationship with God.

When I finally separated from my ex, God showed me that I needed to start reclaiming what I had given up. I had already been allowing God to restore my relationship with Him, as well as my calling, spiritual gifts, ministry, and healing. But my hobbies, health, relationship with friends and family was still not reclaimed. So, as I mentioned in my book Held Hostage, I started dyeing my hair fun colors, got eight (symbolizing new beginnings) piercings, and began to get creative.

Then I also began to reach out and stay connected with good friends, making sure to pray about who God wanted me to connect with. I also began allowing God to show me how to let Him redeem and restore relationships in my family in grace.

I listened to what I wanted to listen to, I watched what I wanted to watch, and I gave myself the freedom to say no to things. I redecorated my room and reclaimed it as a place of peace where God is with me, instead of a place of abuse. I learned how to shoot a gun. I wrote my book 'Held Hostage' with God's leading, fourteen years after He first told me I would write a book.

There is so much more that I will be doing to reclaim myself, but I started out small, and now as I write this it's November 2022, which celebrates a year and four months since my divorce, and I am ready now for big, BIG, steps to reclaim myself.

As I mentioned in week 13, I greatly struggled to get pregnant, and perhaps even stay pregnant. There was so much pain and hurt from the lack of a child. There was so much guilt and shame when people asked why I didn't have kids yet. But God reclaimed this area in my life. My ex and I moved back to South Dakota from Utah when my nephew was a year old. I began to help raise him. I took care of him when he was sick, and I would pick him up from daycare and watch him until my sister got off from work. As he got older, I became the assistant teacher in his preschool class for a couple of years and we spent a lot of time together. I never missed a program, a party, and tried to be there for every big event. When he was six, I had to pull back due to his family situation at the time and covered him as a spiritual mom instead.

Then when he was eight years old, my sister gave birth to a baby girl. As I mentioned before, I needed a shift in my work, so God led me to provide care for my niece, and I started when she was six weeks old. My ex-husband was against it, because it meant less money coming in, but it was exactly what I needed. For almost three years I took care of her Monday-Friday, ten hours a day. If I were to add up the time we were apart, it would only be a couple of months, because on my days off we did things as a family, so I took care of her then too. We would also see each other weeknights and weekends. When my niece was sick, I was with her; when I was sick, I was with her. I took her to all her appointments. I was there for most of her firsts.

I would have my nephew before school and after school and then during summer break. During covid, I ended up homeschooling him for five months. I was the kids' second mom. God in His great love gave me the opportunity to be a mother. The hardest thing I had to do when God told me I would be going into ministry and traveling around the world was letting go of my kids. I had to release them back into their parents' hands, and step back from everyday care so they could have a healthy transition and get used to my absence.

Before I can go further into this process, I am going to jump to another story and then come back to this. Growing up, my grandma and grandpa on my mom's side passed away when I was around six years old. My grandma and grandpa on my dad's side passed away in my late teens and early twenties, but we had so many cousins who needed them, we didn't have many of the normal grandparent and grandchild experiences. God gave one of my mom's sisters a beautiful role in my life. Not only did she take on the role of aunt and show everyone a beautiful heart fully devoted to God, but she also took on the role of grandma. In fact, when people tell me different stories about their grandparents, she comes to my mind. We would have sleepovers, go to movies, enjoy family meals, especially holidays, and she would have us come and decorate her house for Christmas and bake cookies together.

She encouraged me in my walk with God. She believed in me. When she found out I had eloped with my ex-husband, she called me up to congratulate me and did not hide the fact that she knew about it. She was there for us at every big event and often used her gifts to bless us. She was an amazing cook.

When my ex and I moved back after his drinking caused us to lose our apartment on our one-year anniversary, I was not ready for what that summer would bring. One morning I received a call from my aunt. My ex had been on an abusive roll the week before and we were finally having a good day. She told me she was in the hospital and had been for a couple of days and she wanted me to let my mom know so she would come to her. I didn't stay on the phone long but said I would pray for her, and that I loved her. Heart surgery followed, and we were not allowed to go up to visit because they wanted to keep things low key for her healing. But no one was prepared for her to leave this world and go home to heaven. Only two days later, I was at work and received a call that my brother had an accident at work and had fallen from a 32-foot ladder. I reached the hospital to find that he had broken his arm in three places, as well as a couple of bones in his back. He was rushed to surgery, stayed a couple of days, and when he was released, he required constant aid. Due to a cast on his arm and a back brace, he needed help day and night to get out of bed or out of chairs. It was hard watching him go through the unknown.

But what no one knew was that deep down, my heart was broken, and I was living in regret that I had chosen one good day with my ex instead of a day with my aunt who I loved and who loved me. The pain of knowing I had missed my chance to see her one last time, to talk to her one last time, to be with her, filled me with great regret. It was not until God told me to release the physical role of mother to my nephew and niece and step back into the role of spiritual mother that He began to show me why I carried guilt and regret about my aunt. I finally faced my failure and fault and began to heal. God used it to remind me that even though my heart is being broken and torn apart and I'm mourning the release of my son and daughter, I could not pull away, run away, or distance myself to protect my heart. He reminded me that I did not want to waste my opportunities with my kids. So, while I am around them, I see them once a week. They are worth my broken heart. They are worth hurting for. I share this because sometimes reclaiming missed opportunities and reclaiming ourselves will also be painful and hurt deeply but in the long run, we won't have regrets or missed blessings.

Day 7: Self-Reflection

~Prayer~

Heavenly Father,

We come before You and we take time today to hear Your voice. Please direct this time of fellowship with You. Reveal to us what You are wanting to say and direct us. Speak to us very clearly and reveal to us what we need to know.

In Jesus' Name, Amen.

Today I will be asking hard questions and I want you to write down your answers of what God truthfully and honestly has revealed to you.

Where have you lost yourself, your ministry, and your purpose?

Is your identity found in God?

Write down what your identity in God is.

What relationships do you need to invest in again?

What are the hobbies you no longer do but God wants to give back to you?

What clothes, makeup, hair, etc. did you give up, but God wants to give back to you?

What are ways you can create a safe and peaceful environment for your healing?

What spiritual gifts are you no longer using that God is giving back to you?

Pray and ask God to reveal your dreams that have been dead for a long time.

What steps is God telling you to take to reclaim yourself?

Are you going to reclaim yourself?

~Prayer~
Heavenly Father,
We thank You for revealing to us the calling and gifting You have given to us. We are so blessed that You have not only saved us and restored us, but You have also realigned us so we do not miss our callings and gifting anymore. Today we say YES to You!
In Jesus' Name, Amen.

Week 16: Break Free

"[17] Now the Lord is the Spirit, and where the Spirit of the Lord is, there is freedom. [18] And we all, who with unveiled faces contemplate the Lord's glory, are being transformed into his image with ever-increasing glory, which comes from the Lord, who is the Spirit."
(2 Corinthians 3:17-18 NIV)

Day 1: Break Free

This week we will be talking about breaking free and what that looks like. We will also be taking time throughout this week to self-reflect and allow God to show us the journey we have been on the last fifteen weeks. We will be able to see how far we have grown, how much we have healed, and how much breakthrough we already experienced.

True freedom is where the Spirit of the Lord is. John 8:36 (RSV) says, "[36] So if the Son makes you free, you will be free indeed."

Our freedom should be used to help others. We should be diligently looking for ways to share our testimonies and encourage others in the race. Not only that, but our actions should be done in love, with a servant's heart. (Galatians 5:13-14) It is good to note that God has given us laws to live by that we cannot keep on our own, but our righteousness comes from faith in Jesus. (Galatians 3:21-22) I especially love what Galatians 5:1 (RSV) says, "[1] For freedom Christ has set us free; stand fast therefore, and do not submit again to a yoke of slavery."

I am sure that many of you right now are already healthier, breathe easier, and have seen victory over your past. Each step has led to this moment of breakthrough. So do not stop; keep going, and run the race set before you. Take a minute to **read Psalm 119:41-48**. It beautifully describes what our heart's response to God should be.

Read Today: Galatians 5

~Prayer~

Heavenly Father, we come before You, and we ask that You begin to reveal to us how we have overcome, where You have brought us, and what the future holds. Lead us deeper into You and all that You have for us.

In Jesus' Name, Amen.

Day 2: What Is Our Role on Earth

~Prayer~

Heavenly Father,

Today we come before You with great expectancy and longing for You and Your ways. We are so excited to be a part of what You are doing in this world. We get to be Your hands and feet, and we are ready, Father.   In Jesus' Name, Amen.

Today we will be talking about what our role on earth is all about. We will answer the questions of what our role on earth is, how that was taken away, how Jesus reclaimed it, and how do we get it back and use it.

We will begin with the question of what our role in earth is. The answer is found in Genesis 1:28 (NIV) which says, "^{28} God blessed them and said to them, "Be fruitful and increase in number; fill the earth and subdue it. Rule over the fish in the sea and the birds in the sky and over every living creature that moves on the ground."

God says here that that we are made in His image. In fact, it says "OUR" image, which means the Father, Son, and Holy Spirit. From there He says we are to rule, or as other translations put it, to have dominion and responsibility, or govern over everything in the sea, the sky, and the animals on land. He then charges man to bear fruit and increase in number, so that humans will cover the earth and subdue it, or bring under control. Then, again, He tells man to rule. We were created for fellowship with the Father, but the responsibility He gave us is to rule over the world.

When you look at the world, it is clear to see that has not been the way it worked out. So, then the question comes, how was our role taken away, and who took it? The answer is found in Genesis 2:15-17 (NKJV) says, "^{15} Then the LORD God took the man and put him in the garden of Eden to tend and keep it. ^{16} And the LORD God commanded the man, saying, "Of every tree of the garden you may freely eat; ^{17} but of the tree of the knowledge of good and evil you shall not eat, for in the day that you eat of it you shall surely die."

God commanded them not to eat of a specific tree that would teach them the different between good and bad. I find it very interesting how there was another special tree in the garden as well. Genesis 2:9 (NKJV) says, "^{9} And out of the ground the LORD God made every tree grow that is pleasant to the sight and good for food. The tree of life was also in the midst of the garden, and the tree of the knowledge of good and evil."

This tree was called the tree of life. Yet God did not tell them they could not eat from this tree. Imagine that; He made two trees, one that gives life and one that gives understanding of good and evil. And only one out of the two trees were forbidden to eat.

Read Genesis 3:1-5.

What did the serpent say?

What was the woman's response?

What was the serpent's response?

Satan used a snake to deceive and speak lies about what God had said, and woman and man willfully chose sin. In this moment, satan took the control, the power of ruling, away from man. I love how Paula White-Cain talked about this topic. Here are some of the notes I took from a sermon she gave on February 6, 2022, that spoke about this. Psalm 115:16 (NIV) says, "[16] The highest heavens belong to the LORD, but the earth he has given to mankind."

In other words, the highest heavens are God's, the second atmosphere is satan's, and the earth belongs to us. That is why God uses us, because we are over the earth. Here are a couple of points that she made concerning this.

1. Man was given dominion and license over the earth.
2. Satan, through deceiving Adam, stole man's authority over the earth and the lease changed hands.
3. Satan's operation here on earth is illegal.
4. Our lease is for an appointed time and our time is not yet up.

This leads us into the next question: how did Jesus reclaim it? Matthew 27:35 (RSV) says, "[35] And when they had crucified him, they divided his garments among them by casting lots;"

Matthew 27:45-46, 50 (RSV) says, "[45] Now from the sixth hour there was darkness over all the land until the ninth hour. [46] And about the ninth hour Jesus cried with a loud voice, "Eli, Eli, lama sabach-thani?" that is, "My God, my God, why hast thou forsaken me?"

"[50] And Jesus cried again with a loud voice and yielded up his spirit."

Matthew 28:5-7 (RSV) says, "[5] But the angel said to the women, "Do not be afraid; for I know that you seek Jesus who was crucified. [6] He is not here; for he has risen, as he said. Come, see the place where he lay. [7] Then go quickly and tell his disciples that he has risen from the dead, and behold, he is going before you to Galilee; there you will see him. Lo, I have told you."

Revelations 1:17-18 (RSV) says, "[17] When I saw him, I fell at his feet as though dead. But he laid his right hand upon me, saying, "Fear not, I am the first and the last, [18] and the living one; I died, and behold I am alive for evermore, and I have the keys of Death and Hades."

Jesus used His very life to get the keys back. He gave up His Spirit and went into hades (hell) and took the keys that satan had stolen. In other words, Jesus took back the lease that satan had illegally obtained.

Now the next question is how do you get back what satan stole and how do you use it? It is through covenant relationship with Jesus that we can have the authority once again over the earth. Here is a note I took from Paula White-Cain's sermon: "Through belief in Jesus and the work of the cross, we can use scripture to defeat satanic weapons and unseat satanic strongmen, strongholds, and destroy or recover stolen goods. Satan is still able to execute illegal authority here on earth until Jesus brings complete victory over him. For man to preempt satanic authority he must appropriate and execute the terms of the cross and what is written in the scripture." That means that everything we have been learning and putting into practice for the last fifteen weeks is how we take back our authority and begin to bring breakthrough to the world. Because of what Jesus did on the cross, we can be used to bring the Kingdom of God to this world.

Read Today: Genesis 1

~My prayer for you today~
Heavenly Father,
I come before You, and I pray for Your child reading this. I pray that they would begin to hear Your voice leading them in how to take back all that satan has stolen. You are longing to give double, no, triple back for everything satan has stolen, but that requires us to be in covenant relationship with You and walk out what the Bible says to do. So today, let them hear, let them understand, and may they choose to obey.
In Jesus' Name, Amen.

Day 3: My Story

For me, breaking free has been extremely rapid. In fact, people could see a difference the day after my ex-husband moved out. During the following four months of healing, I began to apply everything we have learned about from week 1 through week 15. By the time my divorce rolled around four and a half months after my ex moved out, I was applying all of it at the same time and seeing amazing victory in my life.

Things that had held me in bondage were gone. I found myself standing firm in truth, unswayed even when satan attacked. Temptations no longer held power, darkness and depression could not stay in the presence of God, and everyone commented about my joy and the peace that flowed from me. So many would say that I finally looked like the old me from my teens, full of hope, joy, and dreams.

I found great breakthrough in my PTSD. The symptoms became less and less, and the triggers no longer controlled my responses. In fact, most triggers have become very small. Now I am working on insomnia and pushing myself to face my fears and anxiety. The areas where strong triggers still arise is when similar situations happen to my kids (nephew and niece) or family. It is when things happen to them that I am extremely triggered, but even then, through God's power, I do not sin in it, but calm myself down, and then I pray through it before I discuss the situation that led to the trigger.

I decided that before I officially publish this book in three days, even though I already have the proof version, that I would take time to share one last example of breakthrough. Two weeks ago, I felt God leading me to meet with my ex-husband. We met in a public place, and my friend was in the car, while we stood outside talking. I asked him one last time about the affairs, etc. But in hearing his answer I understood that he had not changed. In fact, he was struggling with guilt and regret, and it was holding him hostage. God told me to pray for him, and right there in a public parking lot, completely unaware of who was around, I began to pray over him. I spoke to the areas he needed to heal in and grow in, and in my prayer, I encouraged him to take the steps needed to grow in his relationship with God. I prayed that he would use his testimony to help other men know what to do and what not to do, and that God would bring him a wife, only when he was healed and grown. After my prayer I looked at him and declared clearly into the heavens, "I have already forgiven you. So don't live in regret. Do what you need to do for a better future." In that moment I knew I was completely healed and free, and that God had given me the authority to speak not only to those who are hurt, but those who cause the hurt as well. FREE INDEED!!!!!!!!

Day 4: Self-Reflection

~Prayer~

Heavenly Father,

We come before You and we take time today to hear Your voice. Please direct this time of fellowship with You. Reveal to us what You want to say, and direct us. Speak to us very clearly and reveal to us what we need to know.

In Jesus' Name, Amen.

Today I will be asking hard questions and I want you to write down your truthful answers of what God has revealed to you.

What were your thoughts about God the Father in the beginning?

What are your thoughts about God the Father now?

What were your thoughts about Jesus the Son in the beginning?

What are your thoughts about Jesus the Son now?

What were your thoughts about the Holy Spirit in the beginning?

What are your thoughts about the Holy Spirit now?

What was your covenant relationship with the Trinity before?

What is your covenant relationship with the Trinity like now?

Day 5: Self-Reflection

~Prayer~

Heavenly Father,

We come before You and we take time today to hear Your voice. Please direct this time of fellowship with You. Direct us and reveal what You want to say. Speak to us very clearly and show us what we need to know.

In Jesus' Name, Amen.

Today I will be asking hard questions and I want you to write down your answers of what God truthfully and honestly has revealed to you.

Have your fears and the lies spoken about hearing Him been broken off of you?

Do you feel confident that you can hear Him?

How have you heard God's voice?

What is God speaking to You?

Are you able to discern the spirits around you?

How are you walking in your spiritual Gifts now?

In what ways do you need to continue to grow in using them?

Have you found your tribe and support system?

What has God said about them?

In what ways have you been bold?

What is God asking you to be bold in next?

Day 6: Self-Reflection

~Prayer~

Heavenly Father,

We come before You and we take time today to hear Your voice. Please direct this time of fellowship with You. Direct us and reveal what you want to say. Speak to us very clearly and reveal what we need to know.

In Jesus' Name, Amen.

Today I will be asking hard questions and I want you to write down your answers of what God truthfully and honestly has revealed to you.

What has God been speaking to you concerning His vision for you?

What is your gifting He wants you to use?

How is God calling you to get involved?

What are the situations where you failed to walk in the opposite spirit?

What are the situations where you were able to walk in the opposite spirit?

Going forward, how does God want you to implement walking in the opposite spirit?

What steps are you going to take to put the flesh down?

What is your perspective of God now?

What is your perspective of yourself now?

What is your perspective about relationships past and present?

What areas do you still need God to renew your mind in?

Are you thanking God daily?

Are you keeping your body, mind, and spirit healthy?

Day 7: Self-Reflection

~Prayer~

Heavenly Father,

We come before You and we take time today to hear Your voice. Please direct this time of fellowship with You. Reveal to us what You want to say. Speak to us very clearly and show us what we need to know.

In Jesus' Name, Amen.

Today the questions and steps can be used as spiritual warfare to help you break free and reclaim yourself and your calling.

Step 1: Pray and ask God to reveal who you need to forgive and what you need to repent of, and then follow through with it immediately.

Step 2: Begin to worship and praise God for who He is, what He has done and who you are in Him. Give thanks to Him.

Step 3: Pray and ask the Holy Spirit to lead this time of prayer. Pray in tongues and then pray against the demonic agenda. Submit yourself to the Holy Spirit and release what you want to hear to Him. Surrender the time to Him.

Step 4: Continue to pray in tongues and let Him lead you in what to pray about and how to pray about it. Speak forth or write down what God gives you.

Take time to pray in tongues concerning it, cast satan and his demons out, and ask the Holy Spirit to come and help you fight this battle. Pray and speak the Word over that spiritual attack. When you feel released, write down what God is saying about this situation and declare forth what He gives you.

Right now, what is an area that you are struggling with (whether it's a sin, a mistake, abuse, trauma, person, etc.)?

What are you feeling about the memory or the situation?

What is the spirit, demonic agenda, or spiritual battle connected to this area?

What is the lie that satan is saying about it?

What is the truth that God says about it?

What steps does God want you take to overcome this?

Final Thoughts:

I pray that the last sixteen weeks has propelled you forward into new beginnings with God. Everything that you have learned, and what God has taken you through is meant to be applied for the rest of your life. These are not just steps for breakthrough, but they are a lifestyle of relationship with God. I want to leave you with a prophetic word God gave me (for those who would read the first book), when writing Held Hostage. You can find it in Chapter 9 of Held Hostage.

February 27, 2022

Today is the day to say YES to Me. Put aside your fears, doubts, and need to be in control. You need to come to this understanding, you will never have all the understanding of Me, and yet as you say yes to a covenant relationship with Me, I will reveal Myself to you more and more. Step out in faith, believe that I will heal you. Let go of the victim mentality, the need to remain where you are. I have created you, and you have so much more than this death. I have a fulfilling, blessed, and anointed purpose and calling on your life. You are meant to be free, loved, and prosperous. Today meet with Me, surrender yourself to Me, and begin to forgive and repent. When you choose Me and are obedient to Me, I will radically change your life and in a very short time you will find yourself in a new place. The old will be gone and you will be walking in FREEDOM and RESTORATION. I want to realign you and bring you back to your original design. Release it all to Me. Release your anger, resentment, pain, and past. Let us walk this new path together. You will not be alone. If you look for Me each day you will see Me and how I am moving in your life. Today, today is the day for your VICTORY! Claim your future. Reclaim yourself, your promises, your ministry, your hopes, and dreams. Reclaim! Stand Firm! Be bold! Activate your courage! Let's go! LET IT BEGIN![13]

---

[13] Aubrey Dawn Weinzetl, "Held Hostage," 2022.

References:

Aubrey Dawn Weinzetl, "Held Hostage," 2022.

CONSTANCE HOLDEN, "Tongues on the Mind," American Association for the Advancement of Science, 2006. https://www.science.org/content/article/tongues-mind

Dawson, Joy. Intercession: Thrilling and Fulfilling. Seattle, Washington. YWAM Publishing, 1997.

Dr. David Jeremiah, "5 Principles for Biblical Decision Making," David Jeremiah Blog, 2023. https://davidjeremiah.blog/5-principles-for-biblical-decision-making/

Dr. George Barna, "Release #6: What Does It Mean When People Say They Are "Christian"?" Arizona Christian University, 2021, https://www.arizonachristian.edu/wp-content/uploads/2021/08/CRC_AWVI2021_Release06_Digital_01_20210831.pdf

"Irrevocable," Merriam Webster Dictionary. 2023. https://www.merriam-webster.com/dictionary/irrevocable

"Knowledge" Marriam Webster Dictionary. 2023. https://www.merriam-webster.com/dictionary/knowledge

Michele Rosenthal, "The Science Behind PTSD Symptoms: How Trauma Changes The Brain," Boston Clinical Trials, June 27, 2019. https://www.bostontrials.com/how-trauma-changes-the-brain/#!/

Wisdom," Merriam Webster Dictionary. 2023. https://www.merriam-webster.com/dictionary/wisdom

Pastor Hank Kunneman, Lord Of Hosts Church. https://lohchurch.org/

Pastor Paula White Cain and Brad Knight, https://paulawhite.org/, https://cityofdestiny.us/, https://www.youtube.com/@paulawhiteministries, https://www.youtube.com/@storylifechurch

Contact:

If you would like to have Aubrey Dawn Weinzetl come and speak at a Bible Study, conference, event, etc., want to know when her next book will come out, hear about opportunities to hear her in person and the events she will be doing; please visit her at:

Website: **www.aubreydw.com**

Facebook: **https://www.facebook.com/AubreyDawnWeinzetl**

Email: **Aubrey.heldhostage@gmail.com**

Book Ideas:

Books on prophecy, spiritual warfare, and healing; they inspired me during my time of healing.

"The Bible," by GOD

"The Wild Ones," by Nate Johnston

"The Armor of God," by Priscilla Shirer

"Stomping Out the Darkness," by Neil T. Anderson and Dave Park

"Live Your Story," by Stephanie N. Hall

"Where is God When It Hurts?" by Philip Yancey

"Spiritual Warfare," by Dean Sherman

"Reclaiming Surrendered Ground," by Jim Logan

"She Will Rise," by Becky Barta Weinzetl

www.ingramcontent.com/pod-product-compliance
Lightning Source LLC
Chambersburg PA
CBHW082144120626
46553CB00010B/2753